D1192024

LIBERAL EDUCATION AT YALE

The Yale College Course of Study 1945-1978

Daniel Catlin, Jr.

UNIVERSITY
PRESS OF
AMERICA

Harriet Irving Library

AUG 18 1983

University of New Brunswick

Copyright © 1982 by **DANIEL CATLIN, JR.**

University Press of America, Inc.

P.O. Box 19101, Washington, D.C. 20036

All rights reserved

Printed in the United States of America

Library of Congress Cataloging in Publication Data

Catlin, Daniel.
Liberal education at Yale.

Bibliography: p.
1. Yale University--Curricula--History. 2. Education, Humanistic--Curricula--History. I. Title.
LD6315.C37 1982   378'.1998'097468   82-17576
ISBN 0-8191-2796-5
ISBN 0-8191-2797-3 (pbk.)

ACKNOWLEDGMENTS

I have found that words are an inadequate vehicle for expressing honest gratitude, particularly to one's teachers of all kinds. Yet I must record my special indebtedness to Philip H. Phenix, without whom the course of study which led to this book would neither have begun nor ended. And the assistance of Douglas M. Sloan has been critical: prodding, guidance, criticism, and encouragement without stint. I also want to thank George W. Pierson, Thomas C. Mendenhall, Maynard Mack, Ralph H. Gabriel, Georges May, and Howard Lamar—all still Yale professors, despite their sometimes high positions within and without the University. Their correspondence and discussions with me provided a perspective, a sense of the moment, and an historical immediacy that I would not otherwise have had. Then, I would like especially to mention Patty Bodak Stark and the rest of the staff at the Yale Archives, who were more helpful than they knew and whose curiosity was more stimulating than they suspected. Finally, Alison Buck Cook, daughter of a Yale Dean and Provost, by reacting as she typed the very first drafts of my work, let me know that someone indeed cared. Although I received the assistance of these and many others, final responsibility for the completed manuscript, defects of fact and interpretation included, is mine alone.

DC

TABLE OF CONTENTS

Chapter I

INTRODUCTION

The search for liberal learning has been a persistent theme in the history of American higher education. Since the founding of Harvard in 1636, one of the traditional functions, perhaps the predominant function, of the college has been to provide a liberal arts education. In the nineteenth century, the explosion of knowledge, the coming of the elective system, the rise of the university, the growth of public higher education, and the inroads made by empirical science into the classical course of study challenged the preeminence of the liberal arts advocates but did not destroy them. At the turn of the century, curricular systems balancing distribution requirements and concentration requirements were widely introduced to promote liberal education. After World War I, Columbia College instituted the now-famous, often-copied general education courses. A whole group of experimental liberal arts colleges was founded between the wars, and during the 1930s a lively debate on the nature and purpose of general education flourished. World War II muted these discussions, but after the War, interest in liberal learning was revived nationwide when Harvard published a much publicized general education curriculum. Concern with liberal education has remained periodically topical ever since.

For nearly three centuries, the ideal of a liberal education has been professed, protected and preserved at Yale. The second oldest university in America was early in introducing scientific and engineering study in the nineteenth century, granted the first American PhD in 1861, and has added eleven graduate and professional schools to the original college. The liberal arts college remains, however, the central concern of the institution that George W. Pierson, Yale's historian, has specifically labeled the "university college." Since Yale's national prominence and her unquestioned position of leadership have led many around the country and even the world to follow its example, it seems worthwhile to examine what has happened at Yale since World War II. This study attempts, therefore, to ascertain to what extent ideal and reality matched, to determine in general the health of liberal education at Yale, and to highlight whatever the past has to say to Yale's present policy makers,[1] who remain articulate champions of the historic cause.

The traditional purpose of a liberal education is to communicate effective ways to make sense of a complex world in the interests of a meaningful life. Plato asserted that the appropriate activity of the mind was to seek knowledge, that pursuing knowledge was inherently satisfying to the mind's proper function and therefore was its distinctive end. It followed that pursuit of knowledge was part of the good life, particularly since in fulfilling the good of the mind, man simultaneously revealed the whole of the Good. Sound knowledge, therefore, was the means of directing the good life. Through study, the mind was able to avoid the deceptive appearances and doubtful beliefs that would lead to erroneous conduct. The mind was the means to both metaphysical and moral knowledge. The idea of liberal education as the pursuit of knowledge as the basis of the good life[2] arises from this ancient constellation of beliefs.

Most conceptions of liberal education have emphasized completeness of knowledge and understanding on the assumption that the more a man knows across as wide a spectrum as possible, the more safely and efficiently he will move through the world and life. Cardinal Newman, for example, pointed out the need

---

[1] George W. Pierson, Yale: The University College: 1921-1937 (New Haven: Yale University, 1950). The basic comprehensive history of Yale is Brooks Mather Kelley, Yale: A History (New Haven and London: Yale University Press, 1974).

[2] Plato, The Republic, translated with introduction and notes by Francis MacDonald Cornford (London: Oxford University Press, 1941); P. H. Hirst, "Liberal Education and the Nature of Knowledge," in Education and Reason, by R. F. Dearden, P. H. Hirst, and R. S. Peters (London: Routledge and Kegan Paul, 1972), pp. 1-3; Sebastian de Grazia, Of Time, Work, and Leisure (Garden City, N.Y.: Anchor Books, Doubleday and Company, 1964), chap. 1.

for an understanding of the interrelationships among the various branches of knowledge and the liberating effect of knowledge taken as a whole. Ortega y Gasset saw every culture as characterized by a "vital system of ideas" and believed that the purpose of education was the teaching of these vital ideas. Deep acquaintance with that interlocking web of knowledge would allow the individual to live "in accordance with the height of the times." The alternative was thought to be brutal barbarism.[1]

Traditionally, liberal education has been distinguished from professional or vocational education or any kind of utilitarian training toward some other, more limited end. As John Stuart Mill put it:

Men are men before they are lawyers, or physicians, or merchants, or manufacturers; and if you make them capable and sensible men, they will make themselves capable and sensible lawyers or physicians. What professional men should carry away with them from a University is not professional knowledge, but what should direct the use of their professional knowledge.[2]

This distinction between liberal and professional education is useful provided one recognizes that it is the matter of purpose and not subject matter per se which permits the distinction, as Alfred North Whitehead has made clear:

No course of study can claim any position of ideal completeness. . . . three main methods . . . are required in a national system of education, namely, the literary curriculum, the scientific curriculum, the technical curriculum.

---

[1]Jose Ortega y Gasset, Mission of the University (New York: W. W. Norton & Company, Inc., 1966); John Henry (Cardinal) Newman, The Uses of Knowledge, ed. Leo L. Ward (Arlington Heights, Ill.: AHM Publishing Corp., 1948).

[2]John Stuart Mill's Inaugeral Address at St. Andrews. Reprinted in F. A. Cavenagh, ed., James and John Stuart Mill on Education (Westport, Conn.: Greenwood Press, Inc., 1979), p. 134 et seq.

3

. . . Every form of education should give the pupil a technique, a science, an assortment of general ideas, and aesthetic appreciation, and . . . each of these sides of his training should be illuminated by the others.[1]

Since Plato, pursuit of a liberal education, what Mill called the making of capable and sensible men, has been presumed to incorporate moral worth. John Dewey, for example, believed that to be liberally educated was ‖to possess virtue . . . to be fully and adequately what one is capable of becoming . . . in all the offices of life.‖ Thus, according to Dewey, the effort to increase human knowledge necessarily increases human meaning. Fortunately, man does have both the interest and capacity to learn in response to his need to pursue meaning so as to give direction to personal existence and purpose to his life.[2]

To live a fully human life today remains as difficult and exhilarating as ever. Mankind's biological existence, which was once restricted to the earth, has touched the moon and moves toward the planets. At the same time, the future of any life in the atomic age is perilous. The definition of life is often obscured by medical technology, which sometimes needs the courts to decide when life actually ends. The faith of individual man is buffeted by existential philosophies or the absence of any philosophy. His mind is subverted by his subconscious, and the structure of the society he inhabits changes rapidly and remorselessly. On the other hand, twentieth century life remains in many ways the same. Man continues to debate the perennial questions: the wonder of his relationship with the ultimate, the discovery of internal purpose, a rationale to discriminate between good and bad, the identification of beauty, an understanding of truth. None of the startling advances of modern science that

---

[1]Alfred North Whitehead, The Aims of Education (New York: The Free Press Division of MacMillan Publishing Company, 1967), p. 48.

[2]John Dewey, Democracy and Education (New York: The Free Press Division of MacMillan Publishing Company, 1966), p. 358.

4

have improved man's physical lot and lengthened his life obviate the need to address these ancient issues that continue to excite man's imagination and govern his choices. And thus, today especially, no goal seems more worthy than achieving a liberal education of the type I have outlined, that is, to learn effective ways to make sense of a complex world in the interests of a meaningful, human life. In any case, it is this conception that I will use to test Yale's conformity to its own ideal.

For the last century and a half, the proponents of liberal education, who once had the field of higher education virtually to themselves, have had to fight a rear-guard action; and the historical trend has not been favorable to many colleges identified with furthering the liberal arts. This trend is due to the rise of industrial, technological civilization, to the public demand for the democratization of the curriculum, to the founding of the land-grant colleges with their utilitarian proclivities, to the rise of the research-oriented universities based on the German model. The revolution in epistemological values which overemphasized naturalism and destroyed the classical curriculum has not been congenial to liberal education. Logical positivism questioned the validity of moral, aesthetic, and religious claims to knowledge, and truncated the scope of the traditional curriculum accordingly. Science, or at least the scientific approach, has been in the ascendent together with a particular kind of specialization derived from empirical techniques. It can plausibly be argued that the governmentally-funded, utility-oriented "multiversity" is the characteristic American institution and the dominant model of the future, one which incorporates the liberal arts but relegates them to a separate area of specialization, often superficial and irrelevant.[1] Yet, as late as 1800, there remained in America a universal consensus about appropriate liberal education. The limited classical curriculum based on the trivium and quadrivium was studied by all as the fullest resource for human intellectual development. Education was general by definition, since it was neither

---

[1]Clark Kerr, The Uses of the University: With a Postscript (Cambridge: Harvard University Press, 1972).

specifically preparatory to a particular profession
nor utilitarian in the strict vocational sense.
This is not to say that a college education was not
frequently a preparation for theological study or
even medical or legal training, for it was; but at
the same time it was intended to be adequate preparation for the politically liberated citizen of the
new nation. In addition to being general and common,
the classical curriculum was expected to be liberating,
in that the knowledge imparted was presumed to be
good for the self-realization and self-fulfillment
of the individual both as an individual human being
and as a free citizen.[1]

In 1828 a famous and widely circulated Yale
Report reasserted the value of a liberal education
and of the traditional classical curriculum in terms
which emphasized the generally preparatory nature
of the fixed course of study, the importance of a
common curriculum to common culture, attitudes and
values, and the necessity to train the mind to function effectively. Often criticized as apparently
unmovable conservatism, this Yale Report is most
accurately conceived as a statement about continuing
educational issues. The Yale Faculty had opted for
liberal education instead of vocational training,
for a core curriculum instead of electives, for scho-
lastic elitism instead of egalitarianism, for common
culture instead of radical pluralism, and for broad
preparation instead of immediate utility.[2]

---

[1]Lawrence A. Cremin, American Education: The
Colonial Experience: 1607-1783 (New York: Harper
and Row, 1970), chaps. 1, 7; Douglas M. Sloan, "Har-
mony, Chaos and Consensus: The American College
Curriculum," Teachers College Record 73 (December
1971): 221-251; Russell Thomas, The Search for a
Common Learning: General Education, 1800-1960 (New
York: McGraw-Hill Book Company, Inc., 1962).

[2]Yale Faculty, "Original Papers in Relation
to a Course of Liberal Education," American Journal
of Science and Arts 15 (January 1829). As Cremin
and Sloan have pointed out, the Yale Report turns
out to be less the conservative bastion it initially
seems if the college is viewed as only one of the
higher educative institutions of the era. Thus,

As the nineteenth century progressed, the limited
classical curriculum was repeatedly and increasingly
attacked as insufficiently broad to allow it to be
the general education common to all the democratic
citizens of the new nation. It was also attacked
as being insufficiently practical and useful. By
mid-century, the traditional consensus reaffirmed
by the Yale Report began to come apart. Francis
Wayland, President of Brown University, for example,
directed his attention to subject matter and was
prepared to sacrifice the commonness of the old curriculum to achieve a breadth the classics could not
provide. This intended breadth would enable the
college to offer a more democratic curriculum, which,
if it moved away from elitism, also tended to be
more utilitarian and less liberally humanistic.
Henry P. Tappan, who headed the University of Michigan,
continued to equate general education with humanistic
liberal education, and this led him to be concerned
not with preparatory education for civic or professional life, but with development of the individual's
faculties to their utmost powers. He therefore concentrated on depth of scholarship, which led him
to believe that the college should be set within
a university. He thought that extending the course
of study beyond the usual four years could be made
to overcome the contradiction between significant
depth of scholarship and the extensive subject matter
of a common general education. The President of
the University of Wisconsin, P. A. Chadbourne, was
concerned to align the traditional liberal arts college to the needs of the contemporary world. He
reasserted the importance of a personally liberating

---

vocational education is being undertaken by the mills,
and egalitarian interests satisfied by the library
or lecture hall. This broader perspective encourages
one to see the Yale Faculty as saying not that all
higher learning should be classical, common, preparatory, etc., but rather that the colleges' distinct
role among the educative opportunities of the era
was to undertake this particular kind of educative
effort for persons particularly concerned to avail
themselves of it. Incidentally, the fact that at
mid-century most proponents of the university did
not object to what the colleges were doing but rather
to the extent of what they were doing supports this
view.

7

education for the individual and refused to be concerned with utilitarian and professional training. Chadbourne had little interst in changing the traditional scope--either in breadth or depth--of the curriculum, but he did suggest that a study of the modern humanities rather than the usual classics might accomplish his purpose more effectively.[1]

Charles W. Eliot of Harvard, the most famous and influential reformer, was interested primarily in education as preparation, both for professional training and for effective life in the "real" world. Eliot believed that knowledge which was useful in this broad sense was liberal because it freed the individual to use knowledge effectively in some sphere of action. Since all students would not have the same role in after-college life, areas of academic endeavor would have to be selected according to individual potentialties. Eliot thus emphasized the role of electives in liberal education and was prepared to sacrifice general common humanistic knowledge to personal goals despite the fact that some of them might end up being narrowly vocational or utilitarian.[2] While the primary purpose of the elective system was to motivate the student by capturing his existing interests, it also permitted a wider course of study than the classical curriculum. Therefore, an elective curriculum could be, and Eliot expected it would be, a more liberating experience for those who wished to use it for that purpose and not for more immediate goals. In any case, the elective system became overwhelmingly popular in the last third of the nineteenth century--though not at Yale. Several factors conspired to assist this triumph of individual needs: First, existing secondary schools were not able to provide a good general education; second, the new science of psychology stressed the needs of the individual in particular methods of learning and in the selection of relevant experiences; third, the

---

[1]Thomas, The Search for a Common Learning: General Education, 1800-1960, pp. 20-30.

[2]Ibid., pp. 24-28, 34-60; Lawrence Veysey, The Emergence of the American University (Chicago: University of Chicago Press, 1965), chap. 2.

universities as institutions were developing along departmental lines according to the discipline and research interests of their faculties. This last fact affected the way professors taught in the college so that often general or liberal arts education became yet another specialized branch of study.

The rigidity of the classical curriculum defended by the Yale Faculty in 1828 lasted in New Haven for almost fifty years. The Reverend Noah Porter, elected President of Yale two years after Eliot was inaugurated at Harvard, was deeply conservative. He was not enthusiastic about the university ideal espoused at Harvard and soon embodied in the newly-founded Johns Hopkins. But competition for students and public approval forced change. In 1876, Yale introduced its first "optionals," or electives; between 1884 and 1893, the Faculty adopted a compromise curriculum, the first half of which was required, the second freely elective. At the turn of the century, under President Hadley, freshmen were, for the first time, allowed to select between "alternative" courses, but not among electives; and the Faculty simultaneously grouped the entire curriculum into three divisions, requiring a major in one and, for balance, minors in each of the other two. Shortly afterwards, the Faculty added a system of hours of distribution and concentration. Thus, by 1903, in a confusing process involving complex compromises among economic pressures, educational philosophies, and intellectual personalties, Yale had adopted a course of study which opposed depth to breadth, concentration to distribution, and specialized to general requirements in order to achieve a liberal education. A similar, but less rigorous, system would be imposed at Harvard several years later.[1]

---

[1]George W. Pierson, "The Elective System and the Difficulties of College Planning, 1870-1940," *Journal of General Education* 4 (April 1950); George W. Pierson, <u>Yale College: An Educational History: 1871-1921</u> (New Haven: Yale University Press, 1952). This history is definitive for a study of the Yale curriculum of the era.

By the end of the nineteenth century, the theory of liberal education had become so neutral as no longer to dictate any specific curriculum content. College administrators interested in liberal education now found it necessary actively to promote a common curriculum emphasizing individual liberation--two assumptions embedded in the classical curriculum that had been prevalent over many years. The label "liberal education" came to be variously applied, and the ideal conceptualized in many ways. During the 1930s Robert M. Hutchins, for example, used it in outlining an educational system with a strong metaphysical base, emphasizing careful study of the great books of the Western tradition. The Harvard faculty, after World War II, focused on the importance of advancing common human values, especially democratic citizenship. In the mid-sixties, Daniel Bell advocated coping with the explosive growth and increasing differentiation of knowledge by concentrating on the centrality of method; and, a decade later, Earl McGrath proposed a curriculum which stressed the importance of ethical issues through the study of problematic social situations. So various have the definitions and implementations of liberal education been, and so persistently and inconclusively have liberal educators reviewed them, that this fact alone is sometimes cited to show that the ideal is invalid.[1]

One succinct, influential conception had been outlined in the 1880s by A. Lawrence Lowell, a Boston lawyer who, twenty years after he wrote, became President of Harvard. Openly criticizing the elective system, Lowell defined the object of a college education to be "a general training of the mind as distinguished from the acquisition of specific information." "Strength and soundness" were to be achieved by

---

[1] Robert M. Hutchins, The Higher Learning in America (New Haven: Yale University Press, 1936); Harvard Committee, General Education in a Free Society (Cambridge: Harvard University Press, 1945); Daniel Bell, The Reforming of General Education: The Columbia College Experience in Its National Setting (New York: Columbia University Press, 1966); Earl J. McGrath, General Education and the Plight of Modern Man (Indianapolis, Ind: The Lilly Endowment, Inc., 1976).

continued hard work in depth in whatever subject
appealed, not for any specialized utilitarian purpose,
but because "this training is much more certainly
obtained by working upon a single subject until one
has thoroughly mastered its principles. . . ." This
type of mental training constituted "one-half of
an education." The other half, for "breadth and
elasticity," the purpose of which was "cultivation"
and "broad and comprehensive" views, was to be
achieved by taking courses in a wide variety of subjects. Lowell's conception of liberal education
as involving both depth of scholarship and breadth
of learning created a set of two crossed criteria,
joined together, however, in an all-too-often-
forgotten, common, liberal purpose. Lowell's scheme
was instituted at Harvard after he was inaugurated
in 1909.[1]

Despite Lowell's reforms, Harvard continued
to be identified with free electives, especially
in New Haven. Having repulsed the nineteenth century
onslaught of the elective system, Yale thereafter
continued to insist that its curriculum manifest
a structure and organization determined by the Faculty.
Throughout the twentieth century, the conceptual
foundation which underlay the Yale College course
of study was the crossed criteria of depth of scholarship and breadth of learning. However, during the
1930s, the Faculty effectively concentrated on developing a more rigorous course of study, largely accomplished by developing more challenging majors, by
instituting comprehensive examinations at the end
of the senior year, and by requiring a significant
piece of independent work known as the Senior Essay.

To briefly outline the events that are the subject matter of this study, one might begin on the
eve of World War II. As Charles Seymour became President and William C. DeVane, Dean, it became apparent that too much emphasis had been placed upon depth
of scholarship. It was time to bolster breadth of
learning. During the war the Yale Faculty debated
and then adopted a program which strengthened the
system of distribution, attempting by means of the

---

[1]A. Lawrence Lowell, "The Choice of Electives,"
in At War with Academic Trdition in America (Cambridge:
Harvard University Press, 1934), pp. 3-11.

Reforms of 1945 to preserve an appropriate breadth and unity to undergraduate study. Thus, Yale commenced the modern era trying, after the stresses of wartime, to recapture the ideal of liberal education in its course of study.[1] The University was not, however, exempt from the effects of the increasing professionalization and departmentalization of the faculty, the explosion of knowledge and the fragmentation of learning, the democratization of a variously prepared student body of differing capabilties and interests, the growth of graduate and professional schools with demanding entrance requirements, and the permeating influence of the "scientific" approach of logical positivism. For valid reasons, the concept of liberal comprehensiveness came under increasing pressure--from the demands of specialization, the research interests of the faculty, the vocational objectives of the students, graduate school interest in the mastery of specified literatures, and the practical needs of the professional schools.[2] So in the mid-fifties, a major reform of the undergraduate curriculum was proposed by President Griswold's Committee on General Education. The Committee's proposals were intended to combat the newly developed stresses upon the traditional ideal of a liberal course of study. During the Faculty debate, which led up to the Reforms of 1955, liberal education eventually came to be equated with the "non-specialized," general education which the President's Committee had proposed for freshman and sophomore years as specifically, appropriately and effectively preparatory to the specialized work of the major. This new, truncated definition of liberal education perverted the formerly avowed purposes of liberal education and made it both possible and reasonable for the Departments to fragment "non-specialized" education into a series of competing pre-specialties. Those trained in and interested in the disciplines

---

[1]Pierson, Yale: The University College: 1921-1937, chaps. 3, 9, 16, 17, 18.

[2]Teachers College Record 80 (February 1979); William C. DeVane, Higher Education in Twentieth Century America (Cambridge: Harvard University Press, 1965); Christopher Jencks and David Riesman, The Academic Revolution (Chicago and London: University of Chicago Press, 1977).

12

asserted their claim to be, and surely were, in the best position to decide just what constituted excellent preparation for their own particular and varying purposes.

At the time of the Reforms of 1945, the Yale College Faculty had also created an exceptionally successful "Planned Experiment in Liberal Education," which involved a small group of students who studied a fixed, required curriculum, philosophically coordinated and interrelated--in many ways a self-conscious attempt to recapture the virtues of an earlier era. Tracing this Experimental Program leads directly to the 1953 recommendations of the President's Committee on General Education, which were largely ignored by the Reforms of 1955. This happened because the curriculum proposals of the mid-fifties, though tied to the Experimental Program and true to the traditional search for a liberal education, were flawed in their theoretical basis and hence indefensible in the face of the continuing pressures of modern specialization. Directed Studies, as the Experimental Program had come to be known, was thereafter quickly transformed into a specialized honors programs in the humanities, an archtypical instance of the collapse of a defined liberal course of study in the face of pressures from those no longer primarily interested in education for the good life. The key point is that once the advocates of liberal education had allowed its purpose to be changed from the preparation of men for the good life, it became impossible for the faculty to define any single course of study which constituted liberal education, even in a special program.

With the traditional purpose absent and at best a sketchy philosophical basis outlined, departmental politics and an interest in departmental protection proliferated. Finally in the mid-sixties, the faculty desisted from the effort to encode the ideal and concluded that it would inevitably disagree about an appropriate common general preparation. The Faculty then acknowledged that the only possible common objective to incorporate within the course of study was a blanket provision which guarded against overspecialization. The negatively expressed distributional requirements which prevented over-concentration were accompanied by the Guidelines of 1966, which

exhorted the students to a vaguely defined liberal
education. This outcome caused no real discomfort
to the advocates of specialization, most of whom
would readily have agreed that too-narrow specialization was bad even for the dedicated specialist.
In the last analysis, the requirements of specialization had been accommodated, though the faculty hoped
not entirely at the expense of liberal education.
Yet the fact was that there remained no way to examine
a particular set of course selections, that is, an
individual student's course of study, and on that
basis alone determine whether the student was aiming
at a fulfilled liberal education or at specialized
excellence (or some lesser objective). The student's
organizing purpose was nowhere revealed, and the
traditional liberal purpose was not insisted upon
by the Faculty. This result was inevitable once
the purpose of liberal education was allowed to shift
from its traditional one to the more limited purposes
of pre-specialization. Accordingly, some observers
might conclude that, despite the Guidelines' rhetoric
which attempted to indicate otherwise, Yale had effectively abandoned the traditional conception of liberal
education.

The insights which this study hopes to offer,
and which are outlined below, challenge this conclusion. To assume that Yale now honors its liberal
ideal only rhetorically is to succumb too easily
to the temptation to equate the formal course of
study with the curriculum in the widest possible
sense. It is so much simpler to cite catalogue descriptions of courses and programs than to identify
the actual content of the students' learning.[1] One
of the key themes of this study is to show that
efforts were made at Yale to assert the liberal ideal
both in the course of study and in areas outside
the course of study. One excellent example involves
Yale's system of residential colleges--essentially
dormitories that were built in a gothic style, with
libraries, dining halls, faculty offices, common
rooms, and a master's house, all grouped around quiet,

---

[1]Lawrence A. Cremin, _Public Education_ (New York:
Basic Books, Inc., 1976); Lawrence A. Cremin, _Tradi-
tions of American Education_ (New York: Basic Books,
Inc., 1977).

14

landscaped courtyards. Thus, it will be necessary to pay close attention to the difference between, and sometimes the confusion between, the curriculum and the course of study.

A second point to note is that the ideal of a liberal education is always accepted at Yale and never overtly questioned or opposed. Thus, it is generally necessary to search further to determine whether the specific proposals made in the name of furthering liberal education are in fact liberal or illiberal. Not surprisingly, some are, and a good many are not.

A third recurring theme involves the extent to which the scientific spirit pervades Yale (and, I suspect, most other universities). Naturalism and logical positivism have made it difficult indeed to discuss purpose and view the curriculum as extending beyond the classroom. At Yale, intention becomes pertinent when curricular planning involves the creation of courses by academic specialists for non-specialist students. What actually is at issue is the purpose of the course, but since the matter of purpose is hard to discuss in empirical terms, the matter is addressed indirectly, tangentially, or not at all.

Closely allied to this is a fourth theme, the difficulty of integrating the sciences into the Yale College course of study in any meaningful way. The science Departments, convinced of the overwhelming importance of their own specialized work, have been first institutionally, then geographically, and always atmospherically, separated from the rest of the College. The scientific spirit of the era merely aids and abets the sciences' self-centeredness and their suspicion that whatever happens elsewhere at Yale is largely irrelevant. That attitude is naturally reciprocated, particularly by the humanities.

The sciences are not alone, however, in their independence from and their resistance to control by Yale College as the supposedly overriding entity with overriding interests. A fifth theme which constantly recurs involves the efforts of the Yale College Deans to counteract the faculty's orientation toward their Departments. These efforts were not

15

aided by the growth of the Faculty to the point where
it could not function as a meaningful body, nor by
departmental control of appointments and budgets,
nor by the merger of the Yale College Faculty with
the Graduate School Faculty, or by the University-
wide emphasis upon research as the vehicle for career
advancement at Yale or elsewhere. Accordingly, the
Faculty resisted all efforts to reform it by instituting separate faculties for teaching and research,
for example, or for general education and specialized
education.

The emphasis on the Departments leads to a sixth
theme, which is the extent to which defining the
required course of study involves departmental politics and maneuvering for preferred position. Establishing exact distributional categories invariably
incites the urge toward departmental advantage.
The incredible proliferation of course offerings,
and even of specialized majors, and the unwillingness
of the Faculty to decide on any basis at all which
of them were key and which not, only contributed
to this insoluble problem.

Part of the eventual fragmentation of the course
of study was due to the inability of the Faculty
to accept, agree upon, or develop any integrating
principle or philosophy. This is a seventh theme.
Interdisciplinary courses were very seldom successful,
and courses emphasizing conceptual integration were
quickly abandoned. The faculty seemed unable to
develop sustained intellectual rigor outside departmental study, and attempt after attempt had to be
abandoned. This forced the Faculty to overrely on
the system of distribution to achieve the integration
of knowledge which all agreed was key to a liberal
education but which they could find no other way
to provide. The Yale faculty, while acknowledging
the importance of making interconnections between
subjects, resisted making them for the students by
the ineffective means, as they saw it, of general
education courses. On the other hand, only rarely,
for example in the early years of the Directed Studies
program, was the faculty able effectively to assist
the undergraduate in making his own synthesis. Generally, the mechanics of the distribution system
were left alone to do the job, and all too often
it remained undone.

This leads to an eighth theme. In the interests of introducing intellectual rigor into interdisciplinary programs that were usually intended to limit departmental overspecialization or promote an integrated understanding of several fields of knowledge, members of the faculty often emphasized expensive, instructional methodology and then equated it with the liberal goals they were trying to achieve. Small seminars, comprehensive examinations, residential college discussion groups, reading lists, supervised independent work were frequently suggested in the interests of a broad liberal training. All too often, the methodology, which was not fundamentally integral to the goals of the interdisciplinary programs, was separated from the programs' objectives and harnessed, in the end, to the objectives of specialized study. Even the device of the major was not unaffected by this tendency, for if the major had once been a vehicle to promote "strength and soundness" of mind as one, but only one, of the key ingredients of a liberal education, it came to be increasingly devoted to extended study of a minute fragment of one or another of the ever-expanding disciplines.

The ninth and tenth themes are not particular to Yale. We shall follow the struggle of the Faculty to control the curriculum against outside pressures, in the face of the reality that no college dictates the previous education of its applicants nor the expectations of those who hire or admit its graduates. Yale College is inescapably caught between the high school, the graduate school, and the "real" world. Its freshmen are both under and over prepared, more or less capable. Veterans in their twenties and youngsters of sixteen arrive in New Haven together. The federal government requires ROTC courses and then decides what shall be taught in them. In planning the curriculum, the Yale Faculty must try to control a situation which is always in some absolute measure beyond its control. Accommodation is, therefore, a recurrent part of curriculum planning. So also, a tenth theme, is the necessity to negotiate in one way or another with the students who are subject to the strictures of the course of study. These negotiations reached great heights of tension and visibility in the sixties, but those troubled years had roots in earlier attempts to regulate extracurricular activities, in Admissions Office concerns about protecting programs that attracted talented

17

students, in the Faculty's increasing involvement in deciding just who would be admitted to Yale and upon which criteria. Student maturity and student motivation were of constant concern to the faculty because the course of study was necessarily affected.

Finally, we will see the extent to which liberal education has come to be seen "in reaction to" or "in contrast with," and not as advocating what really matters. To the ancient Greeks, leisure was the normal state of affairs. The only word for work was "non-leisure." To us, work is the normal state of affairs, and free time its opposite. The Greeks evaluated the conditions of life in terms of leisure, we in terms of work. Thus, the Greeks had leisure, and we have two week vacations.[1] Too often the proponents of liberal education have, in similar fashion, accepted the definitional terms of the opposition, and liberal education has been reduced to nonprofessional, non-specialized, non-utilitarian education. And true liberal education has suffered accordingly. Fortunately, there is some indication that this framework is being challenged, that a wider view of acceptable knowledge is being propounded, and that the matter of purpose is once again subject to consideration.[2] I say fortunately because if one does accept a broader view of the curriculum and a wider conception of what might constitute the course of study and for what particular purposes, it then becomes possible to suggest that Yale, and therefore others, may continue to make possible a liberal education of true breadth and real self-fulfillment.

The liberal education Yale presently offers somewhat inadvertently lies, in part, in the value system of a University dedicated to excellence in scholarship, in teaching, in civic life, and even in the extra-curricular activities that so antagonize some of the faculty. It lies, in part, in the residential college system, which gives undergraduates

---

[1] de Grazia, Of Time, Work, and Leisure, chap. 1.

[2] Douglas Sloan, "The Teaching of Ethics in the American Undergraduate Curriculum, 1876-1976," in Education and Values, ed. Douglas Sloan (New York and London: Teachers College Press, 1980).

the opportunity to know each other, some of their
instructors, and sometimes themselves. It lies,
in part, in the contributions made to the College
by other parts of the University--the art galleries,
the Music School, the architectural beauty of the
whole place--all of which teach aesthetics. It lies,
in part, in the long tradition of the centrality
of the humanities, subjects difficult to pervert
to narrow utilitarian or professional ends. It lies,
in part, in the guidance, formal and informal, of
great professors who are themselves embodiments of
the liberal education they proclaim. It lies, finally,
in the Faculty's determination that the difficulty
or impossibility of articulating a theory of liberal
education in the codes of the course of study will
not be accepted as an excuse for abandoning the traditional ideal. The detailed history which follows
should make this contention clear.

Chapter II

THE REFORMS OF 1945

Traditionally, Yale had always been self-consciously insistent upon the Faculty's structuring its undergraduate curriculum. Since the 1870s, and particularly since the end of the First World War, that ingrained structure had been whittled away at. By the early 1930s, it had virtually, but not entirely, disappeared. Intent on introducing further rigor into the course of study, the Faculty chose to concentrate first upon improving and strengthening the system of concentration, the major. The requirements which were instituted were characterized by a university outlook and certain graduate school techniques. Higher standards, increased specialization and upper-class concentration were the results. By the end of the decade, however, it had become obvious that the strengthening of the major had gone far enough and that a similar strengthening of the system of distribution was indicated. The Faculty's initial attempt to counteract the excessive importance of the major by implementing an expanded system of extensive distributional requirements was blocked by the advent of World War II. The war, which stressed Yale's insistence upon exposure to the liberal arts in previously unimaginable ways, effectively ended up strengthening the Faculty's historic devotion to its liberal ideal. Accordingly, the work of planning, refining and strengthening the liberal course of study continued undiminished during the war, which, ironically, also provided a unique opportunity to revise the whole curriculum in one sweeping change. Thus, the Reforms of 1945 are a clear indication of the depth of the Faculty's commitment to the then largely-ignored humanities and liberal arts. The Reforms of 1945 as implemented were deeply traditional in that they reaffirmed the crossed criteria of depth and breadth that had characterized the Yale curriculum for years. On the other hand, they were tremendously innovative and extensive in that the distributional categories were radically revised and the work of the major strictly limited and clearly defined.

In 1931, the only requirement that remained from a course of study that had once been totally dictated was the Faculty's insistence that every student take at least one course in each of four distributional categories: modern language, science, science with lab, and Greek, Latin or classical civilization. As the Faculty began its efforts to strengthen the major, the required 120 term-hours were replaced by 20 substantial year courses. Reading periods in junior and senior years were delivered into the hands of the various Departments. In January 1935, those same Departments were authorized to institute comprehensive examinations in the major subject, the first of which were actually taken by the class of 1937. Undergraduates were now required to plan the work of their major with the approval of the Department. In the subject of their choice, students were required to take two courses in junior year and in their senior year two further courses plus the equivalent of one course devoted to independent work. The Departments began to introduce discussion courses, seminar-style, which covered small areas of the major field with considerable intensity, and urged students into them. In December 1940, the Faculty voted to require a program of independent study for the BA degree. This meant completing a Senior Essay (previously required only of honors students) under the supervision of the major Department. The goal of this nearly decade-long reform had been

> more effective upper-class work through the mastering by every student of the field of his main interest. This mastery was to consist in part of a more complete knowledge, in part of a better interpretation of that knowledge, and in part, finally, of some exploration of the art of adding to that knowledge.

The major emerged triumphant at the close of the decade.[1]

The attempt to achieve intellectual rigor by means of strengthening the discipline of the major

---

[1]Pierson, <u>Yale: The University College: 1921-1937</u>, Chapter 16 passim; quotation from p. 353. Actually, by 1933, the two science requirements had been merged into one (with or without lab), and the student had but three distributional hurdles to surmount. The system of distribution had reached its nadir.

was rooted in the departmental organization of the Yale faculty which had been instituted during the reorganization of the University following World War I. Since that time, the Departments had grown in integrity and strength, which growth reflected the national trend toward the professionalization of academic life. It was also true that the established, core disciplines have, over time, proved a most effective way to organize knowledge so that it may be clearly conveyed and built upon. That this systematic procedure should be reflected in the undergraduate curriculum was not unreasonable, given any interest in serious intellectual pursuit.

The triumph of the major was not, however, complete conquest. Among other things, the return from Cornell of William C. DeVane, B.A. 1920, as Dean of Yale College indicated that the traditional concern with a structured liberal education was very much alive.[1] In his first report covering the academic year 1939-40, the new Dean was critical of the Departments' administration of the majors: First, DeVane felt course offerings were ill-coordinated with the comprehensive exams; second, the in-depth discussion courses were too loosely tied to the major (they covered very limited portions of the broad academic terrain which was supposedly tested by the comprehensive examination); third, the Dean was unimpressed by the Departments' counseling of students who had elected their majors. In addition to criticizing the implementation of departmentalized specialization, DeVane began to exert pressure to counteract the whole tendency. He advocated the introduction of two new interdisciplinary courses, and he addressed the need for the development of additional interdepartmental majors.[2]

---

[1]Kelley, Yale: A History, p. 394. DeVane had refused the Deanship when offered to him at the end of Angell's presidency and again when first approached by Seymour. Later Seymour asked him to define the function of the Dean and, upon receiving DeVane's reply, invited him to take the job as outlined. Correspondence in Seymour Mss., Box marked Yale College, folder marked William C. DeVane.

[2]Dean's Report, 1939-40, pp. 6, 14, 15.

Besides Dean DeVane, another forceful believer
in the liberal arts appeared on stage at the end
of the 1930s: Ralph H. Gabriel, who was, as of
January 1940, Chairman of the Course of Study Committee,
the faculty group in charge of approving specific
courses for inclusion into the undergraduate program
of study as well as for recommending broad curricular
reforms to the Faculty of Yale College. Gabriel,
an historian who eventually published a book about
Yale's past, had a broad outlook on scholarship,
believing in history and the historical approach
as an effective method for organizing interdisciplinary subject matter. He discovered like-minded individuals in the English Department, and together they
investigated cooperative ventures cutting across
the traditional departmental boundaries. The result
was a seminal course called American Thought and
Civilization, which Gabriel taught with Stanley T.
Williams of the English Department, who later joined
the Course of Study Committee which Gabriel chaired.
American Thought and Civilization had a counterpart
entitled History of England and Great Britain and
later inspired French Thought and Civilization in
the Eighteenth and Nineteenth Centuries. Thus,
Gabriel was intimately involved in the process of
introducing Yale undergraduates, for the first time,
to the systematic study of the history of ideas.
The eventual flowering of these efforts was the establishment, after World War II, of the Department of
American Studies.[1]

The story in the pre-war years of the interdisciplinary program entitled History, the Arts and
Letters is further evidence that the faculty never
entirely forgot its commitment to a structured breadth
while emphasizing specialized concentration in the
interests of academic challenge. HAL, as it was
known, touched the lives of many of the key participants in the history of the Yale curriculum and served
as the basic exemplar for much of what the Course
of Study Committee, at least, was trying to accomplish.

---

[1]Pierson, Yale: The University College: 1921-
1937, pp. 391-392. Faculty Record, 25 January 1940.
Gabriel's book was titled Religion and Learning at
Yale (New Haven: Yale University Press, 1958).

24

DeVane, for example, from the beginning of his term,[1] urged the creation of more programs like HAL.

HAL had its genesis in A. Whitney Griswold's graduate program. When this member of the class of '29 wanted to combine the study of English Literature, American Literature, and American History, a special committee was established to supervise his doctoral program. Shortly thereafter, the Department of History, the Arts, and Letters was formed; and Griswold was awarded its first Ph.D. degree in 1933. That Spring 24 sophomores enrolled as HAL honors candidates--among them Charles Seymour, Jr., son of the Yale Provost, soon to be President. HAL had numerous problems, some institutional and some administrative, most of which conspired against its freeing itself from departmental domination, but in the 1930s, the program was a lively, innovative force both in the Graduate School and in the College. Its vitality led the Faculty to vote, in the winter of 1940-41, that two or more Departments might, under supervision, establish cross-departmental majors. Whereupon an entire group of interdepartmental studies quickly came into being. The reluctance of the Faculty to abandon its traditional conception of a liberal, structured education was clear, and DeVane's urgings in this direction were apparently beginning to have some effect. The Dean had commenced his long battle against the domination of the College by the Departments of the faculty, a trend which he viewed as narrowing to student perspective and destructive to an understanding of the unity of knowledge, an understanding which he personally believed[2] to be at the heart of a liberal education.

As the decade turned, the Faculty moved toward increased emphasis upon breadth of study, which was to be accomplished by increased attention to the system of distribution. In late 1940, the Faculty voted to increase the proportion of work devoted to the major--but upon limiting conditions. The course load of seniors was reduced from five to four,

---

[1]Dean's Report, 1939-40, p. 15.

[2]Pierson, Yale: The University College: 1921-1937, pp. 393-396.

25

two of which were normally devoted to the major area, as was the one course equivalent allotted to independent study. Clearly this amounted to an increase in concentration. However, the Faculty countered this effect by authorizing, as we have seen, the introduction of cross-departmental majors, by strictly limiting the major to a maximum of two courses in both junior and senior years, and by allowing the reintroduction of term courses to encourage breadth and wider exposure in the elective area. The Course of Study Committee clearly expressed its intention that an amount of time equal to the time spent on the major be devoted to distribution, probably by requiring courses in seven categories, with five of the seven mandated courses to be completed before the end of sophomore year. The Course of Study Committee strongly urged the Departments to study how to make "their courses genuine courses in a program of general education, offering a comprehensive view of their subjects and not merely a pre-professional view."[1]

The Yale faculty was wrestling with the increasing departmentalization and professionalization of university life which was rampant. The faculty had been willing to use these forces to promote what it believed to be good, that is, the increased rigor and serious study which they felt an effective major could best provide. The problem was that, pushed to excess, concentrated work, given the limited time undergraduates had available, could result in the student's knowing a lot about very little. This result was at variance with the traditional goals of a liberal education, one of which was some understanding of the various facets of knowledge as well as their fundamental interrelationship. Having perhaps inevitably unleashed the forces of disciplined specialization, for good reasons, the faculty was now seeking some way to control those forces before they destroyed the liberal ideal which was equally or more important to a faculty that had always rejected both unorganized electives and specialized utilitarian preparation.

Dean DeVane was unmistakably on the side of balanced knowledge and understanding. He reported

---

[1]Dean's Report, 1940-41, pp. 5, 8.

to President Seymour "that a good deal of damage
has been done to our students--at least it is clear
that we have not been equipping them, during the
last eight years, with a broad view of the fields
of human knowledge." To his own opinion that the
distribution system should be strengthened, Dean
DeVane added the spur of competition. He informed
the President that Harvard had been studying Yale's
former program of distribution, by which he presumably
meant the pre-1931 curriculum which had been more
or less in effect during his own undergraduate days.
DeVane then went on to predict--and how this must
have flattered and motivated the curricular reformers--
that Harvard would very soon arrive at a modified[1]
program of distribution of its own.

A month before Pearl Harbor, the Course of Study
Committee proposed a program of distribution requiring
students to take at least one course in each of eight
fields. This requirement was to be fulfilled largely
in freshman and sophomore years. Dean DeVane commented that

> the program signalized [sic] the fact that the
> Faculty was ready to take up once again the
> direction of the student's education instead
> of leaving the management of the whole matter
> to the whims of student choice as the free elec-
> tive system (the chief proponent of which was
> Eliot of Harvard) had so disasterously done
> for American collegiate education.

The Declaration of War negated the Faculty's intention
to give direction in this particular fashion, and
it accepted instead a modified plan with distribution
in six categories. The government programs for men
in the military reserves generally incorporated four
of the six.[2]

---

[1]Ibid., p. 8.

[2]Dean's Report, 1941-42, pp. 9-12; quotation
from p. 9. The categories omitted by the armed services were (a) the classics and (b) literature, fine
arts, and music.

Yale College had necessarily to react to the events of war as they unfolded in their rapid, unpredictable fashion. There had been harbingers: More than 100 faculty members had already left to serve the government, and university students had lost the blanket deferment previously extended to them automatically. Some planning by Yale authorities had begun as early as May 1941, so that when Pearl Harbor was attacked, President Seymour immediately announced that the University (and the College) would operate on a year round schedule and award degrees after three years. Since the draft age was twenty at this time, and since the required courses could actually be completed in two years and seven months, the full-time academic schedule was a significant attempt to give the undergraduate a virtually completed education before he was drafted. At first, students above or below draft age who enlisted in the Reserves were permitted to finish their studies in the expectation that they might make higher level contributions to the war effort later on. This so-called Reserve Plan was abused in many colleges across the nation (but not apparently at Yale), and it was terminated at the end of 1942 when the draft age was lowered to eighteen. DeVane saw this change in dark terms:

> Under the Reserve Plan the University controlled the education of the student in large part; under the new program the University administered and taught studies which were prescribed by the Army and Navy. Essentially, our freedom was taken from us; or, to put it more handsomely, we gave our freedom to the great cause of our country.[1]

DeVane's analysis is particularly telling if it is realized that there were both Army and Navy programs, engineering and science programs, pre-medical programs; that all these programs had objectives which were unclearly defined but rapidly altered as war needs changed; and that the students' comings and goings were controlled by military needs and not educational goals. And all this confusion transpired in a wartime atmosphere of rationing, food shortages, and lack

---

[1] Dean's Report, 1943-44, p.1.

of transportation unknown since. By July 1943, "most of the characteristics of undergraduate life had changed or disappeared completely," as DeVane understated it.[1]

The education which Yale had been forced to provide for the armed services was anything but liberal. It was, in fact, totally utilitarian--to maximize the effectiveness of the war effort--and frequently vocational--to train engineers or interpreters. Academic work in the "purposeless" humanities was viewed as irrelevant. In short, Yale's liberal tradition and its ancient purposes were being largely if not entirely ignored. And, as might have been expected, the Yale community rose to their defense. The Corporation issued a ringing declaration in support of the liberal arts:

> The Corporation wishes to impress upon Yale graduates and upon the general public the danger of the impovrishment of the nation's mind and soul, should the less tangible values of our culture be allowed to shrivel while our energies are devoted to the task of winning a war to maintain them. Of what worth is freedom from want, if our minds be on a lower intellectual level; or freedom from fear if we have a less cultured life to defend; or freedom of speech if we have poorer thoughts to express; or freedom of religion if we bring a less enlightened faith to the worship of God?[2]

President Seymour attended a Yale College Faculty meeting and "emphasized the importance of the liberal

---

[1] Kelley, Yale: A History, pp. 396-397. Dean's Report, 1942-43, passim; quotation from p. 3. For two descriptions of Yale during World War II, see an abbreviated history by Loomis Havemeyer, The Story of Undergraduate Yale in the Second World War (New Haven: Yale University, 1960), and an informal reminiscence by Polly Stone Buck (Mrs. Norman S.), We Minded the Store: Yale Life and Letters During World War II (New Haven: Buck, 1975).

[2] Statement of the Yale Corporation, Corporation Records, 12 December 1942.

arts during the emergency,["] particularly the need
to press forward research.[1] A Committee on the Preservation of the Humanities was created, chaired by
Chauncey B. Tinker, a famous, beloved teacher and
perhaps the most prestigious member of the English
department.[2] George W. Pierson, then an associate
professor of history, made, in the dark days of December 1942, a plea that the nation "apply intelligence
as well as patriotism to our human resources." The
university was not being best used, said Pierson,
when its "distinguished talent" among faculty and
undergraduates was converted into "ordinary cannon-
fodder." Nor could the liberal university, steeped
in historic tradition, if it were once destroyed,
be merely reassembled like a machine at the war's
end. The future, Pierson alleged, was being inade-
quately considered in general, and in particular,
in this moment of immediate crisis, the "humane
studies" were, because of their vulnerability to war
pressure, being starved with serious consequences.
Little attention was being given to "a broad background and real social understanding," a condition
he viewed as an ominous trend for happier days.
There is every reason to believe that at Yale at
least this analysis was accurate.[3]

Perhaps the clearest indications of Yale's commitment to its liberal ideals are the continuing efforts

---

[1]Faculty Record, 5 November 1942.

[2]Board of Permanent Officers Record, 8 April
1943. The purpose of this committee was to focus
attention on the plight of the humanities, which
it did, among other ways, by attracting the interest
of the Educational Policy Committee of the Yale Corporation. Eight fellowships of $2500 each were estab-
lished for scholars who had completed graduate work.

[3]Dean's Report, 1942-43, pp. 2, 3; Kelley, Yale:
A History, p. 399; George W. Pierson, "Democratic
War and Our Higher Learning," Yale Alumni Magazine,
December 1942. The members of Tinker's Committee
were, originally, J. M. S. Allison, F. R. Fairchild,
F. S. C. Northrup, H. M. Peyre, and E. W. Sinott,
later joined by Professors Bellinger and Dunn. The
Committee was discharged with thanks on June 7, 1945.
See Board of Permanent Officers Record, June 7, 1945;
also Seymour Mss, folder marked Liberal Arts.

of the faculty to revise the undergraduate curriculum
to further "that vital task of training, in our day,
free, cultivated, and humane views." On May 7, 1943,
after four years' work, Professor Gabriel, on behalf
of the Course of Study Committee, reported to the
Educational Policy Committee of the Yale Corporation,
the University's board of trustees, concerning the
efforts of his group. Professor Pierson, a member
of the Committee, and Dean DeVane were also in attendance. With minor modifications, the revisions in
the course of study outlined that night became the
curriculum reforms of 1945. The key innovation was
a strengthened system of distribution, which was
intended to assure that the undergraduate obtained
a broad and integrated view of most of the fields
of knowledge. The accompanying analysis of the ills
of the existing educational system and the rationale
for the proposed reforms are indeed intriguing, particularly when considered in the light of what wartime
Yale was like, which was a long way from the tradition
of cultured leisure that at one time dominated the
liberal arts college. Professor Gabriel reviewed
"the factors that have brought the liberal arts to
their present unhappy state." He referred to Yale's
old prescribed curriculum, capped by the President's
course in moral philosophy--"a course that put the
institution's final stamp on the student. It was
intended not only to give philosophical integration
to his education but to relate that education to
the problems of life." This curriculum had been
fixed and rigid; electives were not permitted.[1]

Gabriel ascribed the rending of the fixed curriculum (which had been so thoroughly defended by
President Jeremiah Day in 1828) to an increase in
fields of knowledge, to the growing influence of
science and its tendency to undermine old values
and assumptions, and to the rise of naturalism.
The 1920s and 1930s were "a period of the relative
decline of religion and philosophy, of disillusionment
and cynicism, and of the widespread affirmation of
the doctrine of ethical relativity." More specifically, the old liberal arts curriculum was first

---

[1]Records of the Educational Policy Committee,
7 May 1943, Appendix I, p. 1.

31

challenged and then disrupted by President Eliot's elective system; and it was bastardized in the new state universities where the liberal arts college functioned to provide English and history courses at the beckoning of the utilitarian departments of these practicality-oriented institutions. What was needed was "coherence and a definite sense of goals" for the liberal arts.[1]

After four years of systematic study, the Course of Study Committee had reached the conclusion that "coherence is not primarily a matter of curriculum arrangement, though that is necessary, but is rather an aspect of a particular student's education." Gabriel did not elaborate on the meaning of the term "aspect," though one is tempted to think that it may have meant the quality and thoughtfulness with which the particular student's curriculum was arranged. This oversight left hanging the question of just why the broad coherent pattern prescribed by the Course of Study Committee (or for that matter any other) would provide the desired aspect of coherence which constituted the liberality of a liberal education. Accordingly, it necessarily became the responsibility of the student to find and incorporate that aspect within his educational goals, which in turn meant that the student was left to establish his own purpose. If that purpose were narrow and specialized, very little in what the Committee identified as its central principle would alter it:

> In a liberal arts education the necessities of the overall education of the particular student must control. Education must be tailormade and fitted to its particular possesor. The principle combines both flexibility and control. The weakness of the old classics curriculum was its lack of flexibility. The weakness of the elective system was lack of control.

---

[1]Ibid., p. 2. President Seymour had on a number of occasions shown that he understood the virtues of the classical curriculum: First, the hard work of mastering the languages instilled discipline; second, studying the thought of the ancients gave perspective; third, concentration on these authors developed a sense of mastery.

The governing principle applied to the curriculum meant "the development of a coherent educational pattern, or patterns, with definite and easily understandable goals." Such a coherent pattern involved "the development of a program that insists upon distribution of the student's work through several disciplines, concentration in his last two years in a major field, and independent work in conjunction with an aspect of his major field." The governing principle of control also meant that "the faculty must, through its Course of Study Committee, assume active, continuous, and effective supervision of course offerings . . . the departments should be service organizations providing the courses asked for."[1]

Dean DeVane's report to the Educational Policy Committee was more pragmatic and less philosophical in tone than Professor Gabriel's. After his discussion of the importance of integrated distribution, of most interest is his analysis of the shortcomings of education at the high school level. These institutions, he claimed, had been "grossly misled" by "soft educators," an occurrence which DeVane blamed on John Dewey, or at least on his disciples. The Dean did not mention that the insistence upon student-centered education which permeated the new program of liberal education he was recommending, was thoroughly Deweyian and part of a philosophical tradition stretching back to Rousseau.[2] DeVane criticized

---

[1] Ibid., pp. 2-3. The program recommended by the Course of Study Committee did nothing, it may be observed, to address the full range of Gabriel's excellent historical analysis of the reasons for the breakdown of a coherent curriculum. For example, no serious provision was made for the ever increasing number of new, combined, or subdisciplines and the interests of younger professors in developing new courses covering their subject matter.

[2] Dewey, Democracy and Education, particularly Chapter 9. On the other hand, DeVane received an August 12, 1943 letter from Clyde M. Hill, Professor of Education in the Graduate School, which was very Deweyian in tone, emphasizing problem-based education and the importance of curricular relevance to the

the high schools' failure to teach "the fundamental disciplines and tools necessary to further education." College administrators today and at least as far back as the early days of Eliot at Harvard have made the same complaint and tried to force this responsibility downward onto the secondary schools; DeVane was no exception.[1]

During the war, Yale had had firsthand experience with those missing fundamentals. Of the men sent to Yale by the Armed Forces, the insider's rule of thumb was that only 10 percent would have made it in normal times. Trainees assigned to the Engineering School all too frequently required special tutoring in math; the absence of competence in foreign tongues was scandalous, though Yale emerged as a leader in solving this problem; and at the most basic level of all, the standardized test scores were markedly lower. When Yale first administered the required National Examinations, the collective ego of its teaching staff was badly bruised by comparisons

---

student's immediate problems. Hill wrote of the proposed reforms, "I fear, however, that many of the seeds in the general preparatory work in the first two years fall on barren ground because students fail to see any possible relationship between the things they are expected to know and the things that really concern them." DeVane scribbled "yes" in the margin. Also, DeVane acknowledged the debt of the Scholars of the House program to the "so-called progressive movement."

[1]Records of the Educational Policy Committee, 7 May 1943, Appendix II. DeVane defined the missing basic tools as:
"1) the ability to write, speak, and read English
2) the ability to deal in mathemtics, the basis of science and engineering
3) the ability to speak and read a foreign language."
The Dean also stressed the necessity for breadth in the student's education, the necessity for guidance, the necessity for concentration, and the necessity for independent study.

of Yale's scores with those of other colleges. Too
late Yale realized that vastly more students should
have been flunked out of the wartime program, or
never admitted in the first place.[1]

Both Gabriel and DeVane pointed out to the Educational Policy Committee that the health of the
liberal arts at Yale depended, among other things,
upon close collaboration between the colleges and
the schools. DeVane concentrated on the practical
necessity of their interdependence, a reality which
the new program accommodated by permitting the antici-
pation of distributional requirements, particularly
those assuring the acquisition of basic tools. Significantly, Yale's concern with a regeneration of
the liberal arts was in this respect clearly rooted
in a broad perspective. On the other hand, one may
doubt that DeVane and Gabriel fully realized, despite
their wartime experience with the difficulties involving basic studies, the extent to which the democratization of the Yale student body would, after World
War II, challenge their conception of a liberal curriculum. For the problem of inadequate preparation
was basically but one symptom of a far larger problem.
The pluralistic society beyond the familiar New
England prep schools was not agreed about what was
in fact the content of proper preparation, and the
differing academic goals were not always attained
with equal accomplishment, which was partially a
result of the unequal aptitude of students. When

---

[1]Dean's Report, 1943-44, pp. 5-12. DeVane commented, "we discovered that quite a few of our
trainees had never gone beyond commercial arithmetic,
and the great majority had had only one year of high
school algebra, and that had been taken several years
earlier and had been long forgotten" (p. 7). DeVane
also commented, "It is not too much to say that the
work done in the languages . . . at Yale has been
a revelation. . . . The intensive method . . . was
first developed in its modern form at Yale, and bids
fair to become the standard method for beginning
the study of a modern foreign language" (p. 11).
For statistics on low test scores, see p. 7.
Havemeyer, Undergraduate Yale in the Second
World War, passim.

these variously prepared students arrived at Yale, often with differing interests as an added challenge, it would be difficult to design a curricular system which would stress commonly held values and broad concepts of knowledge without ignoring the differences among students, thereby boring some and overchallenging others. Still, in the interests of efficient education, the most effective, and probably the sole approach, was to concentrate on the undeniable interdependency with the secondary schools. Eventually, President Griswold, following this thrust, would participate in the project known as the School and College Study of General Education, which resulted in the report General Education in School and College, which in turn led Griswold in 1953 to appoint his own President's Committee on General Education at Yale.[1]

The reforms which Gabriel, DeVane and Pierson proposd to the Committee on Educational Policy occasioned little discussion, for the Committee adjourned before two hours elapsed. There was no disagreement. That a major reform should be proposed at all at chaotic wartime Yale, its civilian enrollment shrunk to 565, shows the depth of that institution's historic commitment to liberal education.[2] On the other hand, assuming that humane studies, the liberal arts, and general education somehow did survive, those interested in their advancement had a grand opportunity. They were energized by the wartime challenge to liberal education, but piecemeal reform was frustrated by the military's virtually complete control over the College curriculum. After the war, planned, thorough reform would be possible as never before. The Course of Study Committee would face a tabula that was more or less rasa and face it with the knowledge, as DeVane put it, that at war's end, "no self-respecting university or college could afford to

[1]Pres. Report, 1952-53, reprinted in A. Whitney Griswold, Essays on Education (New Haven: Yale University Press, 1954), p. 156; William C. DeVane, "American Education After the War," Yale Review, Autumn 1943, pp. 34-36; William C. DeVane, "Changes in the Curriculum," Yale Alumni Magazine, December 1945.

[2]Kelley, Yale: A History, p. 402.

find itself without a brand-new, novel, and colorful new program of studies."[1] At Yale, as at Harvard and the University of Chicago, the discontinuity in the continuous changing of the curriculum caused by the war made possible a radical revision which at Yale happened to be typically conservative, rooted as so often before in the tried and true.

At the same time that the Course of Study Committee was developing the 1945 Reforms, it was deeply involved in outlining a program known as Studies for Returning Servicemen, Yale Studies for short. Close parallels developed between the two (Professor Gabriel ended up as Director of Yale Studies), and the rationale for Yale Studies, which originated in Yale's patriotic concerns, helps to illuminate the intentions of the reformers. Yale Studies was intended to be a program of great flexibility, an individualized regimen recognizing individual aspirations, individual war experience, and individual levels of previous education. Counseling was of prime concern, particularly if the physical or mental health of the returning servicemen required special treatment. Yale Studies was designed to deal with those who had had no college experience and those who had nearly graduated, those who had attended Yale and those who had not, those who had career objectives clearly in mind as well as those who wanted to cast around. The overall aim was to assist the veteran by giving him the appropriate knowledge to make the transfer from the regimented world of military existence to the life of intelligent choice led by "free, self-reliant, responsible citizens of a democracy." Yet such a program was not, above all, to be a laissez-faire collection of electives selected more or less intelligently by the student himself. Yale insisted on a Program of Orientation:

> The present social and political order must be understood in the long perspective of history. The equally long striving of man to shape events to his own ends must be known and appreciated, as well as the creative expression of human aspirations, ideals and faith in the forms of art, philosophy and religion. All this varied

---

[1]Dean's Report, 1945-46, p. 2.

37

knowledge has to be offered with some measure
of philosophical unity. A program of orientation
is necessary, a program of the organization
of knowledge wherein the fields of knowledge
are studies [sic] in systematic perspective.[1]

There follow, as a guide to the program and
method of Yale Studies, intriguing considerations
on the nature of a liberal education:

> The individual has to school himself by learning
> what the experience of civilized mankind has
> treasured and passed on as cultural heritage--
> the impressive body of rational sciences, the
> sciences of Nature, man and society, and the
> creations of imagination and reason in art,
> literature, ethics, philosophy and religion.
> The self-organization of an individual's mind
> will take place through following a balanced
> and comprehensive organization of studies of
> what is thus worth while in our tradition of
> civilization. It is the contact with reason
> and genius in such well-tried good things and
> great things, the things man has long strug-
> gled to acquire and preserve, that elicits the
> spark of independent mind and originality in
> the individual, that sets him off to ask ques-
> tions of his own and to go about solving them
> in his own way and thus to advance in learning
> and in the power to take care of himself in
> this world."[2]

The vehicle for transmitting the key elements of
this liberal education was to be a full year course,
required of every Yale Studies student. The fields
of knowledge were to be looked at from two systematic
perspectives: philosophical and historical. Lectures
were to carry the brunt of systematizing, and discussion groups were to assure the interaction between
the students and the material. The whole was to
secure "a balanced understanding and judgment" and
achieve a comprehension of the world and man." The

---

[1] Dean's Report, 1942-43, Appendix IV, pp. 2-
3.

[2] Ibid., p. 3.

38

first term was to be uniform in content; the second might accommodate special interests. Naturally the professors were to be "men of maturity and distinction."[1]

As it turned out, most of the servicemen admitted or readmitted to Yale chose to pursue the standard course of study. The collective decision by the veterans, with more experience than the usual crop of freshmen, to invest their time, effort and money in the normal Yale program is in itself testimony to their belief in the importance of a complete liberal education as well as a Yale degree. But equally significant is the fact that Yale was determined that in no case, no matter what the circumstances, no matter how justified the pressures, no student, not one, should graduate without some exposure to the liberal arts. Great principles are sometimes hung on little hooks; it is the consistency with which they are hung that gives them importance and validity.[2]

When listing the causes for the decline of the classical curriculum for the Educational Policy Committee, Professor Gabriel had first mentioned an increase in the fields of knowledge. The war had exacerbated this trend with which the Course of Study Committee had to deal. In addition to the usual accretion of courses, whole new areas of expertise had to be incorporated in the curriculum. An excellent instance is Foreign Area Studies. Dating back to the late 30s, Foreign Area Studies combined, as Graduate School programs, the study of a foreign country and its culture--artistic, historic and social

---

[1]Ibid., pp. 6-11; Pres. Report, 1943-44, pp. 10-11.

[2]Report of the Director, Yale Studies for Returning Servicemen, 1946-47, Yale Archives. Between 1944, when Yale Studies was opened, and the Fall of 1947, when the program was discontinued, only 517 undergraduates were enrolled in some academic capacity. During the academic year 1946-47, there were only 77 men registered as Special Students in Fall term and but 62 in the Spring.

scientific--together with fluent competency in its foreign tongue. Even before the war, student interest in foreign affairs was quickening. After Pearl Harbor, the practical advantages of these programs quickly became apparent to a nation starved for anyone who knew something fairly substantial about the far-off places it was fighting. Foreign Area Studies invaded the undergraduate curriculum during the war, when Yale College gave regular credits for the program's intensive language courses which the military mandated. Later the Yale Faculty tried a two-term experiment within the College itself: French, German and Spanish were to be taught by the new intensive method. At war's end, this experiment was extended yet another year.[1]

As Foreign Area Studies burgeoned, they were presided over by A. Whitney Griswold. Their wartime utility quickly ascertained, the question became whether to and, if so, how to incorporate them as part of peacetime Yale. President Seymour appointed a committee, which Griswold chaired, and that committee not unexpectedly recommended the continuation of the Area Studies both as undergraduate electives and as undergraduate majors. These recommendations turned out to be entirely compatible with the objectives of the Course of Study Committee.[2] Yale had, during the war, considerable experience, first, with the language illiteracy of the American high school graduate; and second, with the efficacy of intensive verbal-auditory instruction in enabling an individual to reach communicative fluency in a foreign tongue. The first experience heightened the Committee's resolve that a liberally educated man be exposed to "the true objects of language study, the literary and cultural values of a foreign language." The second experience seemed to show that a better methodology had been found to achieve this goal. Unfortunately, it became apparent to the faculty after the war that the breakthrough intensity of the wartime effort could not be sustained in conjunction with

---

[1] Faculty Record, 8 June 1944 and 7 June 1945.

[2] Report of the President's Committee on Foreign Area Studies, 18 October 1944, Yale Archives.

other academic pursuits. There were too few hours
in the day. Therefore, the modern language requirement had to be reduced--to achieving the level of
basic competency. Even the exciting new teaching
techniques could not bridge the gap between available
time and the high level of fluency needed for effective access to the literature and culture of a foreign
civilization. The faculty was forced to rely on
<u>encouraging</u> students who had completed the basic
course requirement "to make use of the language in
courses in literature, area courses, in science,
or research in the humanities." This uneasy compromise ended up as the distributional requirement in
foreign languages.[1]

---

[1]Report of the President's Committee on Modern
Foreign Languages, 15 May 1944, Yale Archives. Many
statements about curriculum reform in this period
involve confusion about which studies were instrumental (that is, "basic tools") and which were desired
goals in themselves. Mathematics was often presumed
to encourage "clear, concise reasoning," though it
may be no more effective than a concise critique
of the <u>Mona Lisa</u>. Even when the broadest categories
were sometimes conceived as instrumental (for example,
the study of history to give temporal perspective),
there was little proved connection between subject
matter and the goal. The rationale for the study
of foreign language particularly collapsed into these
contradictions. If the end goal of language study
was knowledge of a foreign culture (which to be maxi-
mally worthwhile had to have the immediacy only a
knowledge of its language could bring), then bare
competence was but a way stage to that end. As late
as May 1944, the Course of Study Committee was reaffirming that the purpose of the modern language
requirement was "to offer the student a facility for
interpretative reading in foreign literature." But
since it was impractical to achieve that goal, basic
competency had been made to sustitute, which made
the purpose of reaching the less-challenging goal
dubious indeed. Unfortunately, requiring the lesser
objective tended to cast doubt on the larger goal,
which in turn may explain, in part, why languages
in general have been so challenged in recent years.
For an excellent analysis of this whole problem with
reference to the Harvard Committee's <u>General Education
in a Free Society</u>, see P. H. Hirst, "Liberal Education
and the Nature of Knowledge," in <u>Education and Reason</u>,

The increase in the Yale College program of study occasioned by the incorporation of Foreign Area Studies into the curriculum was minor compared to that occasioned by a high level, institutional reorganization of the University. In 1943, Charles H. Warren, long-time Dean of the Sheffield Scientific School, perhaps influenced by his pending retirement, perhaps by the coming Yale College curricular reforms, perhaps by the passage of time, or perhaps by all three, proposed, with some bitterness and a sense of regret, to abolish the Scientific School as an undergraduate entity and "let Yale College administer all undergraduate education." By 1945, this had come to pass.[1]

Over the years, the Shefield Scientific School, essentially an undergraduate organization, had operated parallel to, and in fractious rivalry with, Yale College. In the past, it had attracted, in addition to scientists, many candidates who were not interested in the classical curriculum and its remnants or who were unable or unwilling to fulfill the Yale College Latin entrance requirement, which had endured until 1931. The curricular distinction between the two had never been entirely clear cut, for Yale College had always offered science courses and even required them. On the other hand, the Scientific School had once offered a "select" course, which attracted those who wished not to specialize in science but to emphasize it within a broad cultural and educational context. At one time, more "Sheff" students were enrolled in this program than in any other. In 1920, the Corporation had instituted the Common Freshman Year, as, among other things, an attempt to bridge the gap, social and traditional, between "Ac" and "Sheff." Thereafter, the sense

_____

by R. F. Dearden, P. H. Hirst, and R. S. Peters (London: Routledge & Kegan Paul, 1972), pp. 3-9.

[1]Pres. Report, 1943-44, pp. 18-20; Dean's Report, 1942-43, pp. 25-26; Dean of the Sheffield Scientific School Report, 1942-43, pp. 8-23; Board of Permanent Officers Record, 12 October 1944. The early history of the Sheffield Scientific School is recounted in Russell H. Chittenden, History of Sheffield Scientific School (New Haven: Yale University Press, 1928). See also Kelley, Yale: A History, and Pierson, Yale: The University College: 1921-1937.

42

of duplication and unnecessary rivalry grew with
the years, and as late as the Second World War, DeVane,
with an eye to the work of the Course of Study Committee, had refused to "relinquish the vast and important fields of science" from Yale College's undergraduate programs. Interested as he was in a comprehensive liberal training, there was no other position
for DeVane to take.

The merger of "Sheff" into the College gave
impetus to developing more and better science majors
in Yale College since the College science faculty,
which was weak, would be strengthened by the addition
of the Scientific School professors. But to understand what actually happened, it is helpful to make
two conceptual distinctions. Scientists and humanists
may be distinguished rather readily on the basis
of their academic specialties, and a second, unrelated
distinction may be made between any scholar interested
in the broad ramifications of his work for the purposes of liberal education and one concerned merely
with his narrow specialty. In concept, there is
no reason to believe that scientific scholars are
any more or less interested in a liberal education
than, say, art historians. Yale's own early scientists, for instance, were liberally educated and
interested; but, over the years, the separate distinctions had blurred until Yale was, somewhat arbi-
trarily and certainly unthinkingly, divided into
two categories rather than the more conceptually
accurate four, into scientific scholars who were
considered specialists and humanist scholars who
tended to view themselves as generalists.[1] This
odd, conceptually ill-founded division cropped up
in the thinking of the Course of Study Committee,
which, dominated as it was by humanists, intensified
its determination to assert the values of a broad
liberal education in the face of the challenge now
implicit in the influx of numerous "scientific specialists." The three new science courses, Science I,
II, and III, which were to be developed as part of
the 1945 reforms can be seen as a response to the
opportunities to make science more meaningful to

---

[1]This distinction endures at modern Yale. See
A. Bartlett Giamatti, "'Nature Justly Viewed': Yale's
Scientific Heritage," Yale Alumni Magazine, October
1979, p. 19 et seq.

the traditional humanist student in Yale College. On the other hand, they may also be seen as overt resistance to the premature specialization supposedly encouraged by the "illiberal" scientist. The three new science courses, two of which were required of every student, were intentionally designed as general education courses for non-science majors. The scientifically inclined, however, were not offered special courses in the humanities. They, like the returned veterans in Yale Studies, had to have faith that "contact with reason and genius" would "elicit the spark of independent mind" and cause their intellects "to advance in learning."[1]

The assumption was that the liberal education of the young scientist would automatically benefit from the present course offerings of the supposed humanist-generalists of the Yale College Faculty. A corollary assumption was that the existing introductory courses in the sciences were inappropriate for the purposes of a liberal education. Put to the test, the science Departments were not prepared to accept either assumption. Thus they were forced into the easily assumed position of opposed outsiders, championing science Department objectives with little or no regard for the liberal purposes from which they had been excluded by the Course of Study Committee. When DeVane, for example, asked if the new science courses would be acceptable as minor subjects in pre-med programs or as prerequisites in the scientific majors such as chemistry, the answer was not long in coming. The science Departments felt they would not, and the Faculty decided that a full year's work in chemistry or physics could be substituted for the Science I course and that a pre-med student could satisfy both distributional requirements in science by taking introductory biology and introductory chemistry.[2]

---

[1] William C. DeVane, "American Education After the War," Yale Review, Autumn 1943, pp. 42-43.

[2] 1945 Report of the Course of Study Committee, Yale Archives, p. 22; Faculty Record, 29 March 1945. Permission of the Dean was required. The Course of Study Committee debated lowering the two science requirements to one but worried that in doing so they "might not expect to receive the full cooperation

Seen broadly, and more broadly than the participants saw it at the time, what was at issue was the
purpose of the introductory science courses. The
science Departments saw them as prerequisites for
the long and demanding, necessarily carefully graduated study of the particular science at hand. The
making of a scientist was a difficult task, for which
there was insufficient time anyway. The humanists
of the Yale College faculty saw the new science
courses as an appropriate opportunity to expose students to the sciences as part of their general education. One single course could not, however, be organized to serve both purposes. But rather than argue
about their purpose, which the humanist-generalists
probably felt ill-at-ease about in the "scientific"
environment of the era if indeed they formulated
it at all, the Yale College traditionalists ended
up discussing the quality of instruction, the profes-
sorial rank of the instructor and the narrowness
of his interests. That they had made different regulations in their own areas of expertise did little
to add to their creditability among the scientists.

The reforms finally adopted by the Yale College
Faculty in the Spring of 1945 to become effective
for the next year's freshman class were extraordinar-
ily comprehensive. During the two years which had
elapsed since the basis of the reforms had been outlined, the Course of Study Committee had worked
intently with the various Departments to develop and
improve courses which would fit the revised requirements. DeVane described the new curriculum as "no
routine revision or adjustment, such as we see in
the history of the College once every five years,
but rather a major reform which, in my opinion, has
established the basis for a sound liberal education
for the next half century."[1] The Course of Study
Committee was supposed to have read every important

---

of the departments of science." See CSC Minutes,
13 July 1944. For a complete citation of the present
location of the Course of Study Committee Minutes
(abbreviated throughout as CSC Minutes), see Bibliography.

[1]Dean's Report, 1944-45, p. 1.

book on education, ancient and modern, and it acknowledged its debt to Robert Hutchins, Stringfellow Barr, the progressive colleges, Charles W. Eliot, Alfred North Whitehead, and John Dewey.[1] Placing the Reforms in Yale's history, the Committee declared that:

> over the last sixty years the curriculum of
> the College has emphasized successively: first,
> elective opportunity; second, planned breadth
> and distribution; and finally, concentration
> in the major field . . . [the 1945 Reforms]
> have struck a reasonable balance between these
> elements, and have provided plans which will
> preserve our gains in past decades and yet bring
> further order to a situation which has been
> in danger of becoming chaotic.[2]

The "truly distinguished and distinctive program of studies" effectively encompassed three programs: the Standard Program for perhaps 85 percent of the undergraduates; the Scholars of the House Program for a handful of exceptionally mature and able students interested in pursuing totally independent work in their last two years; and an Experimental Program, testing a controlled and integrated education for two score undergraduates. The objective of the Standard Program was "to provide the student, in school and College, with the fundamental studies, to acquaint him with the great fields of knowledge, to make him a reasonably competent person in a limited field, and to bring him to that maturity which ought to distinguish the young graduate of Yale." The program had four aspects: basic studies, distributional requirements, major requirements, and requirements for summer reading. The three basic studies were English, Modern Language and Systematic Thinking. The need for competence in English was propounded without explanation. The required proficiency in Modern Language was justified by the modern world's need for men free from "national provincialism" who had access to "the culture and civilization of another

---

[1]1945 Report of the Course of Study Committee, pp. 4-5.

[2]Ibid., p. 4.

great people." The Systematic Thinking requirement emphasized "the need of the student for the ability to think clearly and correctly in symbols and abstractions." This capacity was said, from a rather elite point of view, to distinguish "the rational citizen from the masses of men in a democracy." The Committee acknowledged predilections among various kinds of students in this skill and provided for a choice among mathematical reasoning, logical reasoning, and linguistic reasoning to be attained by courses in math, philosophy, or linguistics. Each of these courses was seen as instrumental since the emphasis was to be placed not upon content, but upon "formal training in the systematic processes of . . . abstract thought." In developing this section of the Standard Program, the Committee did not address the confusing relationship between the subject matter of a course and those intellectual or personal characteristics it was intended to develop, an oversight which deprived the Committee of the opportunity to comment upon the role of the student's purpose in effecting a liberal education.[1]

The second aspect of the Standard Program was the program of distribution, six categories in number, designed to introduce the student to the great fields of knowledge: first, the science of the inanimate world; second, the science of living organisms; third, the social sciences (except psychology, which was classified with the study of living organisms); fourth, the classics; and fifth, literature, music and art. The sixth distributional requirement was designed to show that "knowledge for all its convenient compartmentalization is essentially one piece, as is the life which supports that knowledge." The disciplines which were expected to convey this realization were philosophical, historical and synoptic. As with the basic skill of Systematic Thinking, this distributional requirement, which was normally to be fulfilled in junior or senior year, was intended to be instrumental, "to pull together the student's learning and show him how syntheses may be made in the modern world." Parenthetically, the Committee, perhaps aware that something in this requirement might resemble a remnant of the old-time moral

---

[1]Ibid., pp. 5-6.

philosophy course, denied any intention to indoctrin-
ate. The overt teaching of values was anathema in
a modern university.[1]

As a defense against "cramping the student's
freedom," and this freedom apparently meant freedom
to pursue his present interests, the Committee made
four points: first, that basic and/or distributional
requirements would be largely fulfilled in freshman
or sophomore year; second, they could be anticipated
by competent work in secondary school; third, that
there were considerable choices among specific courses
in each required category; and fourth, that a prerequisite for any major was quite likely to lie within
one of the distributional requirements. The defensive
tone of these paragraphs indicates the extent to
which the 1945 Reforms were conceived as reforms
against over-concentration in the major field rather
than as a vehicle of liberal education as a viable
end in its own right. Less obviously, perhaps, the
tone also shows the extent to which the breadth and
distribution requirements as well as the basic requirements were conceived as preparatory to the major
rather than as a continuing, balanced counterpoint.[2]

Next, the Committee turned to the requirements
for the major, most of which were, as we have seen,

---

[1]Ibid., pp. 6-8. DeVane from the beginning
realized that any attempt at integration would have
to be either theological or philosophical. He may
have been influenced by Charles W. Hendel, a member
of the Course of Study Committee who was Chairman
of the Philosophy Department and held the chair in
Moral Philosophy. Hendel, who minimized, unlike
Hutchins, the role of metaphysics, believed the purpose of philosophy was to interpret the other forms
of knowledge and thus to be contemporaneous. This
view permeated the Directed Studies Program, whether
or not Hendel was personally responsible. See his
Remarks at Philosophy Club, 31 October 1940, Carroll
Mss, Box 2, folder marked Minutes 1939-41.

[2]1945 Report of the Course of Study Committee,
pp. 8-9; DeVane, "American Education After the War,"
p. 45.

either initiated or strengthened during the 30s.
The war, the Committee surely knew, had eroded some
of these requirements. In early 1943, the Faculty
had allowed the hard-pressed Departments to drop
either the required Senior Essay or the required
departmental exam. Later the same year, men in
uniform--and that was the vast majority--were specifically excused from completing the Senior Essay.
The new regulations reasserted the desirability of
independent work and comprehensive exams. The rule
of thumb was that about half the student's career
was to be devoted to his major, and no student was
permitted to allocate more than three course equiva-
lents to his major in either junior or senior years.
The Committee did not confuse the concept of majoring
with departmentalized specialization, which was coun-
teracted in four ways: first, by the Scholars of
the House Program, which permitted total, if supervised, freedom to make any serious investigation;
second, by interdepartmental majors, which were encouraged; third, by allowing students in the Standard
Program to enroll in the major fields of the Experimental Program; lastly, by permitting the Departments
to require but a single prerequisite in the work
of freshman and sophomore years. In short, the Committee was serious about distinguishing concentrated
work from overspecialization: "The object of concentration is to inculcate the great intellectual virtues
of thoroughness and judgment and to give the student
the sense of mastery which he needs for his further
development," said DeVane.[1]

Perhaps the least known aspect of the 1945
Reforms was the provision for mandatory summer reading.
This requirement had antecedents in a long history
of "reading periods," which over the years were used
or abused, favored by this Department and ignored
by that, suited to English but not, for example,
to chemistry. In concept, the reading periods were
part of the faculty's continuing struggle to raise
academic standards. The war experience with year-
round education had also taught the faculty that

---

[1]Faculty Record, 26 January 1943 and 5 August
1943; 1945 Report of the Course of Study Committee,
p. 9; quotation from DeVane, "American Education
After the War," pp. 45-46.

there were some benefits to be gained from year-round
student effort. Accordingly, all students in each
of their three summer interstices, were expected
to read eight or so books from required lists and
be examined soon after the opening of the Fall term.
For the period between freshman and sophomore year,
the list was specified by the Faculty, presumably
by the Course of Study Committee through the Dean's
Office, and the following two years, by the student's
major Department.[1]

The willingness of the Course of Study Committee
to deliver the second and third of the required reading lists into the hands of the Departments reflects
the difficulty of developing meaningful lists of
suitable titles, as well as the difficulties caused
by the absence of an appropriate academic unit to
enforce the requirement, administer tests, and record
the grades. Still, the "departmentalization" of
the reading lists is evidence of the extent to which
the Committee envisioned the distribution system
as preliminary to concentrated majoring rather than
as a continuing commentary upon it for other purposes.
Were the Committee's view otherwise, it might at
least have specified what was once considered, to
wit: that Departmental reading lists be used (while
the student was majoring) to promote liberal breadth
and general perspective, said lists to be subject
to the approval of the Faculty as a whole.

The ground work had been well laid for the
Reforms of 1945, which had been nearly five years
in the making. They had the full support of the
President, the Provost, the Dean and the Corporation.
Fresh from the experience of wartime and war's dis-
respect for the liberal arts, the Yale Faculty

---

[1] 1945 Report of the Course of Study Committee,
pp. 9-10. Exhibit G, p. 29, lists a sample of twenty
titles in five categories: English and American
Literature; European Literature; Biography and History;
Studies of Society; and Science. The student was
required to read eight titles, at least one and no
more than two from each group. The minutes of the
committee that developed the list of twenty titles
are, unfortunately, not available to historians or
political scientists.

ringingly reaffirmed the traditional ideal of a "sound liberal education." The Faculty coped with the first ripples of the coming wave of post-war students of a new type by instituting a rudimentary system of advanced distributional credits, that is, exemptions from the distributional requirements. The curriculum was broadened to incorporate whole new areas of knowledge, some of which fitted more easily into the new distributional scheme than others. Although an Experimental Program was endorsed, the Standard Program conservatively continued to rely upon the traditional but tricky balance between breadth of learning and depth of scholarship. On the whole, the new curriculum was an effective vehicle to counteract the pre-war trend toward specialization. Yet the failure to bond the science Departments onto the liberal arts College would cause unforeseen problems as would the stress which the expansion of the curriculum would place upon the integration of knowledge, that key category in the distributional scheme. And no one clearly foresaw the far-reaching effects of a larger, more democratic, more pluralistic student body, the mere size of which would, within a scant two years, force the first revisions in the curriculum arrangements that DeVane had predicted would last for half a century.[1]

---

[1]Pres. Report, 1942-43, pp. 12-16; Pres. Report, 1943-44, pp. 31-32, including a nice quotation from Cardinal Newman.

Chapter III

A PLANNED EXPERIMENT IN LIBERAL EDUCATION

The Experimental Program, which was adopted by the Faculty at the same time as the Reforms of 1945, was a deliberate effort to recapture many of the lost virtues of the classical curriculum. Proponents of the Experimental Program, which quickly came to be called Directed Studies once it was implemented and in operation, were primarily interested in creating an integrated, coordinated four-year course of study. Thus, the Experimental Program was intended to revitalize the liberal purpose of the major as well as emphasize the integrating functions of the system of distribution. Clearly identifying the principle of philosophical integration would automatically incorporate a value scheme stressing wholeness of understanding. To accomplish this worthy result, those who designed the Experimental Program were prepared to limit severely the scope of the subject matter to be covered in Directed Studies courses and ignore many of the non-core disciplines. They were also prepared to ignore most individual differences in aptitude, preparation, and interest among the 15-20 students who would enroll in the experiment--all in the interests of a fixed, and therefore necessarily common, curriculum. This approach, like that of the old classical curriculum, was intended to promote common understanding and common values among educated men.

The early successful years of Directed Studies were an exciting and stimulating education for both instructors and students. But the program, which continued to be opposed by many among the faculty, shortly began to encounter difficulties. Philosophical integration, the common intellectual experience, and the purposefully broad orientation became harder and harder to sustain. New subjects insisted upon inclusion into the Directed Studies curriculum, making philosophical integration, or integration of any kind, more and more difficult. As interest and enrollment in Directed Studies increased, forcing all the program's students, who came from varied backgrounds with unequal preparation, to cover identical material made less and less sense. And it became more and more obvious that Directed Studies' claim to be adequate preparation for most any departmental major was subject to effective challenge. In addition, Directed Studies was financially strapped, further proof of its anomalous position in a departmentalized University. Despite all its troubles, however, Directed Studies was sufficiently promising to serve those in the College who were most interested in liberal education as a model for the major reforms which were eventually proposed by the 1953 President's Committee on General Education.

Directed Studies as it had developed was, however, markedly altered from the original Experimental Program; for Directed Studies ended up functioning as a two year program whereas the Planned Experiment in Liberal Education had envisioned a four-year program. For reasons insufficiently examined, and with unforeseen consequences, the last two years of the Experimental Program were never implemented as designed. Thus, Directed Studies ended up not by incorporating majors of its own, but by being controlled by the departmental majors it was necessarily forced to feed—and accommodate. The varying requirements of those "outside" majors eventually fragmented the Directed Studies curriculum beyond recognition and altered the original conception beyond salvage.

The "Planned Experiment in Liberal Education" was written by George W. Pierson on behalf of the conception's initiators, including Thomas C. Mendenhall and Maynard Mack. The experiment's roots went back to the 1828 Report to the Yale Faculty and beyond, to the trivium and quadrivium, and to their roots in the philosophy of ancient Greece. Arguing in 1943 from the context of the crisis the liberal arts faced during World War II, Pierson noted three dissatisfactions with the Yale curriculum: First, it was "geared too closely to the average and not very serious students"; second, insufficient attention was paid to breadth of interest, to the intention "to widen each student's horizon"; third, the system of the majors had slowly and imperceptibly and unconsciously lost sight of the central requirements of a broad, liberal education. The Experimental Program was thus designed to emphasize "the abler man, harder work and broader planning." Its objectives were

to begin with, a better system for breadth or distribution: a better way of orienting freshman:

54

at the same time some way of giving him a sense of direction and purpose in his studies. Next, we need to improve (not discard) our system of the Major. Better beginning courses, a less narrow specialization, above all a return by the faculty to the important disciplines and the core materials of their subjects, are obvious steps. Finally, the student's education, as a consistent whole, is to be considered again.[1]

Pierson went on to analyze the concept of breadth with a succinctness and taut logic which raised profound questions that still remain unanswered. Planned distribution, he said, had two objectives: (1) breadth of information and (2) understanding. "By the first, ignorance and provincialism are avoided. By the second, tolerance--and a grasp of order, relationship, and value--are achieved." Distribution would advance the student toward these goals but too much was being expected.

> Is it really possible to expose any single student to formal course work in all the different "fields of knowledge" or aspects of human experience? Apparently not any longer. . . . In fact the problem of acquainting our youth with the complexities of modern civilization has baffled the whole educational world. This much for information.

Understanding, on the other hand, was a different matter.

> Given the facts, what should a young man make of them? Ah, there is the job of the liberal arts, and of the wise teachers! . . . Will not the humanistic subject matter, especially our courses in literature and history, provide interpretation? Unquestionably they will do much, if taught and studied in a philosophical

[1]George W. Pierson, "A Planned Experiment in Liberal Education," 8 April 1943, pp. 1-5, appended to CSC Minutes, 1 April 1943. Undated letter from Maynard Mack to author, received 1 December 1980; also author's conversation with George W. Pierson, 10 June 1980.

way. Yet are we really persuaded that understanding, and a sense of direction or purpose,
will be sufficiently supplied by variety of
material, by historical perspective, and by
a taste of English literature?[1]

The Course of Study Committee reading Pierson's
proposal had been hard at work on a distribution
program for months. Accordingly, Pierson denied
that he was criticizing any such plan, though he
asked to be "permitted to doubt" whether such a system
would accomplish as much as was expected of it:

> If we really mean that the student should be
> made to seek an understanding of himself and
> of his world, are we not going to have to do
> more than expose him? Are we not going to have
> to ask him the leading questions and start him
> thinking? By whatever means we call the process,
> by whatever devices we carry through this busi-
> ness of analysis and evaluation, <u>are we not
> going to have to see that he gets some philosophy</u>?
> Given some historical perspective, and some
> exercise in philosophy, no small amount of infor-
> mation and of course experience in other fields
> may be forgiven.[2]

This argument, at least that part of it pointing
to the key role of philosophy, was not unfamiliar
to the Course of Study Committee, which had, as we
have seen, established a controversial distributional
category entitled Interrelationships of Knowledge
to accomplish much this same purpose within the Standard Program. Unfortunately, as it eventually turned
out, it was easier to establish the category than
to accomplish its purpose: Both had to be abandoned
after several years' trial.

---

[1]Pierson, "A Planned Experiment in Liberal Education," pp. 6-7. Professor Pierson, in addition
to emphasizing the purposes for which courses were
taught, commented that "our instructors have been
trained as professionals rather than as broad and
understanding counsellors" (p. 7).

[2]Ibid., p. 7.

The "Planned Experiment in Liberal Education,"
unlike the general education offerings at Columbia
and the University of Chicago and those that would
come into being at Harvard, was specifically conceived
as a four-year program. Pierson wanted to recast
the major "to get away from excesive specialization
and balkanization of subject matter." Divisional
majors, interdepartmental majors, majors supported
by strong, required minors--all developed difficulties
in practical application. "In any case," added
Pierson,

> are not all three of these reforms, as ordinarily
> practiced, still founded in faculty administra-
> tive arrangements rather than in intellectual
> reorganization? A common sign of this is failure
> to abandon the specialized departmental courses
> in favor of a newer and broader core of study.

One possible approach was to explore "genuine Field
or Province Majors," which were to be organized around
three principles:

> 1. There should be a core of theoretical
> study, carried on at least in part through group
> discussion courses.
> 2. There should be application of theory,
> and concentration of study, in a limited area
> (geographical or topical).
> 3. General information should be made avail-
> able through a substantial reading list.

Pierson suggested that the requirements of a Field
Major could be expressed in terms of courses falling
into four groups: (a) prerequisites; (b) information
and concentration; (c) theory and interpretation;
and (d) breadth and relation. A final essay would
be required and a two-part comprehensive exam, with
the first part covering the area of concentration
and the second dealing with a concept central to
the major.[1]

_____

[1]Ibid., pp. 7-9; and Document B, attached.
The only Field Major ever to appear in the Course
of Study Bulletin (in 1946-47 and 1947-48) was American Studies. (See also CSC Minutes, 22 May 1945.)
The Major's requirements were listed according to

It is clear that Pierson and his colleagues saw a liberal education curriculum as the entire end of academic efforts and not as a counterpoint to disciplined specialization. In this view, the long range purpose of the "Planned Experiment" was

> to modify the teaching, and to replan the under-graduate study, of the several liberal arts in such a way as to make each particular subject, and the standard academic curriculum as a whole, contribute more than they now regularly do to the liberal education of our students. . . . This means asking ourselves again why we require science; what truth is, and what types of truth there may be; in any case, what is it that litera-ture or history or philosophy can contribute toward the making of a man?[1]

Pierson's four part taxonomy. Thereafter, the concept bifurcated: In 1948, the so-called Divisional Majors picked up the concept of breadth (see Chapter IV) but without the concept of rigor (comprehensive examin-ations, reading lists); the Special Majors and, in 1950, the revised Divisional Majors, emphasized the concept of rigor and interdisciplinary approach (see Chapter IV also) but without the concept of integra-tion beyond the set limits of the interdisciplinary discipline. The concept of a basis in theoretical study got lost entirely. No student who completed the first two years in Directed Studies thus ever got to enroll in the sort of Field Major conceived as part of the Planned Experiment. The Special Majors were basically Area Studies in Chinese, Japanese, and Russian financed by the Rockefeller Foundation. (See CSC Minutes, 22 November 1945.)

One might conclude that the post-1950 Divisional Majors, which were the lineal heirs of Pierson's Field Majors, were really new specialized disciplines with interdisciplinary names rather than "new and broader cores of study." The humanities did not, apparently, have the sciences' facility for naming new disciplines (bio-physics, for example).

[1]Pierson, "A Planned Experiment in Liberal Educa-tion," pp. 10-11.

The "curriculum as a whole" was involved in this questioning, and the fundamental purpose of the "Planned Experiment" was to make explicit "the existence of a pattern in a proper education, despite the fact that the anarchy of the past fifty years has obscured or destroyed it."

> The present method of grouping subjects categorically under Roman numerals is as confusing to all concerned as the dishes in a cafeteria would be if there were not well recognized order and subordination in one's conception of a meal. There is at the present time no such order and subordination in most people's conception of an education, and we must therefore educate them--and possibly in some measure ourselves-- to perceive one.[1]

Pierson's "Planned Experiment" recommended itself to the Course of Study Committee, and shortly thereafter to the Educational Policy Committee of the Corporation. President Seymour publicly endorsed the plan, commenting that "its educational consequences, in my opinion, might prove to be of the highest importance."[2]

In the Fall of 1943, Dean DeVane, who in Gabriel's absence was guiding the Course of Study Committee, appointed Thomas C. Mendenhall, who was an assistant profesor of history, chairman of a subcommittee to flesh out and refine the "Planned Experiment." The detailed program developed by Mendenhall's subcommittee, presented to the Faculty in March 1945 and approved by it, was a full four year program. The "Advanced Phase" in junior and senior years, proposed to offer five Field Majors to any student whether or not he had been enrolled in the first

---

[1]Ibid., Document A, p. 1.

[2]A second experimental program was suggested by John S. Nicholas, a scientist, but the Course of Study Committee felt it was inflexible (and perhaps too weighted, at 25 percent, in science courses). CSC Minutes, 15 April 1943, 30 April 1943; Educational Policy Committee Records, 7 May 1943; Pres. Report, 1942-43, p. 17.

two years of the program. Courses in the "Basic Phase" were rigidly prescribed:

Freshman Year	Sophomore Year
Mathematics	Social Science
Literature	Historical Perspective
Philosophy I	Philosophy II
Language 1	Language II
Science I	Science III

Science I and Science III were the same courses newly developed for the Standard Program, and Language I and Language II were to be standard courses in any modern or ancient language. In the interest of a common experience, it was specifically intended that the language would be a language which the student had not studied before. The other six courses were specifically and especially designed for the experiment, particulary the philosophy courses which, as in Pierson's original conception, continued to be at the heart of the program.[1] The Course of Study Committee had already decided that the Experimental Program would not be called an honors program (though it was "open to a limited number of ambitious students"), that its students would not be veterans but undergraduates coming to Yale directly from

---

[1] 1945 Report of the Committee on the Course of Study, pp. 30-42. The Field Majors which were then contemplated were (1) History of the West; (2) Studies in Society; (3) Literature and the Arts; (4) General Science; and (5) Philosophies and Religions.
There was already some opposition to the Experimental Program at the time of its adoption. Faculty Record, 12 April 1945.
For information on Science I, II and III, see Chapter II. Mendenhall claimed that these courses were originally designed for Directed Studies and then offered to the entire undergraduate body. See T. C. Mendenhall, Report on Sophomore Year of Directed Study, 7 July 1949, Yale Archives.
Mendenhall's subcommittee consisted of Maynard Mack (English Department) and Carl F. Schreiber (German Department).

secondary schools, and that those students would
be representative of the top half of the class.
Maynard Mack of the English Department was selected
to run the first year of the program, Mendenhall
the second. In the Fall of 1946 the first students
were chosen from the applicant-pool, and the Experimental Program was underway. Provost Edgar S. Furniss
told President Seymour that he might anticipate the
full cost of the program, when both years were in
operation, at about $25,000.[1]

In its early years, a certain enthusiasm and
esprit de corps among both faculty and students characterized what was already called Directed Studies.
Though the instructors, like the leaders Mack and
Mendenhall, were not apt to be senior men, among
the group were those, like the leaders and like Robert
Dahl, John Ellsworth, and Louis Martz, whose reputations would someday be outstanding. These men were
enthusiastic, and they were forced to innovate by
the interdisciplinary nature of their efforts. Literature was taught, for example, by members of the
Classics, French and English Departments. History
I, The Individual in Europe and America from the
Middle Ages to the Present, was in turn taught by
a philosopher, a political scientist, an American
historian and a European historian. This history
course, the only one in the program, was based on
two assumptions: that all students had a cursory
knowledge of American history, and that they might
possibly take no more history of any kind. The staff
believed that the course had enough scope in time
to give a sense of the movement of history and enough
scope in space (i.e., the broad western tradition)
to serve as a foundation for a world view of contemporary events. It met twice a week for lectures
and twice in discussion groups. The lectures carried
the brunt of conveying the narrative, while the nature
of the historical process was covered in the discussion groups. History I began by describing man's
relatively unfree condition in medieval society and
traced the forces which had liberated him over the
centuries. Liberal ideas associated with the rise

---

[1]CSC Minutes, 1 February 1945, 7 March 1945,
31 May 1945; Memorandum from Furniss to Seymour in
Seymour Mss., folder marked Experimental Program.

of individual freedom were examined as were the changing philosophies of the state. The course concluded with an analysis of the modern problem of reconciling the freedom of the individual with the need for state-mandated social security.[1]

The presence of a philosopher in a history course allowed political theory and institutions to be treated in historical context. Machiavelli, for example, was "first studied under the historian's guidance as a Renaissance historical phenomenon"; then the political scientist taught "his contribution to the science and philosophy of politics." This was but one example of interdisciplinary coordination. There were others involving economists teaching the Studies in Society course, and still others involving aesthetics and the role of the artist in history. Some of these curricular innovations were later incorporated into the standard courses. Philosophy, which held the central, coordinating role, proved stimulating and at times challenging to the faculty as well as the students. Mack remembered "the free-for-all that resulted . . . when the students asked me (under the malign influence of [their] philosopher) what right Shakespeare's poetry has to be called great, when it violates almost every standard of good expository prose." The social science course involved a case study drawn from contemporary New Haven. One year, in what would today be called a simulation game, students considered whether or not a specific local housing project could and should be expanded. When the "political committee" killed the entire scheme without so much as a straw vote, the participants got an effective lesson in the democratic process. The students in the Experimental Program themselves were well aware of the exciting education they were getting. One of the first of them, reflecting impressively deeply on his two year experience, commented: "It may be that after all this, I know only that I know not. But it would seem that I know more specifically what I do not know, and that I have three valuable criteria to

---

[1]Mendenhall, Report on Sophomore Year of Directed Study, pp. 2-3.

judge the material that comes my way in the future.
. . ."[1]

When, after its third year, Mendenhall evaluated
Directed Studies for Dean DeVane, he too commented
on the program's _esprit de corps_ and motivation,
and on the fine performance of the students in the
course of their "common intellectual experience."
The instructors found this "emancipating," the final
result being "the best kind of intellectual curiosity."
Mendenhall and his group obviously responded to the
teaching challenge which the inauguration of Directed
Studies was, and their commitment inspired the students, who, on the whole, tested better than their
classmates at the end of sophomore year. Mendenhall's
evaluation of the curriculum suggested that some
courses in the fine arts might replace either mathematics, the second science course, or possibly Language II. In sum, the "informal chairman" of the
Directed Studies "faculty" recommended (1) that the
program be continued and expanded to reach 70-80
students per class; (2) that the curriculum be
restudied; and (3) that "increasing attention be devoted
to the continued procurement of a devoted and able
faculty." Ironically, in view of things to come,
Mendenhall felt that "the size of the university
and its traditions certainly preclude any thought
of extending such a program to the entire student
body."[2]

---

[1]Maynard Mack, "Directed Studies," _Yale Alumni
Magazine_, May 1949, pp. 8-10; Richard E. Crocker,
"The Directed Studies Program: An Experiment in
Education," _Et Veritas_, April 1948, pp. 6-9. Maynard
Mack was one of the magazine's faculty advisors.
Mendenhall, Report on Sophomore Year of Directed
Study, pp. 4, 9.

[2]Mendenhall, Report on Sophomore Year of Directed
Study, pp. 21-25. In 1950, _Science I_ was replaced,
in the first year of Directed Studies, by _History
of Art 12_. This move was part of the Faculty's revolt
against _Science I_ which will be detailed in Chapter
IV. See CSC Minutes, 8 February 1950. Actually,
the Directed Studies "faculty" wanted to develop
a new course in fine arts/music, but funds were not
available, and the standard course in history of

The initial success of Directed Studies is testimony not only to some of the virtues of the discarded classical curriculum, but to the virtues of good teaching, particularly innovative teaching. The early history of Directed Studies also shows that it is possible, though very difficult, to achieve academic rigor and intellectual stimulation outside the core disciplines usually used to develop a similar sense of mastery. Directed Studies was, at the beginning, an excellent, if not perfect, vehicle for promoting the rounded and integrated understanding which was taken to characterize a liberal understanding. Yet beneath the rosy, idealistic glow which suffused Directed Studies, the first problems had already begun to appear. The quality of the instruction in the philosophy courses was one of the more troublesome. The Philosophy Department had hired "two young men to carry the new programs," perhaps because their experimental nature kept them from being perceived as central to the Department's task. Professor Beardsley taught Philosophy I in the program's first year and then left Yale for Swarthmore. His successor, Professor Hoopes, stayed three years, as did Professor Roelofs, who initiated Philosophy II. None of these men were tenured. The head of the Philosophy Department, Professor Blanshard, at the same time that Mendenhall was being so enthusiastic in his evaluation, commented that the key philosophy section of Directed Studies had been "in the doldrums" during the 1948-49 academic year. Blanshard expressed his hope that "fresh blood" in the person of a recently hired instructor, Robert Cohen, would help.[1]

One is struck by the disparity of the inexperienced scholarly talent assigned to Directed Studies

art had to be substituted. See letter from Maynard Mack to Edgar S. Furniss, Griswold Mss., Box 32, folder marked Directed Studies.

[1]Dean's Report, 1944-45, p. 14; Dean's Report, 1945-46, p. 5; letter from Brand Blanshard to R. C. Carroll, 21 June 1949, Carroll Mss., Box 8, folder marked Directed Studies Program. A listing of instructors in Directed Studies, 1946-53, is also in this folder.

by the Philosophy Department and the magnitude of the expectations the program had for philosophical discipline. For example, there had been problems establishing relations with some of the social scientists, "largely because ultimate questions of value are so frequently (and deliberately) avoided by these gentlemen." DeVane commented that the Department had not consistently appreciated the opportunity offered by its courses in Directed Studies and believed that a senior individual should be found to take "permanent" charge of this work. Pierson had said in the original draft of the "Planned Experiment" that

> Most people concerned with education are willing to pay lip-service to this central study [philosophy], provided they may in practice relegate it to the periphery or beyond. Doubtless one reason for this attitude is the departmentalized habit of thinking of philosophy, as of every other subject, as one among several competing studies all of which are equally important.

This departmentalized habit had, apparently, extended to Yale's Philosophy Department. On the other hand, it may be that the coordinating and integrating functions which philosophy was asked to undertake were too ambitious--for the philosophers or anyone else.[1]

By 1949, Directed Studies was beginning to experience its first dropouts, that is, students who, after completing freshman year, elected in sophomore year to pursue the Standard Program. The first few instances of this pattern were carefully investigated by the Dean's Office since, if this tendency indicated a trend, it would doom the whole concept of a prescribed curriculum which was central to Directed Studies. Students who sought permission to transfer

---

[1]Mendenhall, Report on Sophomore Year of Directed Study, p. 6 (quotation re: questions of value); Dean's Report, 1951-52, p. 9; Pierson, "A Planned Experiment in Liberal Education," Document A, p. 1. A senior professor, T. M. Greene, who wrote about liberal education, supervised the Philosophy Department's efforts in Directed Studies, but he did not have time to teach in the program. Letter to author from T. C. Mendenhall, 29 November 1980.

were asked to explain their reasons in writing, and they did, often cogently. The difficulty of pursuing a major outside the liberal arts or humanities was cited; so were the afternoon class meetings which cut into athletic practices and bursary jobs. One thoughtful student criticized the philosophy course for failing to live up to its central, coordinating role, preferring, instead to undertake his own synthesis. Another criticized <u>Mathematics I</u> as too easy for graduates of independent schools and too hard for those from high school. Still another, commenting on the prevalence of theory, wanted the opportunity to concentrate on subjects that particularly appealed. Virtually all the dropouts, incidentally, commented on the high quality of the courses they had taken, and the frankness of their expressions makes it clear that they were not discontent with individual teachers, work loads, or other relatively superficial problems. What the dropouts were questioning were the fundamental bases of the program: the central role of philosophy, the common intellectual experience (of a math course that was suited to none), and the determined orientation toward a broad, general education covering the basic, core curriculum.[1]

Directed Studies was also in financial trouble. The program was funded by a special budget controlled by the Dean's Office as specified by the initial recommendations of the Course of Study Committee. These funds were largely used to purchase teaching time from the various Departments, though it was also hoped that they would, in the way of money everywhere, provide some leverage--in this case by Yale College. DeVane wanted, in the interests of effective teaching, more influence over faculty appointments, which were made by the Departments. Unfortunately, the University had for two years run budget deficits, and a deficit of $1,600,000 was projected for 1950-51. DeVane supported Directed Studies as a "great success [which] has achieved a renown throughout the country. [It adds] spice and variety and frequently sets standards of achievement which other parts of the curriculum may envy or aspire to."

---

[1]See letters attached to letter from Blanshard to Carroll.

Nevertheless, Directed Studies had "highly-placed" enemies who wanted to abolish it, and the budget problems were an obvious opportunity and excuse.[1]

In April 1950, Provost Furniss, who also headed the Graduate School, wrote to Dean DeVane, expressing, not for the first time, his belief "that this interesting experiment should be terminated in view of the serious financial emergency." Furniss went on to claim that Yale's newly-selected President, A. Whitney Griswold, shared this view. When DeVane read this letter to the faculty group in charge of Directed Studies, Maynard Mack reacted strongly: He wrote directly to Griswold, who was vacationing in England before formally taking office, expressing his belief that Directed Studies should be preserved, even if it had to bear its fair share of the budget cutting:

> When hard times hit, no business house would liquidate first its most vigorous and (in the outside world) best known branch. It tries to prune out the dead wood, not the green. Directed Studies belongs to the green.[2]

Griswold's response, also sent to Furniss and DeVane, was largely self-protective, though it cast considerable doubt on the Provost's claim that the President had agreed with him. Griswold was irked to have been involved at all and reminded Mack that any and every program would have to come under financial scrutiny. He had agreed with Furniss that Directed Studies "might" have to be suspended. On the other hand, in the past Mendenhall's and Mack's arguments on its behalf had restored his faith "whenever I thought about it." They still did, "provided

---

[1]Dean's Report, 1949-50, p. 19; quotation from pp. 11-12; Dean's Report, 1950-51, p. 2.

[2]Mack expressed much the same views to Furniss and at the same time questioned the extent of the savings to be achieved, estimated by him at $9,000. Letter from Furniss to DeVane, 28 April 1950; letter from Mack to Griswold, 11 May 1950; and letter from Mack to Furniss, 13 May 1950; Griswold Mss., Box, 32, folder marked Directed Studies.

(a) the program has the full confidence of the faculty, and (b) we can afford it." From this neutral stance Griswold instructed Mack, Furniss and DeVane to see that the program received full consideration from both its partisans and its critics, and suggested that Furniss and he would abide by the result. Mack immediately thanked Griswold for foregoing a decision until the matter was fully considered, and Furniss communicated his assumption "that we will not do anything more drastic than try to cut the cost. It's evident that none of those involved . . . will agree to give it up entirely; and I am hardly in a position to order them to do so." Despite Furniss' capitulation, his attitude and the whole incident demonstrate the extent to which Directed Studies was distrusted around the University. The post-war trends toward departmentalization, toward the publication of research for faculty promotion, and toward increased emphasis upon graduate school instruction were none of them favorable to Directed Studies and its objectives.[1]

As the Course of Study Committee set out to review Directed Studies in the late Fall of 1950, it was confronted with two contradictory indications: the financial crunch and Mendenhall's recommendation that the program be expanded to accommodate virtually double the number of present students. This recommendation would not have doubled the cost of the program, because it was intended, in part, to make more effective use of that portion of the teaching which was done in lecture format, and which could easily handle more students. The number of discussion groups would have to be increased, but on the other hand additional students absorbed into Directed Studies would not have to be accommodated in the Standard Program. Thus, Mendenhall's recommendation was not as preposterous as it appeared at first glance. Better yet, DeVane was able to report to the Committee that outside financial help was on the way. The Carnegie Corporation had decided

---

[1]Letter from Griswold to Mack, 11 May 1950; letter from Mack to Griswold, 30 May 1950; and letter from Furniss to Griswold, 23 May 1958, Griswold Mss, Box 32, folder marked Directed Studies.

to finance a program of Internships in General Education. A selected group of interns, that is, young, untenured instructors at the college level, who wished to learn more about teaching the liberal arts, were invited to do so at Brown, Chicago, Columbia, Harvard and Yale. They would be expected to teach one third of their time and spend the balance observing classroom procedure and teaching techniques. The salaries of these men, three of whom were assigned to Yale, were underwritten by the foundation, Yale's share being $22,000 for the 1951-52 academic year. This teaching talent--junior as it was--was immediately assigned, when it arrived, to the Directed Studies program. The Internships in General Education programs were expected to and did last for several years, through most of the decade.[1]

The Ford Foundation also provided needed succor, but it chose to finance students, not professors. Yale had joined several other colleges to ask for assistance, during the Korean emergency, in preserving the liberal arts, which had, in recent memory, been so neglected during World War II. The means was an experiment which would save time for young men by taking them into college at an earlier age and by more closely integrating the early, college years, which were to be devoted to liberal study. Fifty freshman places were to be reserved for pre-induction scholars (it was wartime again, as the term suggests). Some of the pre-induction scholars would lack the customary preparation, all were to be basically less than 16-1/2 years of age, and most were to be high school students. No more than 40 percent were to have completed the twelfth grade. Pre-induction scholars would pay no tuition and in some cases would be granted additional support. Yale received approximately $300,000 from the Ford Foundation for a three-year trial of this program. All fifty of Yale's pre-induction scholars, sometimes called Ford students,

---

[1] Yale University News Bureau Release 530, 9 April 1951; correspondence between Griswold and various officials of the Carnegie Corporation; and later press releases covering years until 1956-57, Griswold Mss., Box 32, folder marked Directed Studies. See also pamphlet, "Joint Program for Internships in General Education," Yale Archives.

were assigned to the Directed Studies program, thereby bringing it approximately to the enrollment level recommended by Mendenhall and to a financial prosperity hitherto unknown.[1]

If "wartime" carried this great financial boon, it also brought the curricular problem of ROTC. At this time universal military training was much discussed and generally anticipated. If it were not mandated by legislation, the draft and the average age of college students would combine, as they had in World War II, to arrive at much the same result. ROTC was the available way to delay military service and complete one's college education. The Course of Study Committee could not ignore the problems of ROTC, and if it wished to preserve, even expand, Directed Studies, the program could not continue to be closed to those who wished to enroll in ROTC. The Committee had already elected to force one science

---

[1]Undated memorandum from W. C. DeVane received by Griswold 20 February 1951, and Yale University News Bureau releases of 19 April 1951 and 22 April 1951, Griswold Mss., Box 37, folder marked Ford Foundation: Fund for Advancement of Education; Columbia, Chicago, Wisconsin, Yale (1951-53; 1956-58), passim. This program was resisted by the Admissions Office and some high school educators. Yale terminated the program in the Spring of 1953 for financial reasons. The Ford Foundation had assumed that the pre-induction scholars would be drafted after sophomore year and that the balance of their college years would be paid for by the GI bill. When this assumption proved erroneous, Yale was stuck with the costs until the Foundation helped out with a further grant of $100,000. When Yale terminated the program, an "Early Admissions Program" was substituted. This program simply financed, to the extent of $32,000, students who were qualified in every normal way but who were unusually young. One of the happier results of the pre-induction experiment was that it led John M. Kemper, Headmaster of Andover, to apply to the Foundation for funds to underwrite the School and College Study of Liberal Education (see Chapter IV). Letter from Kemper to Dr. Clarence Faust at the Ford Foundation, 29 May 1951, in folder cited above.

course out of the program to make way for the Arts, and it had recently acknowledged that Directed Studies was not appropriate for those who wished to major in music or pursue pre-medical studies. The concept of total curricular prescription (though the language courses had in practice never conformed), the concept of a common experience, and the concept that Directed Studies was a basic preparation for most any departmental major were all fundamental to the program. To what extent was deviation in the interests of accommodating ROTC possible before the basic concept itself was extended to the point of destruction?[1]

The result of the Committee's discussion was that two Directed Studies programs were effectively established, one for ROTC students and one for "regular" students. ROTC courses replaced Language I in the freshman year, and applicants to this variation of the Directed Studies program were essentially required to have completed basic language study in secondary school. This alteration was quite a step away from the original conception, which had contemplated that all students in Directed Studies would be beginning the study of some language together, as well as from the original practice, which was that the student study some language at the appropriate level. The revised requirement also kept the "average" freshman who did not happen to have advanced placement in language from enrolling in Directed Studies. Once this "rubicon" was crossed for ROTC students, the same advanced placement principle was applied to the "regular" program. This

[1]Undergraduate Course of Study Bulletin, 1951-52, pp. 12-13. From the very beginning, Directed Studies had been considered suitable preparation only for B.A. majors as distinct from B.S. majors. In point of fact, the vast majority of Directed Studies "graduates" majored in the humanities, in the Divisional Majors, or in the Scholar of the House program. For the class of 1950, the figure was 68 percent (5 percent in Sciences, 27 percent in Social Science). For 1951, 82 percent (7 percent in Science, 11 percent in Social Science). For 1952, also 82 percent (0 percent in Science and 18 percent in Social Science). See CSC Minutes, 15 February 1951.

enabled "regular" Directed Studies students to take both a second science and art in their sophomore year. ROTC students necessarily dropped one of these two, and it was the art course. The solution of requiring that the language requirement be anticipated had been preferred to the alternative of extending the program to six courses.[1]

What was actually involved was a revision of the original intention to limit the scope of the Directed Studies curriculum. Already the program had had to choose between science and art. Now it was being forced to incorporate a further course, ROTC, at the expense of language. In the broadest sense, this development questioned whether it had been wise, or even possible, for the founders of Directed Studies to define what constituted the key curriculum, the ever-elusive "what every educated man should know." In earlier days, the classics were the acknowledged core, and no one basically disagreed. Now the claimants were too numerous, and their claims too good to be relegated, as the Directed Studies faculty had chosen to do, to the periphery. A second difficulty with the resolution of the ROTC problem became apparent almost as quickly. The incipient tendency in the program to favor "ambitious" students at the expense of the common intellectual community was not only acknowledged but strongly encouraged. Only the ablest students, and of those only the ones who had had the right opportunities, would have anticipated the language requirements of Yale College. In other words, it was harder to gain admission to Directed Studies than to Yale. As it turned out, once the process of favoring the brightest began, and it decidedly began in the original decision to favor applicants from the top half of the class, it accelerated. Then, joined with other forces, it eventually destroyed Directed Studies, not in name but as a general program in liberal education. Those developments were, however, far in the future and not at all apparent to the Course of Study Committee who saw more clearly the opulent funding and the chance to expand a successful program

---

[1]CSC Minutes, 15 February 1951, 22 February 1951.

which had generated considerable excitement and lots of enthusiasm. The Committee happily voted to extend Directed Studies for a period of four years, and the Faculty concurred.[1]

President Griswold's initial ambivalence about Directed Studies did not last long. Its attraction for a liberal arts enthusiast like Griswold was simply too great. And the financial support of the Ford Foundation and Carnegie Corporation, which the President had been involved in obtaining, made it easier to support anyone's conviction that Directed Studies was outstanding liberal education. Surely the program had to be included in any major reinvigoration of the liberal arts which quickly became a priority concern of Griswold's, once he was inaugurated and acclimatized to his new position and power. The key was funding. Neither Ford's pre-induction program nor the Carnegie Internships were permanent sources of financing. So Griswold turned to his wealthy classmate and friend Paul Mellon and obtained his support for A Plan for General Education in Yale University. This ambitious effort called, among other things, for the expansion of Directed Studies.[2]

---

[1] Faculty Record, 1 March 1951.

[2] The plan also proposed the establishment of sophomore seminars, which were to be offered within the residential colleges, and the provision of additional discussion courses for juniors and seniors. Finally, and somewhat tangentially, the plan envisioned the reconstruction of Connecticut Hall, "the sole physical remnant of colonial Yale," as the center of student and faculty activity for liberal education. The designs for Connecticut Hall, which had had to be abandoned a couple of years earlier as structurally unsafe, included a faculty meeting room on the ground floor, seminar rooms on the second. On the third floor, there were to be offices for faculty involved in Directed Studies, Divisional Majors, and Scholars of the House. The fourth floor was devoted to guest suites for visiting professors and distinguished guests. DeVane did the first draft of the letter sent to Mellon, but the evidence is that the project had been discussed previously with Provost Furniss and Mellon himself. See letter from Griswold to

In approaching Mellon, Griswold described the program
basically as a "successful experiment" whose purpose
was to "correct conditions created by the elective
system on the one hand and the narrow and too-early
specialization of the majoring system on the other."
Griswold's more detailed description of "The Program
of Directed Studies in the Liberal Arts and Sciences"
was somewhat inflated. It was not exactly true that
students took special courses in languages or in
history of art (the first were standard courses,
the second a modified course), and one must doubt
that the philosophy course, Forms of Reason, was
entirely successful in "tying together the other
courses . . . in this program and showing [the stu-
dent] the characteristic methods of thinking in his
several studies." The redundant title Griswold had
applied to the program could also be considered mis-
leading since despite the use of the word "science,"
the Directed Studies program was generally and increasingly adequate preparation only for BA majors. One
could not, however, quibble with Griswold's forthright
statement that "the outstanding and universally
attested success of this program argues strongly for
its expansion," from 40 students per year to 150,
at an annual cost of $110,000.[1]

Mellon responded handsomely: He gave $5,000,000
to Yale's endowment. When Griswold announced his
generosity at Alumni Day, the President was inter-
rupted, as he wrote his friend, by loud and prolonged
applause. The huge gift was qualified in only two
important ways: First, the income was to be used
specifically for general education; and second, the
the funds were to be a net increment to the present

Mellon, 8 October 1951, and attachments, Griswold
Mss., Box 60, folder marked Old Dominion Foundation:
Plan for General Education (Paul Mellon) (1951, 1952,
1954).

[1]To capitalize this need at a 4 percent income-
rate, Griswold was asking Mellon for $2,750,000 for
the program. Ibid. Also Course of Study Bulletin,
1951-52. The liberal arts, as originally defined,
included the sciences of mathematics, geometry, and
astronomy, thus making the term "Liberal Arts and
Sciences" a redundancy.

funds of Yale College and were not to be used to recapture other funds of the College for use in other parts of the University or for other purposes. It was understood that all of the educational facets of the plan Mellon was endorsing were subject to the approval of the Faculty.[1] Directed Studies had made a major breakthrough, been given a permanent financial base and an opportunity, perhaps, to dominate the College. The future lay, or seemed to lie, with general education. It did not, however, for by this time Directed Studies had been subtly, but entirely, transformed along the way without anyone's quite realizing it.

Over the years, the tendency to narrow the function of the major had increased. The difficulty with any major, and with the concentrated specialization that usually goes with it, is that the same course of study, the same collection of identifying catalogue members, can be so readily used, if the student or teacher is so inclined, for utilitarian or professional ends. Mastery of chemistry is as helpful, and more practical, for the would-be doctor as it is to the human being he initially was. It was much the same situation which was encountered at nineteenth century Harvard when the elective system was increasingly abused to achieve limited professional and vocational goals. The original design of Directed Studies, which had been clearly conceived as a four year program, had included an effort to reverse this trend. Specifically, it will be remembered, the "Planned Experiment" had called for the establishment of Field Majors, and it had been envisioned that "graduates" of the "Basic Phase" of Directed Studies would proceed in junior and senior years to the "Advanced Phase," to the Field Majors.[2]

---

[1]Letter from Mellon to Griswold, 19 February 1952; letter from Griswold to Mellon, 26 February 1952; letter from Griswold to Furniss, 4 March 1952, Griswold Mss, Box 60, folder marked Old Dominion Foundation: Plan for General Education. See also Yale Alumni Magazine, March 1952, pp. 21-25; Faculty Record, 6 March 1952.

[2]Technically, sophomore "graduates" of the first two years of the program were free to opt to pursue the Departmental Majors in the Standard Program,

The founders of the Experimental Program had hoped that the "Basic" and "Advanced Phases" of Directed Studies, when combined, would constitute a new kind of liberal education, though it might have been said to much resemble the earlier version and the broad liberal purposes of A. Lawrence Lowell. This type of liberal education would effectively, it was hoped, subordinate the discipline of the major to its larger, overall purpose.

What actually happened, as we shall see, is that the Field Majors as originally proposed were modified (and renamed Divisional Majors) in order to achieve entirely different purposes which originated in unrelated practical problems. In the process they were stripped of their intellectual rigor, though not of their interdisciplinary nature, and grafted onto the Standard Program alongside the Departmental Majors. Thus, the Field Majors never ever operated according to their original design and purpose. While everyone was looking at the practical problems which the transformation of the Field Majors into Divisional Majors helped to solve, Directed Studies was simultaneously, subliminally, but effectively transformed into a two year program, which necessarily fed a whole complex of majors, none of them organically connected to the "Basic Phase" of Directed Studies. This meant that Directed Studies had now become a liberal education program which, though happenstance, was solely preparatory to the various majors in the Standard Program. This particular definition of liberal education is fraught with difficulties, as we shall see. Thus, when Directed Studies, or a version thereof, was eventually proposed as a model for the entire freshman and sophomore classes, it was unacceptable to the faculty for many reasons, but for one of particular importance: The assumption that Directed Studies as it then operated was adequate preparation for any of the Departmental Majors as then implemented was simply not credited. In the crunch, the faculty would prefer the demands and existing functions of the Departmental Major to the needs and hard-to-define purposes of liberal education. It was too bad, in the end, that the

---

just as any qualified sophomore who had been in the Standard Program was free to apply for admission to a Field Major.

Planned Experiment in Liberal Education was inadvertantly deprived of an opportunity to function, at
least for a while, as initially conceived. The history of liberal education at Yale might have been
very different.

Chapter IV

GRISWOLD'S INITIATIVE: THE 1953 REPORT OF THE

PRESIDENT'S COMMITTEE ON GENERAL EDUCATION

The 1945 Reforms, designed to last a half-century, did nothing of the kind, since they had to be adapted, and rather immediately, to the realities of post-war Yale. One of these realities, rooted in the expansion of and the increasing heterogeneity of the undergraduate body, was the need better to coordinate the student's transition between secondary school and college. Yale readily participated in this effort, which resulted in, among other things, the advanced placement program that gave (and still gives) the well prepared applicant college credit for any college-level work he might have completed in secondary school. While Yale was redesigning programs to effect its half of the "bargain" with the feeder schools, that effort merged with the interests of Yale's new President, A. Whitney Griswold, in advancing liberal education. Griswold was well aware that the Korean War, the University's financial crisis, the expanding curriculum, the growing importance of the sciences, the pressures created by increased interest in post-graduate study, and the further orientation of the faculty toward their professional objectives were all stressing Yale's--and his--traditional conception of a liberal undergraduate program. Directed Studies, a seemingly unqualified success, lay at hand as an experiment which could be adapted to advance his purpose. And this purpose merged with the work of integrating college program and secondary school program when Griswold created the President's Committee on General Education and charged it to accomplish both ends. After a year's work, a widely hailed Report was issued, and to those who did not or could not examine its recommendations too carefully, it seemed as if Yale had found an exciting, new, and effective course of study that would assure that the undergraduates received, in modern times, a true liberal education.

All of Yale life, now that the wartime emergency was concluded, resisted reverting to its traditional pattern. Enrollment was at 9000 compared to the pre-war normal of 5200; there were housing

79

shortages for both students and faculty; classrooms, dining halls, and libraries were overcrowded. Rooms in the residential colleges designed for two now accommodated four. Waitress-service was no longer the mealtime norm, a fact particularly and generally lamented not only because cafeteria chow-lines lacked an aura of leisure and gracefulness, but because tin-tray efficiency did so little to provide the close faculty-student relationships the residential colleges were designed to foster. If it were no longer wartime Yale, no longer was it pre-war Yale.[1]

Seventeen hundred fifty members of the class of 1950 were the first undergraduates to enroll in the Standard Program of the new curriculum. This class was, as might be expected of a group including so many older men who had seen war service, highly motivated. Academic work was of excellent quality, and the numbers of men dropped for unsatisfactory grades unusually low. By and large, the new curriculum worked well for these freshmen. However, the Course of Study Committee was not long in realizing that the unanticipated crowding of post-war Yale and the stress those numbers would place on the administration of the major, particularly the Senior Essay, would require modifications in the recently reformed curriculum. On December 20, 1947, the Committee proposed a further curriculum revision which openly acknowledged two motives: "first, to break across departmental lines and make more meaningful combinations of studies for the general student than single departments can usually supply; and, second, to devote a greater share of the attention and care of the Faculty than is given at present to the superior student." The first motive eventually created the so-called Divisional Major, the second, an honors major known as the Intensive Major.[2] The reforms

---

[1]Pres. Report, 1946-47, p. 1 and passim.

[2]Dean's Report, 1946-47. p. 6. Egalitarianism at Yale had tended over the years to make difficult the creation of an honors system. In addition, creating an honors course and an easier standard course made it possible for honors-capable students to enroll in the standard course and emphasize extra-curricular activities which were held at Yale (and elsewhere) in very high esteem. Less cynically, the emphasis

were to take effect in September 1948, thereby
enabling the faculty to cope with the "tremendous"
size of the class of 1950.[1]

The revised curriculum did not alter the basic
studies or distributional requirements of the 1945
Reforms, but it did envision four types of majors
in place of the single major in the previous Standard
Program: the Departmental Major, shorn of the Senior
Essay but confirmed in the comprehensive exams; the
Intensive Major, which required departmental permission for admission, departmental exams, and a Senior
Essay, and which alone among the alternatives, enabled
the student to obtain departmental honors. Then
there were the Special Majors, a catch-all category
which included HAL and American Studies, and the
Interdepartmental Majors such as French and Philosophy,
and Physics and Philosophy. Last and most innovative
were the Divisional Majors, whose roots were in the
Field Majors. These seventeen organized groupings
of courses had names like The Role of Ideas in Literature and the Arts, The Theory and Practice of International Organization Since 1876, and General Studies
in Pre-Medicine. Four of these "Divisional Programs
in General Studies" were in the humanities, ten in
the social sciences, and three in the sciences.
Students who enrolled were required to take five
courses, mostly lecture courses, in both junior and
senior years, and a preponderance of these courses
were to be devoted to the major. Neither a Senior
Essay nor departmental exams were required, but the
major courses were to be, with the advice of a coun-
sellor, arranged with reference to a closer time

---

upon purely intellectual achievement implied by honors
programs and degrees were at variance with Yale's
policy of attempting to educate the whole man.

[1]1947 Report of the Course of Study Committee,
20 December 1947, p. 1, Yale Archives; Faculty Record,
15 January 1948. The Senior Essay had essentially
been dropped the year before when the Faculty allowed
each Department to choose whether or not to require
independent work. This solution to the immediate
problem of class size promised to lighten the Departments' overall work load and to make it possible
to give more attention to better students.

frame, say the ancient world or the nineteenth century.
The chairman of the committee of counsellors, whose
duties included the supervision and coordination
of the Divisional Majors, was ex-officio a member
of the Course of Study Committee.[1]

The Yale faculty tended to view the reforms
of 1947, as Dean DeVane had hinted that they might,
as a way of introducing an honors program under
another name, specifically, the Intensive Major, which
the Departments were gearing up to offer to 25 percent
of the undergraduates. However, the faculty were
also groping for a major for the less able which
would honor the principle of concentration, which
was part of their fundamental concept of liberal
education, without using the expensive and hard to
administer tools of seminars, departmental exams,
Senior Essays and individual counseling. They found
what they were searching for in the as yet untried

---

[1]1947 Report of the Course of Study Committee,
20 December 1947, pp. 2-4. The Faculty, perhaps
aware of the irony of a general studies program
entitled "Studies in Pre-Medicine," when it examined
the typical programs attached to the Course of Study
Committee's Report, probably noticed that the area
of concentration in the humanities included seven
courses, one in sophomore year; in the social sciences,
it included eight, two of them in sophomore year;
and in the sciences nine courses were required, two
in every year but junior year, when three were
required. Determined as the faculty was to avoid the
mere appearance of the elective system it despised,
it was no less attracted to premature concentration
toward specialized studies. Accordingly, the Faculty
voted to limit all "Divisional Programs in General
Studies" to seven full-year courses or the equivalent,
these seven courses to be in addition to the stipulated basic and distributional requirements already
in effect. They also dropped all three of the proposed Divisional Majors in the sciences, probably
because there were not enough students interested
in majoring in the sciences to warrant both Departmental and Divisional Majors in that area. Report
of the Course of Study Committee, 20 January 1948,
pp. 8-15, Seymour Mss, folder marked Course of Study;
Faculty Record, 22 January 1948, 27 January 1948.

"Advanced Phase" of Directed Studies. The Field Majors, which had initially been outlined as the "Advanced Phase" of that program seemed perfect, and the interdisciplinary portion of their character fitted into the Course of Study Committee's intention to break across departmental lines. The original concept of the Field Major was now drastically modified to serve a purpose--accommodating large numbers of students--entirely different from its original purpose and was renamed the Divisional Major. In the process, probably inadvertantly, the Faculty linked the goal of breadth of academic interest, which the new Divisional Majors were intended to promote, with a diminished intellectual aptitude, or at least interest. It was impossible for a student to be honors-bright and achieve his due by means of the Divisional Major. Consequently, the intelligent tended to get pushed toward departmentalized concentration. More significantly, the student with a plethora of academic interests was not encouraged to pursue those interests in quality fashion. Not surprisingly, the curriculum thus organized proved unstable since it played two of the College's traditional goals, breadth of scholarship and intellectual achievement, against one another.

On February 11, 1950, A. Whitney Griswold was elected the sixteenth President of Yale. Griswold, an acknowledged spokesman for Yale College and the liberal arts, had interested himself in curricular matters as a member of the Faculty. Once Seymour had passed into retirement, his successor would surely take an active interest in the undergraduate curriculum. Thus, the academic year 1950-51 was characterized by a clear need to achieve closure, an urgency that often appears when a major transition offers the prospect of new initiatives toward significant innovations. The Course of Study Committee was specifically committed to review the status of Directed Studies and the broad range, relatively unchallenging Divisional Majors, both of which had been undertaken as "experiments." DeVane appointed himself Chairman of the Committee and undertook the job. His evaluation of the existing state of affairs was mixed. He readily acknowledged the breakdown of Yale's efforts "to adopt and use the sciences for the purposes of a liberal education." On the other hand, Directed Studies was a great success. DeVane reasoned that

to abandon the experiment would "leave the first
two years of the student's curriculum without any
special feature . . . ."[1] The Divisional Majors
established in 1948 had proved highly and increasingly
popular. However, the faculty suspected, quite
rightly, that some very able men were enrolling in
the academically easier Divisional Majors, and not
in the Departmental Majors, in order to have more
time for extracurricular activities; and the faculty
was not altogether pleased that, except in the strong
Departments like history and English, the Departmental
Majors were losing students. The Divisional Majors,
which crossed departmental lines, in all honesty
did offer "a fuller and richer course of study" than
many a lesser Departmental Major, and DeVane confi-
dentially admitted that he had helped sponsor the
Divisional Majors "to diminish departmental control
of the education of the student during his last two
years, and to restore that control to the College."[2]

The way out of the difficulty was to combine
the educationally advantageous breadth of the Divisional Major with the stricter, though narrower training of the Departmental Major. This was accomplished
by reducing the number of inter-disciplinary Divisional Majors from ten to four (not including American
Studies) and generally limiting the compass of the
program. The remaindermen turned out to be History,
the Arts and Letters; Philosophy, Politics and
Economics; and Culture and Behavior.[3] The requisite

---

[1]Dean's Report, 1949-50, pp. 11-12.

[2]Ibid., pp. 13-14. The Divisional Majors
attracted 43 percent of the class of 1950, 51 percent
of the class of 1951, and 53 percent of the class
of 1952.

[3]The fourth Divisional Major was supposed to
be a science program, but it never came to fruition
for institutional reasons. When the Sheffield Scientific School was merged into Yale College, there
were actually two Course of Study Committees, one
for the BA degree, one for the BS degree. In early
1948, both Committees agreed that the three Divisional
Majors in the sciences would be the responsibility
of the BS Committee (see CSC Minutes, 21 January

intellectual vigor was assured by a comprehensive exam at the end of the senior year, and for the first time, a Divisional honors program was created. Divisional honors required a Senior Essay and participation in a discussion seminar as well as honors quality work. DeVane, as always, did not confuse the intellectual rigor he sought with over-concentration in one field or subject. Sounding a bit like John Stuart Mill, the Dean saw that the increasing trend among undergraduates to go on to professional or graduate school, where concentration was very heavy, made it all the more important that the undergraduate not miss "the broadening effects of adjacent subjects which he will really need to be a good teacher or research man, lawyer, or businessman." Thus, DeVane felt the newly revised and academically strengthened Divisional Majors were "intrinsically more valuable" than the normal Departmental Majors.[1]

Reporting to President-elect Griswold the following summer, Dean DeVane succinctly and accurately summarized the broad outlines of the "excellent educational system" which was in effect in 1950-51 for Yale candidates for the BA degree:

> (1) The Basic Studies, four in number, from which the entering student may be exempted if he has done good work in school and on the entrance examinations in the subject; (2) The Distributional Studies, five in number, of which the student must elect four, spread through the sciences, the social sciences, and the humanities; (3) The Standard [or Departmental] Major, consisting of five courses in a single subject

---

1948). The Committees were combined in the Fall of 1950 (see Dean's Report, 1950-51, p. 2), and the matter of Divisional Majors in the sciences was left hanging, since these majors were unpopular anyway and the overall numbers enrolled in the science Departments did not warrant additional new, and expensive, alternatives.

[1]Report of the Course of Study Committee, 22 November 1950, Griswold Mss, Box 20, folder marked Yale College Course of Study; Faculty Record, 14 December 1950; Dean's Report, 1950-51, pp. 16-17.

in junior and senior years and concluded by
a Departmental Examination; (4) The Intensive
(or Honors) Major in a single subject, consisting
of instruction in a seminar, a Senior Essay,
and a Departmental Examination; and (5) The
divisional Majors.

The Dean went on,

> If we could afford it, all our students should
> be Intensive or Divisional Majors and receive
> accordingly the seminar instruction and the
> benefits of the Senior Essay. If we could afford
> it, we should introduce the close instruction
> provided by seminars to the Sophomore and Fresh-
> man Classes--at least in one of the five courses
> which the students take in each of three years.
> The latter suggestion . . . would pay handsome
> dividends in the difficult problem of engaging
> and holding the interest of the students in
> their studies during these early years.

Thus, the Seymour era came to an end.[1]

The inaugural address of A. Whitney Griswold,
interdisciplinary PhD of eclectic intellectual interests and articulate advocate of the liberal arts,
defended the historic worth and continuing value
of a liberal education:

> [The fundamental purpose of the liberal arts]
> lies, not in their specific content, but in
> their stimulus to the individual student's powers
> of reason, judgment, and imagination. . . .
> they give that individual vision. They enlarge
> his capacity for self-knowledge and expand his
> opportunities for self-improvement. . . . Are
> the liberal arts irrelevant to a mechanic? . . .
> No one is born to drudgery in a democracy, and
> if drudgery is thrust upon any of us (as it
> is in some form or other upon all of us) the
> liberal arts are its antidote. . . . As men
> and women living in a state of civilization,

---

[1]Dean's Report, 1950-51, pp. 17-18.

the lives and welfare of all of us are identified with Man Thinking.[1]

As Griswold spoke, the nation was deeply involved in the Korean War. Griswold remembered what the last war had done to the liberal arts at Yale, and he was making clear his intention that it should not happen again.[2] His concern for the future of the University was increased by the desperate need in the College and elsewhere for more money. His response was a strong effort to assert Yale's traditional role in a hazardous era and a vigorous search for major new financial resources. These two objectives joined in the Plan for General Education, which Paul Mellon had so generously funded. These monies had been donated not only to expand the Directed Studies program, but to staff the new Divisional Majors, to assist the Scholars of the House program, to improve the quality of Departmental Majors by financing discussion seminars for juniors and seniors within these majors, and, most innovatively, to finance new sophomore seminars—twenty-nine courses to be taught in discussion groups within the ten residential colleges in lieu of the more traditional classrooms. It was hoped that these sophomore discussion courses would eventually take on some of the integrative functions of the more-successful Directed Studies courses as well as make for better teaching and more intellectual challenge in the problematic sophomore year. They would also stimulate academic life within the residential colleges.[3]

_____

[1]Inaugueral Address of A. Whitney Griswold, Yale Alumni Magazine, November 1950, p. 9.

[2]For example, shoftly after his inauguration Griswold wrote to Paul Mellon: "My particular concern is for our undergraduate liberal arts curriculum. I think we are all going to have to do some heroic work to keep it from total extinction. . . . These are worrisome times, yet I believe we can win through them. . . ." Letter from Griswold to Mellon, 8 January 1951, Griswold Mss, Box 55, folder marked Mellon, Paul (1950, 1951, 1954-1963).

[3]Dean's report, 1951-52, pp.11-15; Yale Alumni Magazine, March 1952, pp. 21-25.

While Griswold was undertaking this bold initiative at Yale, the Ford Foundation was underwriting a study of general education, the progress of which was closely watched by many educators. Charles Seymour, Jr., the art historian, was Yale's representative on the so-called Andover Study Committee, but other Yale professors acted as guest consultants, notable among them T. C. Mendenhall. The Committee met throughout the 1951-52 academic year in Andover, New York, New Haven, Princeton and Cambridge. Considerable scholarly talent joined with notable educators, and a report was issued and circulated in the Spring of 1952. This undertaking quickly merged with Griswold's own purposes for Yale.[1]

The Andover Report, <u>General Education in School and College</u>, was primarily a pragmatic rather than a philosophic document. Its statistical base was the 344 members of the class of 1951 at Harvard, Yale and Princeton, who had prepared at Andover, Exeter and Lawrenceville. The broad purpose of the study was "to integrate the work of school and college in the area of general education. . . ." More specifically, the Committee defined three purposes:

1. To design an effective program of studies embodying the essentials of a liberal education and eliminating wasteful duplication and overlap.
2. To discover every possible device open to education to increase the student's desire to grow in knowledge and understanding.
3. To see whether, by planning these years as a whole, sound methods could be found whereby the conventional process leading to the BA degree might be shortened for superior, well-trained students.[2]

---

[1]Interim Report of School and College Study of General Education, April 1952; Griswold Mss., Box 65, folder marked "President's Committee on General Education (1952): Interim Report School and College Study of General Education (1952) Appendix I." Incidentally, McGeorge Bundy, a Groton graduate, represented Harvard on the committee. Mendenhall was an Andover graduate.

[2]Ibid., p. 1.

These purposes, an observer might have noticed, were listed in the reverse order of the ease with which they might be expected to be accomplished, and the effort to eliminate "wasteful duplication and overlap" was more properly a necessary part of the effort to accelerate the "conventional process leading to a BA degree" than of the attempt to design an effective liberal education curriculum.[1]

The Committee was more articulate in its reasoning about developing the student's desire "to grow in knowledge and understanding." Three proposals, all of which found their way into Griswold's President's Committee's Report in one form or another, were outlined. The first was to allow students to move ahead as fast as their interests and abilities permitted. "Wallowing in difficulties" was less to be feared than the frustration of being held back. Second, the Committee counseled that students should be made to solve problems rather than passively absorb material. Apparently, the Committee agreed with numerous students who responded to its questionnaire and criticized "the lack of stimulus to active,

---

[1]Ibid., pp. 13-17. Citing statistics showing that the academic aptitude of the top half of the classes in their respective colleges equated with the top 1-1/2 percent nationally, the Andover Committee explained its concern with accelerating the route to the BA by pointing out that many bright students went on to graduate school after several years of compulsory military service, thereby delaying their careers until age twenty-seven or twenty-eight. Even the need to adjust emotional and social and intellectual development to outstanding aptitude and performance did not warrant such a long procedure. The brightest must be made available to the country and to "humanity" sooner. Strangely, the Committee went on to expound favorably on the experience of army service or practical work between school and college. The maturing effects of this type of experience have often been noted (and was clearly observed at post-war Yale), but the Committee did not make explicit why such a beneficial interruption would not do much to disturb the complex testing and placement efforts it was proposing in the interests of efficiency.

independent thinking in both school and college."
Third, the Committee felt students wanted "an integrated, coherent plan of studies, providing both
for general education in major fields and the possibility of acceleration in at least one." Student
after student mentioned that good teaching, without
relying on "assembly-line" methods, was central to
all attempts to increase motivation in the learner.[1]

Unhappily, the Andover Committee simply abdicated
in the matter of defining the essentials of a liberal
education, citing a "wide agreement among educated
people," frequently the terminology for an imprecise
expression which everyone could agree upon. Specifically, "The Committee has felt no need to attempt
a redefinition of a liberal education. It has no
original contribution to make towards determining
the areas of knowledge and the various skills, attitudes, habits of mind and values with which a liberal
education is concerned." Lamely, the Committee
rehearsed what it "unoriginally" knew by defining
six core areas of study, by commenting upon the importance of interrelating knowledge and by stating this
purpose of liberal education:

> [to] develop habits of mind, attitudes and values
> which will enlarge the mind and help to "achieve
> the excellence of human nature." . . . Among
> the most important are intellectual curiosity
> and zest for learning coupled with the power
> of self-discipline; a love for excellence; inner-
> strength and stability; integrity, both moral
> and intellectual; concern for others and appre-
> ciation of the value of human differences; and
> the capacity for self-education, perhaps the
> supreme test of the effectiveness of a general
> education.

"Zest for learning" is straight Alfred North Whitehead
but otherwise there is little evidence of contributions from philosophers.[2]

---

[1]Ibid., pp. 4-6.

[2]Ibid., pp. 6-8.

One might or might not choose to quibble over
the philosophical inconsistencies of the Andover
Report. To do so is to be distracted from its major
difficulty, which is the unquestioned and publicly
unjustified assumption that pragmatic efficiencies
of placement and scheduling, improved teaching methodologies, and greater motivation of students are
necessarily tied to a better liberal education for
the laudable purposes which are its goal. Virtually
every suggestion made by the Andover Committee would
have resulted in a better, more streamlined,
specialist-oriented education as quickly, or perhaps
more quickly, than in its liberal goals. For example,
could not any student be more highly motivated by
allowing him to select his area of interest earlier
(as Griswold's President's Committee ended up recommending) or by allowing him to pursue his courses
with specific professional or vocational goals in
mind? Neither course of action would appear to promote general education however it was defined. Better
education from an administrative and practical point
of view simply did not directly and necessarily equate
with the liberal arts education Yale espoused.

Griswold did not announce the appointment of
the President's Committee on General Education until
November 11, 1952, though the project had been in
its initial phase for over six months. The previous
May, the President had reviewed his ideas and plans
with the Educational Policy Committee of the Corporation. He had also discussed them informally with
the Faculty of Yale College and the Faculty of the
Freshman Year—all before the first informal meeting
of the still-unnamed President's Committee on General
Education. Of the eight men who finally became the
official committee members, five were in attendance:
Griswold, Mendenhall, Seymour Jr., George Van
Santvoord (a Fellow of the Corporation and Headmaster
of Griswold's alma mater, the Hotchkiss School),
and A. S. Foord of the History Department. The executive secretary at the first meeting, Professor Harold
G. Cassidy, had planned to go on leave the following
year, so he was shortly replaced by Douglas M. Knight
of the English Department. From the very beginning,
Griswold and the other members of the President's
Committee were concerned with planning strategy toward
getting their report a favorable reception. Whether
or not it would be better for Griswold to chair the

committee was carefully evaluated, and considerable
effort was made to add to the committee scientists
who would be both cooperative and effective spokesmen.
J. G. Kirkwood, a chemist, was finally recruited,
and J. W. Fessler, a political scientist, was added
over the summer. Both were relative newcomers to
Yale.[1]

It was important to include the scientists in
any effort to reinvigorate the liberal arts at Yale
because the science Departments tended, as we have
seen, to be separated from the rest of the College
community and because they had consequently been
ineffectively involved in implementing the 1945
Reforms. In 1950, President Seymour had created,
in the University-wide Faculty of the Arts and Sciences, a Division of the Humanities, headed by Dean
DeVane, and a Division of the Sciences, headed by
Edmund W. Sinnott, who had been chairman of the Course
of Study Committee of the Sheffield Scientific School
and then Dean. Seymour took pains lest it be thought
that the creation of the two Divisions would revive
the old dichotomies. He pointed out that the Dean
of Yale College had made a brilliant record in a
scientific field, and that the Director of the Sheffield Scientific School was a noteworthy humanist.
"As a result we have achieved a fine harmony between
the sciences and humanities at Yale and it is emi-
nently appropriate that we should assume a leadership
in bringing these two fields of knowledge more closely
together."[2] Although DeVane and Sinnott agreed in

---

[1]Educational Policy Committee Records, 9 May
1952; Griswold Mss., Box 65, folder marked "President's Committee on General Education: General Matters (1952)," passim; Yale Daily News, November 11,
1952. Incidentally, Griswold was not sufficiently
familiar with members of the science faculty to make
selections without maneuvering for advice from others
more knowledgeable.

[2]Pres. Report, 1946-47, p. 6, pp. 12-13; quotation from p. 6. There was also created a Division
of the Arts, under Charles H. Sawyer, Dean of the
School of Fine Arts. And eventually, the Division
of the Humanities was itself subdivided, and the
Division of the Social Sciences created under the
leadership of Professor Arnold Wolfers. The Division

general terms upon the importance of a broad view
of the fields of knowledge and the importance of
a liberal education, in the area where their practical
interests met, namely the required science offerings
in Yale College, they were not in touch with each
other about a situation they saw quite differently.
DeVane commented, "[The Sciences] are properly in
the care of Director Sinnott," and went on to say,
"With a few notable exceptions the teaching in the
sciences must be regarded as mediocre, and at some
points it is distinctly bad."[1] On the other hand,
Sinnott believed that undergraduate instruction "is
not a primary responsibility of the [Scientific]
School but undergraduate problems in the sciences
necessarily concern us all very closely." Sinnott
went on to express his feeling that on the whole
Science I, Science II and Science III were well taught
considering the inexperience of the staff. He
believed that "the young men who leave Yale having
majored in other fields than the sciences, will now
have a much better conception of the content and
spirit of the sciences. . . ." In fact, plans were
afoot to give a new course the following year in
the history and methods of the sciences.[2] But DeVane
continued to address the matter in unflattering terms:

> The short and simple truth is that our elementary
> courses in the sciences are, with a few notable
> exceptions, comparatively badly taught.

---

of the Sciences was basically the graduate portion
of the old Sheffield Scientific School. See Pres.
Report, 1948-49, p. 21.

[1]Dean's Report, 1947-48, pp. 17-18. Science
I had had to be abandoned entirely, because the chemistry instructors had simply jammed a full year's course
into their half-year time allotment; worse they were
hostile to their students, determined "to rub the
noses of the reluctant schoolboys in the subject."
Yale College retaliated by no longer requiring the
course. See Dean's Report, 1949-50, pp. 10-11.

[2]Report of the Dean of the Sheffield Scientific
School, 1947-48, p. 11.

It is a stout young fellow who can push past
the first course in several of our sciences
at Yale, and many students whose aptitudes are
strongly scientific turn at this point to other
fields where they are less competent. . . .
[Without help from the Division of Science and
Department chairmen], the College cannot do
a great deal about it.[1]

Sinnott had been under intense pressure and
had been working uphill, mostly by himself, to build
the University science Departments, expand their
physical facilities, and enlarge their scholarly
reputations.[2] He might well have wondered why DeVane
was looking to him to oversee the science instruction
in Yale College, which was, after all, DeVane's own
bailiwick. Probably the personal compatibility
between the men tended to paper over these divisive
problems, and it may just be that only the impending
departure of Professor Humphreys, the popular and
successful instructor of the physics section of Science I, decided DeVane to bring the matter to a head.[3]
DeVane and the Course of Study Committee had, in
designing the 1945 Reforms, considered the possibility
of reducing the required science distributional categories from two to one at that time. They did not,
in deference to the hoped-for cooperation of the
science Departments in effecting the new curriculum.
Apparently, from the humanists' point of view, that
cooperation had not been forthcoming. So when, in

---

[1]Dean's Report, 1948-49, p. 4.

[2]Sinnott's reports of this period make this
abundantly clear, and he did not get unstinted cooperation from the University. For example, Yale was
newly entitled to some income from a major bequest
(the Huggins Trust). The Corporation, since there
was a budget deficit, decided that the sciences,
who had to be given that income, would be required
to "give back" a like amount for other uses. Thus,
the windfall disappeared, and Sinnott had run very
hard indeed just to remain where he had been.

[3]Report of the Dean of the Sheffield Scientific
School, 1948-49, pp. 2-3.

1948, the Course of Study Committee turned from the problems of majoring to the distributional require- ments, the Faculty voted a minor wording change-- with significant meaning behind it: The number of distributional categories was reduced from six to five. In effect, this one category reduction meant that most students would decide to avoid either a second course in science or any course in classical civilization since these distributional subdivisions were least popular among the undergraduates. DeVane commented:

> the students' programs had become overcrowded
> with hours and requirements. Another reason
> for the change was the hope that by breaking
> the virtual monopoly of the science departments
> and the Classics department a better grade of
> teaching would be obtained. The scientists,
> as was expected, fought the change with some
> bitterness on the floor of the Faculty.[1]

---

[1]Dean's Report, 1948-49, p. 14, Appendix; Faculty Record, 6 January 1949. One of the following sub- divisions could now be ignored:
    I--The Humanities
        1. The Classical Languages, Literature,
           and Civilization
        2. Modern Literature, the Fine Arts, and
           Music
    II--The Social Sciences
        1. Anthropology, Economics, Political
           Science, Psychology, Sociology
        2. History, Philosophy, Religion
    III--The Physical and Natural Sciences
        1. Science I, Chemistry, Physics
        2. Science II, Science III
The terms distributional requirements and distribu- tional categories (or areas) tend to be used inter- changeably to describe the mechanics of the distri- bution(al) system (or program). The requirement technically is to complete one year course in the specified category, for which distributional credit is awarded. A distributional credit automatically becomes a college credit. An advanced placement credit (awarded before admission to Yale) also serves as a distributional credit and therefore a college credit, one of a specified number required for the BA degree. Just after World War II, advanced

Yale's difficulty in the science courses for generalist purposes was, according to DeVane, part of a nationwide trend which had several causes: First, scientific research enjoyed great prestige outside the university because of its beneficial applications in daily life; second, scientists were banded into national or international organizations which minimized their attachments to any particular institution; third, the scientist was "strongly convinced of the overwhelming importance of his own field, and the great necessity for a thorough training in it." Yale was attempting, at the university level, not only to join the trend, but to find a position of leadership. This meant attention to academic reputation, publication, research, and Graduate School teaching. When he was not concentrating on the College, Griswold actively supported these objectives. The result, said DeVane, was "that scientists have customarily failed to see their subjects as part of a total liberal education, and are usually incapable of subjecting [sic] their interests to the total conception."[1] In defense of the sciences at Yale, they alone were being asked to make the effort to design wholly new courses "for the purpose of a general education," a purpose foreign to their overriding university goals. Other clusters of Departments who tried to make similar efforts, for example in Directed Studies, were frequently just as unsuccessful. Perhaps the "failure" of the sciences is explained by the difficulty, oft noted by the members of the Course of Study Committee when criticizing Harvard's General Education program, of designing

---

placement credits, and those distributional credits which were synonymous with them, were awarded conditionally. Upon completion of satisfactory college work during the freshman year in other areas of study, the conditional credits were transformed into full college credits. The distinctions, except for the automatic corollation of distributional credits with advanced placement credits, are not particularly key to an understanding of curriculum planning or design.

[1]Dean's Report, 1949-50, pp. 9-10. Earlier, DeVane had said, "The small scientist is notoriously the most reactionary person in a modern university faculty." See Dean's Report, 1946-47, p. 5.

any course for the purposes of general education, [1] particularly when the instructors are disinterested.

Once its existence was announced, the President's Committee on General Education began to receive numerous and varied suggestions. For example, it was proposed that graduate school training should be revised to be less specialized and to include practice teaching. It was also proposed that the Yale College, Freshman, and Graduate Faculties be combined to destroy or minimize the hierarchy within them. A corollary suggestion was that all Graduate School faculty be required to teach at least one freshman course. Amid the welter of advice, the Committee set about its work by means of systematic interviews. Unlike Gabriel's Course of Study Committee in the 1940s, little reading was undertaken: The only philosophical work on a preliminary list was Whitehead's Aims of Education. The whole process had something of an administrative, pragmatic approach rather than the synoptic, historical, philosophical approach adopted during the war. If the Reforms of 1945 were attempting to better a Yale education by means of an improved, philosophic vision of the curriculum,

---

[1]For examples from Directed Studies, see Appendix to the Dean's Report, 1948-49. President Seymour commented:
"The chief disappointment of the postwar years has been the failure effectively to adapt and utilize the scientific studies on the undergraduate level for the purposes of a general education. . . . The crying need of making scientific studies an essential part of general education has been stressed by Director Sinnott of the Sheffield Scientific School; but despite his enthusiasm and that of Dean DeVane we have not yet approached this ideal in the operation of our new curriculum."
Of the implied assumption that the other disciplines had courses which were already suited or could easily be made suited to the purpose of a liberal education, one can only say that that assumption was entirely traditional at Yale, where the humanities were too often automatically equated with the liberal education of which they are a necessary but not self-sufficient component. See Pres. Report, 1949-50, p. 10.

the President's Committee intended to accomplish
the same goal by means of practical, operational,
performance-based efficiencies such as enrolling
better prepared students, using their time more effectively, and examining them in ways that would raise
their academic standards and challenge them to expand
their intellectual interests and horizons.[1]

In many ways, the unpublished directive of the
President's Committee was to figure out how to make
the agreed conclusions of the Andover Report effective
at Yale. And by deciding to adopt the main focus
of that report, namely the coordination and inter-
relation of school and college, the President's Committee was also inadvertantly failing either to
examine the Andover Committee's flawed philosphy or
to develop a new conceptual basis of its own. The
inherited inconsistency which equated an efficient
course of study with the purposes of liberal education
eventually could not be concealed from opponents
of the work of the President's Committee. The ironic
result was that the majority of the faculty who were
not in agreement with the President's Committee
adopted the same framework of effective interrelationship to promote "illiberal" ends which the President's
Committee would have abhorred.

Tom Mendenhall, Griswold's former colleague
in the History Department, was also a personal friend.
The two men were scheduled to make a tour of England
the summer before the President's Committee began
its interviews. As it happened, Griswold was forced
to drop out, and Mendenhall went alone. The report
which he made on his observations among the British
universities influenced the President's Committee
as a comparison between it and the Committee's final
effort shows. British schoolboys, Mendenhall found,
made an efficient transition to the university because
schoolwork in the last two years for those few who
could hope to make the transfer was directed mainly

---

[1]Griswold Mss., Box 65, folder marked President's
Committee on General Education: General Matters
(1952), passim. Also letter from Stephen B. Jones
to A. Whitney Griswold, 24 October 1952, in same
folder.

toward fulfilling the entrance requirements which
were set by the universities to satisfy their own
needs. The system, though ruthlessly selective,
had a unity of purpose which impressed Mendenhall.
It had a dedication to intellectual excellence as
the first priority which the Yale professor envied.
British universities acknowledged the primacy of
the teaching function (whatever the hazards to scholarship) and accordingly had refined teaching methods
in an admirable (and expensive) way. Their reliance
upon the tutorial system, with voluntary lectures
and a mandatory weekly essay, made for independent,
non-rote learning with an emphasis upon clarity of
thought and expression. The examination system,
which stressed written essays read by faculty readers
rather than standardized, "scientific" tests, assumed
self-integration of material, always under the guiding
hand of the tutor. British schoolboys began to specialize in the last two years of high school, but
it was specialization within the subject areas
designed to develop the intellectual abilities of wholeness of character which the British system so overtly
prized. The student was "put to using his mind with
increasing specialization on just those subjects
which best show what man was, is and ought to be
in the fullness of his powers." It was a very Lockean
approach, which, at its best, indicated that "if
the British experience is worth anything, there seems
to be another approach to general education through
proper specialization." Whether that approach could
survive in the America of Jamesian psychology, democratic pressure for wide access to college training,
economic considerations about keeping teaching costs,
and hence tuitions, on the low side, and a body of
knowledge that somehow continued to explode was
dubious.[1]

---

[1]T. C. Mendenhall, Report on British Schools
and Colleges, Summer 1952, Yale Archives; Griswold
Mss. Box 65, folder marked President's Committee
on General Education: General Matters (1952); quotations from pp. 26, 25. It turned out that Griswold,
whose father had died, was not able to join Mendenhall
on the trip, but Griswold had been in England during
the summer of 1950 before his inauguration. The
1953 trip was financed by a $3500 grant from the
Carnegie Corporation.

The President's Committee began by collecting
statistics and interviewing Deans. The Admissions
Office proffered a rather unfavorable view of the
state of secondary education across the nation and
the curricular pressures that that deteriorating
situation created. Mr. Noyes, Chairman of the Admissions Board, suggested that Yale was not getting
its share of the very brightest applicants, perhaps
because the Freshman Year did not provide a suitable
range of offerings which matched the varied needs
of the students, one of which was the possibility
of a three year BA degree.[1] Dean of the Freshman
Year Norman S. Buck felt that the problems students
encountered in their first year were apt to be moti-
vational or disciplinary in character, though obviously much should be done to attract more capable,
academically minded students. After considering
the administrative and organizational advantages
and disadvantages of a separate Freshman Year and
Freshman Faculty, a tentative consensus emerged that
the present arrangement was logically less defen-
sible than some kind of two-year grouping, despite
Dean Buck's feelings that such a set-up would dis-
courage the all-important teaching of new students.[2]
The President's Committee ranged far and wide with
Dean DeVane, from admissions to the problem of the
sciences to DeVane's persistent concern that extra-
curricular activities were overemphasized at the
expense of intellectual achievement. Specific distributional requirements were reviewed at some length.
When discussion turned to the desired character of
a Yale education, DeVane was emphatic about the necessity of viewing all four years whole. He was specific

[1]Minutes, 5 November 1952; Griswold Mss., Box
65, folder marked President's Committee on General
Education: Minutes of Meetings (1952-55).

[2]Minutes, 1 December 1952; Griswold Mss., Box
65, folder marked President's Committee on General
Education: Minutes of Meetings (1952-55). The two-
year Directed Studies program, which had been introduced with the approval of the Freshman Office, had
already partially undermined the conception of the
Freshman Year and had left its proponents vulnerable
to the kind of argument that making any exception
always occasions.

that the Freshman Year had outlived its purpose,
and he strongly suggested that educational policy
be consolidated in one place under the watchful concern of one faculty. DeVane made the point that
to divide any faculty into a teaching group for the
first two years and a scholarly group for the last
two would be disastrous, as it had proved to be at
the University of Chicago: "Without some chance
to do independent work, good men will die intellectually." At one point, DeVane suggested starting
specialization earlier and using the last year in
part for a reintegration of the student's work, a
concept which apparently originated in some program
at Princeton. The President's Committee did not
pursue the idea.[1]

One can only speculate why this conceptual seed-
ling fell upon such barren ground, though it suffered
much the same fate when a similar suggestion was
proposed at Columbia in the 1960s. In the first
place, the President's Committee was operating within
the 11-14 grade framework it had inherited from the
Andover Study. Second, the general education concept
which had taken root at Harvard, Columbia and Chicago
in varied ways was linked in all three colleges to
the first two years. Third, the President's Committee
was approaching the whole matter of revising general
education with the two-year Directed Studies program as a probable model. Lastly, Yale had recently
experimented unsuccessfully with a minor variation
of this concept. The six areas of distribution created by the 1945 Reforms, it will be remembered,
included one called Interrelationships of Knowledge.
Designed to integrate in either junior or senior
year the information to which the student had been
exposed in the other five distributional categories,
this synoptic category was easier to require than
fill with effective courses. The ones which were
supposed to, at least on the official transcripts,
carried names like Liberal and Collectivist

---

[1]Minutes, 18 December 1952; Griswold Mss., Box
65, folder marked President's Committee on General
Education: Minutes of Meetings (1952-55); quotations
from pp. 7, 9.

Movements in Modern Europe; Science, Philosophy and Culture; Ideologies of the Modern State; and so on. Courses were added to or subtracted from, offered or not offered in this distributional area year by year without coherent pattern or apparent purpose. In 1950, at the time when the Divisional Majors were strengthened and reorganized, the distributional category and the integration concept were quietly dropped by restructuring the areas of distribution.[1]

For whatever reasons, the failure of the President's Committee to appreciate DeVane's insistence on viewing Yale College as a four year educational whole would eventually permit it to outline a very limited kind of general education with the wrong purpose at its heart. The same shortsightedness had been evidenced in the unwitting transformation of Directed Studies from a four-year to a two-year program. At one time, President Griswold did remind the President's Committee that the needs for general education had to be met without jeopardizing the needs of the entire University, that the Committee must look forward to the graduate schools as well as back to the secondary schools. But for some reason, the university outlook was never able to grasp Yale College whole. The Deans of several of the graduate schools were, for example, unilluminating: Better coordination was necessary, more communication desirable, and a sound training in method, "a knowledge of how to work in a specific field," virtually a prerequisite. One Dean expressed a concern for the lack of "broad cultural background" which, in medicine, was coming to be viewed as important to the best training. Another, however, confessed to a sense that he should understand the undergraduate curriculum better. The Dean of the Law School went so far as to suggest more work in the social sciences, training in method in small classes, and even some casebook teaching. President Griswold, perhaps a bit bored,

---

[1]Undergraduate Course of Study Bulletins, 1947-48, 1948-49, 1949-50, 1950-51, Yale Archives. The proposal made at Columbia was Daniel Bell's The Reforming of general Education: The Columbia College Experience in Its National Setting (New York: Columbia University Press, 1966).

summed up the sense of the interview by commenting
that "the solution to the problem . . . lies in the
improvement of non-specialized education so that
it develops motivation and maturity as well as pre-
professional skills." The ardent advocate of liberal
education did not explain how specialized training
for specialized goals differed from non-specialized
training for specialized goals. In any case, the
President's Committee ceased interviewing, spent
the Spring drafting, and distributed its report in
September 1953.[1]

The President's Committee's analysis of the
problems facing Yale College and its criticisms of
present practices were clear, succinct and tersely
witty, the last probably the contribution of Whit
Griswold, who had a deserved reputation as a clever,
spontaneous humorist. Some of the clarity of the
President's Committee's presentation stemmed from
its decision that by limiting its field of discussion
to Yale, more service would be rendered to the public.
"The most pressing problems of non-specialized education" which Yale faced were four in number. The
first was the "enormous diversity in the background,
motivation and previous training of students"; second,
"the necessity to teach basic but not college work
on the one hand . . . and to include training programs
like ROTC on the other." Both difficulties originated
beyond Yale's control. The other two problems, both
internal, were the "failure of the student to commit
himself to the work Yale offers" and "the great and
complex problem of student maturity--or lack of it."
By failing to challenge new students appropriately,
Yale invited them to lose interest, seek refuge from
boredom in extra-curricular activities, never to
return to the main academic purpose of college life.
There was a further problem having to do with the
curriculum:

> Students and faculty alike tend to feel that
> the major is the crucial part of the undergradu-
> ate curriculum, and that the rest of the four
> years merely prepare for or adorn it. This
> feeling has two effects. The students tend

---

[1]Minutes, 7 January 1953; Griswold Mss., Box
65, folder marked President's Committee on General
Education: Minutes of Meetings (1952-55).

to go along passively but plaintively from
requirement to requirement, often asking nothing
more than to be carried by the conveyor belt.
And the faculty either give less time to the
planning and teaching of the first years, or
work hard at a departmental course but expect
it to have no primary purpose beyond that of
feeding the major.[1]

To counteract these difficulties, the program of
distribution, like basic studies, was strongly reaffirmed, though the "need for coordination" was clearly
noted. In the most telling paragraph of this section
of the report, the President's Committee said:

> There is, furthermore, no intellectual sequence
> or correlation in the program of distribution;
> it describes a series of courses in different
> areas, but they may be selected in any order,
> and they form a staggering and perhaps useless
> variety of possibilities. The common result
> is that all the courses move on the same intel-
> lectual plane--a plane determined by the abili-
> ties and training of freshmen. The causes of
> indifference among sophomores are many, but
> one for which the faculty should hold themselves
> responsible is the failure to provide intellec-
> tual demands which grow from and beyond the
> work of the freshman year. At the moment every
> course used by sophomores to satisfy a distri-
> butional requirement can be taken as an elective
> by freshmen. When one adds the fact that many
> men do not complete their requirements until
> junior year, it becomes apparent that elementary
> and often repetitious study dulls more than
> half the education Yale gives.[2]

Fundamentally, the President's Committee was
wrestling with several familiar problems. The heterogeneity of the student body and the diversity of

---

[1]Report of the President's Committee on General
Education, 1953, pp. 1-5; Griswold Mss., Box 65,
folder marked Report of the President's Committee
on General Education, 1953 (Final Draft).

[2]Ibid., pp. 5-7.

their training had only grown since the Course of
Study Committee tried to cope with this same problem
in 1945 by introducing the first advanced placement
credits. More important, the President's Committee
was faced with the acknowledged primacy, among both
students and faculty, of the major, and the inadequacy
of the distribution system as a corrective. As the
original outline of Directed Studies, the "Planned
Experiment in Liberal Education," had mentioned,
a distribution system in and of itself will not assure
coordinated breadth of understanding on the part
of the student. The key is not merely exposure to
a wide variety of information across several of the
fields of knowledge, but the happy facility to make
connections, as William James might have put it,
to relate or interrelate what is known--and the more
diversity in what is known, the better. In that
a distribution system tends to broaden and diversify
the areas where something is known, it facilitates
this process, though one can also imagine one single
course whose subject matter would be so broadly based
and whose instructor would be so widely knowledgeable
that that one course alone would constitute a liberal
education. Something of this sort sometimes fortui-
tously transpired with the classical curriculum.
On the other hand, if the courses selected among
the distributional offerings were offered, as the
President's Committee felt they were being offered,
merely as prerequisites or way stations on the conveyor belt to the BA degree, unsteeped in the traditional purpose of liberal education, the student
would be left wholly to his own devices to make,
or apparently not make, the interconnections which
would illuminate the whole. Traditionally, Yale
had never been willing to transfer the responsibility
for making these connections from the student to
the faculty, a characteristic of many general education programs, but the student's liberal education
was best fostered when the faculty overtly assisted
the process, as in the early years of the Directed
Studies program. What made the difference was that
Directed Studies was imbued with a strident liberal
purpose whereas the rest of the introductory curriculum was mostly left to the devices of the various
Departments.

The President's Committee believed that a potential solution to these problems lay in a "redefinition

of the first two years." A carefully coordinated
course of study was needed to serve five purposes:

1. to make possible a genuine continuity of
courses within given curricular areas--
continuity perhaps more necessary to non-
majors than to majors.

2. to increase steadily the difficulty of work
before students committed themselves to
their majors.

3. to assure the required basic training necessary to a complete Yale education.

4. to make a radical break with the "daily
prodding of the schools" and thereby increase
a student's responsibility for his own work.

5. to fulfill the "general need for development
in the university of the importance of coherent non-specialized study."[1]

The wording of this last purpose, in particular
the phrase "need for development of the importance,"
is unclear if not meaningless, probably the result
of authorship by committee. More significantly,
the President's Committee asserted that this unclear
purpose was implicit in the other four. The Committee
was grasping for a way to assert the importance of
liberal education, but without reference to the matter
of purpose, which is, ultimately, what distinguishes
it. This reluctance to deal in these terms has been
noted before.

Nevertheless, the President's Committee plunged
ahead. If the first two years of college could be
effectively organized "to make full use of student
interest and skill," then "solid grounds" would exist
for "asking whether a course giving highly specific
training in a single field is the only valid preparation for a major in that field." The experience
of Directed Studies indicated that it was not.
Several of the members of the President's Committee
had been involved in that program--Mendenhall

---

[1]Ibid., pp. 7-9.

especially--and one might see the work of the President's Committee as an effort to extend the "proven" benefits of Directed Studies to all Yale undergraduates. If this intention was thoroughly worthy, it was also ill-thought out and hazardous. First, there is always some danger that any small success will not survive the transformation into a large, general program with the resulting differences in scale; second, the same incipient problem existed in expanding the devoted core of instructors, some of whom were numbered among those Yale humanists who considered themselves (and indeed turned out to be) generalists, and who are always in too short supply; and third, any experimental, or off-line, program immediately loses its sense of being special as soon as it is "mainstreamed." This was particularly so in the case of Directed Studies where Yale had managed succesfully to tie a selected opportunity, and one perceived as such, with stiff intellectual entrance requirements. In short, that Directed Studies had worked for the capable in the top half of a class was no guarantee, or even an indication, that it would work for everyone, as Mendenhall had once pointed out. Still, the Committee had brought itself face to face with the key question: Is the major itself, the President's Committee asked, "designed to be an appropriate exercise ground for the mind, or is it patterned as a kind of junior graduate school?" Unfortunately, the President's Committee absolved itself from the responsibility of answering these questions, though "they deserve careful consideration if Yale's four year education is to justify itself as a whole." In so doing, the Committee avoided the crux of the matter, failing to realize that their two-year mind-set would inevitably undermine the liberal goals they were trying so hard to establish.[1]

The President's Committee proposed two plans to achieve its objectives. Plan A could be one means to achieve Plan B, or Plan B could be adopted immediately. Both were based on the division of knowledge into three logical "areas of instruction": the natural sciences and mathematics, the social sciences and history, and the arts. Plan A set aside one

---

[1]Ibid., p. 9.

of the student's five courses in both freshman and
sophomore year for language, ROTC, or basic skills
training. The other four courses were to be devoted,
in freshman year, to one introductory course in each
of the three "areas of instruction" and a second
in the "area of concentration" selected by the student.
In sophomore year, all four introductory courses
were to be followed by "second level" courses. This
approach was intended to achieve a "progression in
strength," which led, in the "area of concentration,"
to a comprehensive exam. Plan B adopted the same
basic framework and really differed from Plan A in
the organization within the four "areas of instruction."
Plan B was intended to introduce both continuity
and direction into the freshman-sophomore curriculum:

> Central in the program is a general examination
> at the end of the second year. Within each
> area of the curriculum would be created a spe-
> cific number of examination syllabi, based on
> reading of set books or the coverage of certain
> fields or levels of knowledge, depending upon
> the nature of the material. The entering student,
> advised in his choices on the basis of placement
> tests, would select the syllabi upon which he
> is to be examined. The work of his first two
> years then consists of a study of the syllabi
> in preparation for the general examination.

The arduous job of constructing the examination syllabi was to be undertaken by a board representing
those instructing in the first two years, those supervising the majoring years, and some outside examiners
from the Graduate School or a neighboring university.
The President's Committee wanted every student to
have "direct and sustained experience with the kind
of intellectual operation demanded by the three great
areas of study . . . a man is not educated merely
because he is exposed to the work of the three different kinds; he is educated if he has used his mind
in the different ways."[1]

In effect, the President's Committee was trying
to put some meaning and some organization into the
distributional system. They were electing to do
this by building in "progression but not

---

[1]Ibid., pp. 10-11, 23-25.

specialization." But there was a price: The student was required to select his "area of concentration" before enrolling in his first freshman course. This result was at variance with one of the original purposes of the Freshman Year and later of the whole distributional system, which was to act as a delaying mechanism to give the student an opportunity to survey the alternatives before choosing a specialty. This broad purpose had been repeatedly reaffirmed by the Course of Study Committee in its regulations involving the number of major prerequisites it allowed. The President's Committee had drifted into a position at variance with Yale's traditional posture.[1]

The President's Committee moved beyond curricular matters to make recommendations regarding the organization of the University. It proposed, as expected, the modification of the Freshman Year into a "social rather than an educational" unit, with Yale College made responsible for all four years of undergraduate education. More controversially, it also recommended establishing a Faculty for the First Two Years, which was to be subdivided into four parts "corresponding to one of the three areas of instruction or to the category of training subjects." On all four subfaculties, which together constituted the Faculty in General Education, membership would be automatically extended to anyone teaching in the first two years, though such membership was not considered a disqualification for service upon any other Yale faculty. The Dean of Yale College was the ultimate authority, with power to appoint faculty chairmen. The chief purpose of the four subfaculties would be "to organize the courses and supervise the general examinations" in the appropriate "areas of instruction." All courses were to be subject, as with departmental courses, to the approval of the Course of Study Committee. Relations between the Faculty in General Education and the Departments were carefully spelled out. To staff the courses designed by the general education faculties, the Departments would be asked to assign instructors. The Departments were supposed to place

---

[1]"Progression but not specialization" quote from the Report of the President's Committee on General Education, p. 12.

one third of their teaching time at the disposal
of general education, the balance going to graduate
work and the undergraduate major. All instructors
in general education would hold departmental appointments, but the four faculties of general education
would be entitled to suggest appointments. How the
faculties of general education would enforce their
suggestions upon the Departments who, under this
scheme, would continue to hold the whip hand in terms
of money and professional future was unclear.[1]

It was clear that the President's Committee
had not heeded DeVane's warning about dividing the
Faculty according to the teaching and research functions. The Committee was, however, endorsing in
a dramatic way the Dean's continuing efforts to curb
the University Departments' influence over the College
and particularly its curriculum. The proposed creation of a Faculty in General Education, a device
used in many other institutions, was an overt effort
to stem the tide of the increasing departmentalization
of an increasingly professional faculty. This new
effort had roots in DeVane's efforts in the late
thirties to introduce interdisciplinary majors, in
the strengthening of the distributional system in
the mid-1940s and the creation of the interdisciplinary Divisional Majors shortly thereafter. None of
these devices had been entirely successful, and certainly none of them had reversed the prevailing trend.
It was therefore questionable whether the President's
Committee's suggestion would appeal to a faculty
well aware that its professional future lay not in
containing research efforts, but in publicizing them,
particulary if that future involved an appointment
at some other university than Yale.

The most significant difficulty with the Report
of the President's Committee was a matter of nomenclature, a thorny problem in the whole field of
liberal education, sometimes known as general education,
sometimes known as the liberal arts. Sometimes the
term general education is synonymous with liberal
education, as for example in the title of the Harvard
Redbook. Then again, general education sometimes
refers to a pattern of sweeping, survey-type courses,

---

[1]Report of the President's Committee on General
Education, pp. 16-18.

like those at Columbia College. The humanities are often confused with the liberal arts by those who do not realize that astronomy, mathematics, and geometry were three of the original seven; and the phrase "liberal arts and sciences" compounds this particular confusion. Griswold began his term of office using the phrase liberal arts (as did Seymour before him). Then he started slipping now and again into "the liberal arts and sciences." About the time of the Andover Study, he seems to have combined the "liberal" of "liberal arts" with the "education" of "general education in school and college" and arrived at "liberal education," which he defined by means of its purpose, which was "to expand to the limit the individual's capacity--and desire--for self-education, for seeking and finding meaning, truth, and enjoyment in everything he does."[1] In 1945 the Course of Study Committee had talked about Yale's liberal education in contrast to Harvard's general education program which was perceived as a collection of general survey courses. The "general education" of the Andover Study was, however, the "general education" of the Redbook title, the synonym for Yale's 1945 "liberal education," which included (as had A. Lawrence Lowell's) the basic studies, the distributional system, and the majoring requirements. DeVane, for example, when he testified before the President's Committee on General Education was really talking about Yale's traditional liberal education, as his proposal for earlier specialization and later integrtion shows. When the Andover Study was concluded and its framework transferred to Yale, the term general (for the more traditional liberal) seems to have come with it. But over the next months, probably in the process of drafting and redrafting, the President's Committee failed to maintain any distinct terminology in its own writings. "General education" was used to mean both the totality of a four-year liberal arts education (for example in describing the 1945 Course of Study Committee's definition of liberal education) and also a two-year general studies program antecedent to the major (for example in the phrase which urged "intellectual continuity between the years of general education and the years of the major").

---

[1]A. Whitney Griswold quotation from Pres. Report, 1955-56, p. 10.

The confusion was not simply a question of seman-
tics, for two major reasons. First, if general education meant liberal education and its purpose was
"to expand to the limit the individual's capacity,
[etc.]," then the purpose of general education could
not be, as the Report stated, "[to develop] motivation
and maturity as well as particular professional skills."
The second reason was that by confusing a freshman
and sophomore year general education program with
Yale's traditional liberal education and by advocating
the first under the guise of the second, the President's Committee was misusing Yale's historic, traditional ideal without admitting it--and worse without
realizing it. For these two reasons, as well as
the still unquestioned assumption inherited from
the Andover Study that intellectual rigor and liberal
arts subject matter went hand in hand, the President's
Committee was, at the most fundamental level, on
dangerously shaky conceptual ground and therefore
terribly vulnerable to reasoned attack.

The public response to the final report of the
President's Committee on General Education was enthusiastic. The New York Times commented favorably
upon it, as did numerous alumni, educators, and interested citizens who wrote directly to President
Griswold. Copies of the report were formally requested
by Harvard, Princeton, and many other institutions,
some of them abroad. Liberal education had a devoted,
often articulate and sometimes uncritical following
which instinctively rallied to support a fervent
enthusiast like Yale's President. Actually, the
response was so overwhelmingly favorable that Griswold
cautiously fell to reminding his correspondents that
the President's Committee's work was unofficial.
Its report had been submitted to the Yale College
Faculty which alone had power to make official changes
in the curriculum. The Educational Policy Committee
of the Yale Corporation had to be reminded of this
salient fact, but the Faculty did not.[1]

----

[1]Griswold Mss., Box 65, folder marked President's
Committee on General Education: Press Comments (1),
Requests for Copies (3); also Pres. Report, 1953-
54, pp. 7-8; Educational Policy Committee Records,
9 October 1953.

Chapter V

THE FACULTY'S REPONSE: THE REFORMS OF 1955

As far back as memory stretched, initiatives regarding the curriculum had originated with the Faculty, normally within the Course of Study Committee. The creation of the President's Committee on General Education, though it was not intentionally conceived as a deliberate challenge to this tradition, did not follow the customary pattern of procedure. Yale Presidents as Presidents had never ever interfered with this Faculty prerogative, though each of them had been, as important individuals who remained individual members of the Faculty, very influential in Faculty meeting debates. In this particular case, because the President's name was affixed to the Committee, that fact alone assured that the Faculty would examine its Report and analyze the recommendations with suspicion and extra care. That examination exposed some of the fallacious assumptions that underlay the Committee's work, and it became apparent that the faculty did not agree with many of them. For example, the faculty was not willing to focus solely on freshman and sophomore years, though it did have to accept the administrative reorganization of the Freshman Year as a given. Neither did the faculty generally accept the notion of changing the distribution system entirely in order to reflect the notion of "progression through strength," since that conception was clearly more applicable to disciplines such as chemistry with clear upward sequences than to those without them, such as philosophy. Nor did the faculty believe that Yale alone would solve the national problem of restructuring grades 11 through 14 as a consistent whole. In more practical areas, the faculty proved unconvinced of the signal virtues of Directed Studies and unwilling to abandon its existing departmental structure in favor of the suggested four subfaculties of the Faculty in General Education. The comfortable system of interdepartmental negotiation centering around and about the distributional system was preferable to any such drastic reorganization, particularly when it might hazard professional futures. Finally, the faculty was perfectly prepared to sever the supposed connection between the recommended methodologies which promoted intellectual rigor and the general education objectives of the President's Committee.

113

Once severed, it was the more efficient techniques which survived along with those recommendations which effectively promoted earlier and increased specialization. And the most significant legacy of the President's Committee was the unexamined equation of liberal education with the "non-specialized" education in the two undergraduate years which preceded the major. Thus, in the end, the President's Committee proved to be out of touch with the Faculty as a whole, perhaps because that Faculty, which had increased in size enormously over the past decade, was not in any agreement, tacit or otherwise, about the key elements constituting a liberal education, nor, even, about the importance of defining and purveying such an education. The President's Committee's vision was clearly not the Faculty's, but on the other hand, there is no evidence that the Faculty had any vision of its own.

The Faculty of Yale College had agreed previously to refer the Report of the President's Committee to the Course of Study Committee and had asked the Dean to appoint several subcommittees to comment upon various sections of the Report. Since DeVane was away on a sabbatical, Alfred R. Bellinger, a classicist, was acting as Dean, and T. C. Mendenhall was, somewhat ambiguously, appointed Chairman of the Course of Study Committee. Mendenhall had served on this Committee as far back as the 1940s, and from this point of view was well qualified. On the other hand, he had been a leading member of the President's Committee.[1]

_____

[1] Faculty Record, 5 June 1953. The subcommittees appointed were: Committee on the Common Freshman Year; Committee on the School of Engineering; Committee on Examinations; Committee on ROTC; Committee on Languages and Literature; Committee on History, Economics and Political Science; Committee on Music and Fine Arts; Committee on Science. Incidentally, the signficance given to ROTC is explained not only (1) by the recent Korean War and (2) by its relative independence from control by the Yale Faculty but (3) the fact that forty students received full scholarship assistance from the government through ROTC (see CSC Minutes, 24 February 1955).

At the first Faculty meeting in the Fall of 1953, the Report of the President's Committee was duly transmitted and received. Before referring it to the Course of Study Committee, Acting Dean Bellinger reminded the Faculty of the considerable efforts of the President's Committee and urged careful consideration of the result. Specifically, he mentioned the danger of comparing the advantages of one system with the disadvantages of another. The Dean went on to note the hazards of assuming that the norms of one discipline were the norms of all, and he closed by reminding the Faculty, if such reminder was actually necessary, that though the President's Report must be treated with respect, it was not a _fait accompli_: The Faculty had the ultimate responsibility. Accordingly, comment from professors to the Course of Study Committee, both individually and through the appointed subcommittees, was entirely appropriate and actively invited. This method of considering the President's Report was probably designed by Dean DeVane, who had told President Griswold over the summer that he foresaw "a good deal of resistance from many vested interests. I trust that the larger purposes may prevail. It is hardly necessary to say that the battle will not be entirely won if the Faculty votes favorably. It will take years of detailed work. . . ." Clearly the Administration was trying by means of the procedure of consideration to build a constituency which favored the report and would, after its hoped-for adoption, work to implement it.

This procedure for consideration was challenged as soon as the Faculty moved into a committee of the whole. Professor John Schroeder, of the Department of Religion, a supporter of liberal education, suggested a series of hearings in which the President's Committee would answer questions and explain the rationale for its proposals and recommendations, but this motion was not carried.[1] More than

---

[1] _Faculty Record_, 1 October 1953; _Dean's Report,_ 1952-53, p. 8. See also memo by Charles W. Hendel, Chairman of the Philosophy Department, entitled "Information and Report Concerning the Discussion of the President's Committee's Report in the Meeting of

parliamentary rules were at stake. The matter was
potentially an explosive "constitutional" issue as
well as a political one. To show what was really
involved, Mendenhall had earlier referred in a draft
to the President's Committee as "extra-legal" and
"ad hoc." In a private communication to his friend,
Griswold took exception, not to the "ad hoc" but
to the "extra-legal," citing his overall responsibility as President, his right to appoint committees,
his previous consultation with Deans and Faculties.
In this case, the President's position was even
stronger, said Griswold, because it was clearly envisioned in advance that the President's Committee's
work would lead to the academic merger of the Freshman
Year with Yale College, and accomplishing that particular objective clearly exceeded the authority
of the Yale College Faculty. Mendenhall promptly
replied that "illegal" was the wrong word to describe
"the extraordinary, almost unprecedented nature of
the Committee, from the point of view of Yale College
tradition and practice."[1]

---

the Faculty of Yale College," Griswold Mss., Box
65, folder marked President's Committee on General
Education: General Matters (1953, 54). Incidentally,
Hendel was perfectly prepared to see philosophy
absented from its place in the distributional scheme
because he quickly realized it would play a key role
in integrating the new arrangement. Hendel had been
a member of the Course of Study Committee at the
time of the 1945 reforms.

Professor Schroeder expressed his views on
liberal education to the Course of Study Committee
in a thoughtful memo. See attachments to CSC Minutes,
14 January 1954.

[1]Mendenhall, admitting that it was to no one's
advantage to argue the constitutional issue in theory,
went on to tell Griswold that the position was not
as clear cut as the President had claimed. Mendenhall
had "no doubt that the President possesses the blanket,
over-all investigating authority" but that "the Yale
College Faculty always . . . reigned supreme over
its own curriculum." Griswold responded, "If I were
really going to court about it, I would challenge
this contention (of the Faculty) as only one side
of an unresolved conflict which has never been, and,
I hope, never will be fought out." See letter from
Griswold to Mendenhall, 4 August 1954; letter from

Once procedural matters were agreed upon, Mendenhall scheduled weekly meetings of the Course of Study Committee, which rapidly lost direction and focus. Part of the problem was that the President's Report overtly invited revision, having been structured as two suggestions among many possibilities. Another complication was that the Report was part diagnosis and part solution, and comment tended to shift from one to the other. This tendency was reinforced because the opening diagnosis was not factually substantiated and was thus open to immediate challenge. Further, the logical inconsistencies of the Report began to appear and create opportunities for digression. For example, on December 3, 1953, the Committee debated the conceptions and definitions of general education programs versus general education courses. On October 8, Professor Leonard Doob asked "on what evidence many factual statements in the early part of the report are based." Two weeks later it was reported that the Berkeley College Fellows felt that the Report was unrealistic in its estimate of the teaching time that would be required of all instructors. All the while letters from individual faculty members were being received and considered, either formally or informally, together with preliminary subcommittee reports or comments. Tentative positions and "strawmen" statements were drawn up by members of the Committee, revised and re-revised. If there was nothing else handy to debate, there was always the perennial question of how best to divide the unified body of knowledge among the three "areas of instruction." On December 10, Professor Robert Dahl reported hearing two quite contradictory rumors: (1) that the Course of Study Committee was being pressured by the Administration to report by February; and (2) that the Course of Study Committee had just barely defeated a motion to refer the proposed curriculum revision back to the President's Committee. The first rumor did not take realistic account of the state of the Committee's deliberations, and the second was simply untrue.[1]

Mendenhall to Griswold, 14 August 1954; letter from Griswold to Mendenhall, 20 August 1954; Griswold Mss., Box 20, folder marked Yale College: Courses of Study (1945, Seymour, 1950-58).

[1]A complete file of the Minutes of the Course of Study Committee for this period can be found in Carroll Mss., Box 2.

Although President Griswold was anxious for action, there is some indication that Mendenhall deliberately fostered the relatively chaotic nature and random pattern of the Course of Study Committee's deliberations. The slowness of progres is indicated by the Chairman's interim report made to the Faculty in February:

Mr. Mendenhall stated that the Committee had held many meetings discussing aspects of the President's report dealing with curriculum but not with administration. He noted that the Committee agreed with the statements of the Report regarding diversity of preparation of students and their motivation. He noted that high school graduates were extended by the work of the first two years, a situation not always true of graduates of independent schools. He emphasized that the Committee deals with the problems of Yale College as located in the middle of the University with a Faculty that has interests and responsibilities outside the College; that the Committee is taking budget problems into serious consideration; and that the Committee is studying the relation between the work of the first two years and the last two years. He noted that many sessions have dealt with Plan A. . . . He stated that the Committee[1] has not approved any part . . . of the Report.

---

[1]Faculty Record, 25 February 1954. Acting Dean Bellinger wrote to Griswold in early January 1954 about a conversation with Mendenhall that Griswold had been urging him to have, presumably to nudge Mendenhall along:
"Long and entirely amicable discussion. His position is (1) a committee has to do this amount of talking before it gets down to making progress, as the Committee did last year (the President's Committee); (2) relying on this experience and conviction, he has allowed the Course of Study Committee to find its own way through the bushes without much attempt to direct it . . . ; (4) the time has now come when we can begin to see results, and he can safely push the committee somewhat and will. If he is right about 4,

Griswold was not, as President of Yale, entirely forced to wait upon the Faculty's deliberations. There were many things he could do in support of the Report of his Committee on General Education and its recommendations, and some of these he did. The first was to seek broad public support by means of his 1952-53 Report to the Alumni. Griswold devoted all of this document to a discussion of the Liberal Arts, in twenty-five oft-quoted pages, succinctly outlining the crisis in the secondary schools and how that affected Yale, the decline of the liberal arts in American education and the tragedy this represented, and the steps Yale was undertaking to reverse this downward spiral. There was no doubting Griswold's sincerity or his articulate intensity:

> the purpose of the liberal arts is not to teach businessmen business or grammarians grammar, or college students Greek and Latin. . . . It is to awaken and develop the intellectual and spiritual powers in the individual before he enters upon his chosen career, so that he may bring to that career the greatest possible assets of intelligence, resourcefulness, judgment and character . . . "men are men," Mill said, "before they are lawyers or physicians or manufacturers; and if you make them capable and sensible men, you will make them capable and sensible lawyers or physicians." I know of no better statement of the purpose of the liberal arts nor any that so firmly establishes their place in a national education system that is dedicated, as ours is, to the preparation of men and women not just for intellectual pursuits but for life.[1]

the problem is pretty well taken care of." Griswold Mss., Box 65, folder marked President's Committee on General Education: General Matters (1953-54).

[1] Pres. Report, 1952-53, pp. 1-13; quotation pp. 10-11. This Report was reprinted in A. W. Griswold, Essays on Education (New Haven: Yale University Press, 1954).

Griswold briefly reviewed Yale's recent historic involvement with the liberal arts--the Reforms of 1945, the Mellon grant for the liberal arts, Yale's participation in the Andover Study leading to the work and report of the President's Committee, now before the Faculty. Yale's President offered this progression to the alumni as proof "that Yale is 'alive to the major movements in undergraduate education today.'" The Course of Study Committee was, it should be remembered, already meeting to discuss the Report of the President's Committee when Griswold's Report to the Alumni was circulated to the Yale community. Apparently Griswold was still confident about the outcome of its deliberations.[1]

The President's Committee on General Education also continued to function, noticeably and publicly. It investigated the curriculum of the Engineering School and instigated a major reform of it. The Committee also got involved with the Music School, the Drama School, and the School of Fine Arts (soon to be the School of Architecture and Design). While worthwhile reforms did arise from this second phase of the President's Committee's work, one can conclude that a major unspoken purpose of its efforts was to demonstrate to the Yale College Faculty the depth of the President's conviction and the intensity of his purpose. When that Faculty did act in 1955, the efforts of the President's Committee were allowed to drag to an end.[2]

When Griswold had the chance to exercise power directly, he did. The President promptly recommended to the Corporation, which concurred, that the curricular responsibilties of the Freshman Year be transferred to the Dean of Yale College. The Report of the President's Committee had consistently viewed the first two years of college education as a unit,

---

[1]Pres. Report, 1952-53, pp. 13-20; quotation pp. 19-20. Griswold returned to the whole subject in the Fall of 1954 in his 1953-54 Report, commenting on progress to date and urging yet again his ultimate goals. See Pres. Report, 1953-54, pp. 5-12.

[2]Pres. Report, 1953-54, pp. 10-12; Pres. Report, 1954-55, pp. 9-15.

following the pattern established by the Directed
Studies program. Freshman Year was at variance with
this position. So was the separate Freshman Faculty,
which was to be consolidated with the Yale College
Faculty. Griswold credited the Report of the President's Committee with delineating clear, educational
rationales for these changes, but since Freshman
Year probably had outlived its original function
and purpose, it was easy to view its institutionali-
zation as an obstacle to coordinated curriculum planning of any kind. Yet in surmounting this obstacle,
Griswold also destroyed the Freshman Faculty, which
tended to be less departmentalized than the Yale
College Faculty, and which honored good teaching
above all. He also significantly increased the size
of the Yale College Faculty, perhaps beyond the point
where it was possible for that group to view itself
as a meaningful, functioning unit.[1]

The Course of Study Committee continued its
weekly meetings during the late Winter and Spring
of 1954. Lacking, in the Report of the President's
Committee, a clear line of argument to follow, it
wandered, getting not very far not very fast. The
Committee argued whether it was wise to ask freshmen
to commit themselves to an "area of concentration"
before getting to Yale; that concern drifted into
a discussion of appropriate prerequisites for admission and the methods, if they existed, for testing
applicants to ascertain their levels of accomplishment.

---

[1]Pres. Report, 1953-54, pp. 8-10. Mendenhall,
incidentally, was a member of the Freshman Faculty.
    The Freshman Year, at the instigation of its
Dean Norman S. Buck, annually allowed students to
comment upon the abilities of their teachers. These
surveys were used to determine promotions from instructor to assistant professor as well as to allow the
Dean to emphasize the teaching he felt was so important. After reorganization, the Freshman Year continued to function as a counselling and administrative
unit, since freshmen did not live in residential
colleges but were assigned as a group to the Old
Campus. Dean Buck moved on to become Associate Provost (and later Provost) of the University and was
succeeded by his assistant Harold B. Whiteman, Jr.

Periodically, the Departments were urged to provide introductory courses that would serve concentrator and non-concentrator alike (as if the hardships of the experience with Science I, II, and III could be urged away!). However, since the Committee had agreed that some distribution system was essential, and since they had agreed, for some illogical reason, that basic studies were to be combined with distributional credits for curriculum planning purposes, the major problem of defining the distributional "rubric" recurred over and over. It was a conceptual problem to be sure; but more practically, if all the Departments were not included in the distributional scheme, then some time for electives had to be allowed in order to keep these "outside" Departments alive. Just where to draw the distributional line was apt to vary depending on whether one's discipline was probably within or probably without the boundary.[1]

In April 1954, the Course of Study Committee concluded that its "present line of approach was not effective." And the Committee agreed to proceed by looking "at the present course of study with an eye to its effectivenes and its weak points." Although the Committee may not have fully realized it, the President's Committee's Report had just been irrevocably altered from a plan of action into a strong influence on business-as-usual. The proposals to create a Faculty of General Education thus became moot, as did the concept of comprehensive examinations at the end of sophomore year. Mendenhall, as chairman, did ask each committee member "to be prepared to compare the proposals of the Report with the present educational program of Yale College," but never again was the President's Committee's Report to be the focus of the Course of Study Committee's efforts, though it was often considered and sometimes dealt with. It was far simpler to discuss the "program of distribution," which the Committee happily did for the balance of the academic year.[2]

---

[1] CSC Minutes, 11 March 1954, are an excellent example.

[2] CSC Minutes, 8 April 1954.

Mendenhall reported orally to the Faculty in
May 1954, and over the summer he prepared a more
formal, written report for President Griswold. This
document, in retrospect, is full of forewarnings.
The Course of Study Committee, for example, "could
never wholeheartedly subscribe" to the Report's focus
on the unity of the last two years of school and
the first two years of college, emphasizing instead
the four years of college. Similarly, the Committee
questioned the Report's concept of "progress in
strength," being more impressed with the variations
in possible sequence in different disciplines: What
was clear progression in science was not, perhaps,
so clear in history. More pointedly, the Committee
had investigated Directed Studies, and talked a little
about Plan B, and it concluded that Directed Studies
was "incapable of being extended to the whole class,
even were that desirable." Mendenhall also commented
upon "the possible inconsistency of asking the young
academic to embark upon time-consuming, new courses
while making it clear to him that his progress at
Yale, or especially his chances of getting a post
elsewhere, would depend so heavily on his scholarly
output." In each instance, the Course of Study Committee was questioning a fundamental premise of the
President's Report.[1]

Since Mendenhall was acutely aware of his "dual
position" as a former member of the President's Committee and now Chairman of the Course of Study Committee, he added to his report a more hopeful section
covering his personal impressions, an action which
implied his efforts to be impartial in the balance
of the official report. Mendenhall expressed his
belief that the Faculty would have voted down the
President's Committee's Report had it been considered
on a take it or leave it basis. Thus, he saw no
alternative to the procedure the Course of Study
Committee had adopted. Mendenhall pointed out that
his Committee had not yet really considered "the
very closely interrelated ideas of progress in
strength, area concentration, and interdepartmental

---

[1]Report to the President by the chairman of
the Committee on the Course of Study, Yale College,
particularly Section III, pp. 4-13; attached to CSC
Minutes, 14 October 1954.

courses." Nor had it debated the many good ideas
of Plan B, particularly "the de-emphasis of the course
unit, the two-year sequences, the comprehensive examination at the end of the sophomore year, the general
emphasis on more responsibility for the individual
student." Mednenhall told Griswold, "I see no reason
why the Committee will not get to these matters next
Fall and why the strategy already adopted will not
still prove to be the most effective one." And he
closed a bit defensively, by saying "To me the worst
and most rragic [sic] outcome of our present inquiry
would be to lose the battle to preserve what is useful
and adaptable to the Report for Yale while its national reputation continues to grow." The situation
was more serious than Mendenhall was conveying, either
because Mendenhall was making the best of it for
his enthusiastic friend or because he genuinely did
not realize how shaky the Report's future was, or
both. In any case, to his copy of the minutes of
the Fall's first Faculty meeting, Griswold attached
a handwritten note: "When, oh when will they ever
get to the Report on General Education?" Would he
have been so anxious if he had correctly appraised
the situation?[1]

When the Fall came, Dean DeVane returned from
his first sabbatical in more than fifteen years to
his traditional place on the Course of Study Committee.
The "program of distribution" had always been the
bulwark with which DeVane shored up his belief in
liberal education. Strengthening it was his major
contribution to the Reforms of 1945, and the Dean
had been refining the system ever since. DeVane
was no friend of general education courses, having
once commented that their chief virtue lay in making
it impossible for secondary schools to imitate college
work. So it should have been no surprise that from
the very beginning, discussion in the Course of Study
Committee centered around DeVane's new proposal of
three distributional areas and not around the concepts

---

[1]Ibid., pp. 13-17. Griswold's note can be found
in Griswold Mss., Box 20, folder marked Yale College:
General Faculty Minutes (1950-63).

of "areas of concentration," interdepartmental courses, and "progress in strength."[1]

Every proponent of distribution favors "breadth," usually as a corrective against over or premature specialization. Thereafter, complications quickly arise, because there are two conceptions of breadth sharing the same label. Advocates of the first conception see distribution as a way of maximizing a student's exposure to the great fields of knowledge, of assuring that every student learns those minimum facts that every educated person should know and that all educated men should hold in common. They talk about keeping options open to undecided freshmen. Advocates of the second conception interpret breadth as meaning competence which extends beyond one narrow area of concentration. They argue the importance of sequence within majors and one or two minors, and they are apt to disparage survey courses and see wide distribution requirements as promoting superficiality. The distribution system and Yale's 1945 Reforms are an example of the first conception; the concept of "progress in strength" of the President's Committee's Report is an example of the second. The point is that these conceptions, both under the one nomenclature of breadth, and both opposed to specialization, are mutually contradictory. If the purpose of distribution is to whet the student's appetite for knowledge, to keep options open, to force maximum exposure to all the fields of knowledge, the student will then be encouraged to experiment over as wide an area as possible. If, on the other hand, the student is forced into deeper involvement in one, two, or three areas of knowledge, the width of his exposure will necessarily be less wide. Given that the student has time to digest only a finite amount of curriculum, a student could not organize his schedule to maximize both conceptions of breadth.

---

[2]CSC Minutes, 14 October 1954, 28 October, 1954, 4 November 1954, 11 November 1954. DeVane's exact comment was "Perhaps the only good argument for so-called general education is that it devises new courses and combinations of courses--courses which the preparatory schools cannot imitate--for Freshmen and Sophomores." See Dean's Report, 1950-51, p. 12.

A line must be drawn somewhere between the two opposed ends, and no paper compromise obviates this necessity. The Course of Study Committee essentially spent the whole Fall of 1954 arguing where best to draw the line. This process reinvolved the Committee in the problem of the sciences. The Subcommittee on the Natural Sciences had lengthily recommended a two-year sequence in accord with the concept of "progress in strength," thereby doubling the existing, unpopular one course distributional requirement. This recommendation reopened the whole problem of the teaching of science in Yale College and its unfortunate history. And the whole problem of specialized courses for non-specialists, not only in science but in social science, cropped up once more and as inconclusively as ever. In its 1955 Report, the Course of Study Committee ended up supporting the two year sequence, soliciting once again, as in 1945, the favor of the science Departments Griswold had been so careful to include among his President's Committee.[1]

The Course of Study Committee got so involved in the matter of distribution and concentration that Mendenhall, who was already drafting its report, was forced to remind the group that it would have, in one way or another, to deal with the President's Committee's Report in front of the whole Faculty-- and by extension the interested public. The glaring omission was Plan B, which to date had not been debated. When it appeared on the agenda, on January 20, 1955, DeVane recommended that Plan B be modified and adopted as an honors major. The Dean, who had often advocated honors programs as a way of raising intellectual standards in the College, was deftly handling a potential political issue, but he was also assuring a safe future for Directed Studies and protecting the Mellon-funded sophomore seminars against an untried plan, which seemed to him not

---

[1]See Report of the Committee on the Natural Sciences and the Report of the Committee History-Social Sciences Working Group included in 1953-54 Minutes of the Course of Study Committee folder, Carroll Mss., Box 2.

entirely in accord with Yale's venerable traditions.[1]
The Committee promptly followed DeVane's leadership.

Mendenhall then established a timetable requiring
his Committee to report to the faculty in the Spring
and continued working on his draft report. Perhaps
this procedure was copied from the President's Committee, which was, in comparison to the Course of
Study Committee, a small homogeneous group. The
larger group was, however, far from agreement--even
tacit. A month before Mendenhall submitted his

---

[1]CSC Minutes, 20 January 1955, 27 January 1955.
DeVane's thought was parallel to, if not inspired
by an insightful critique of the Report of the President's Committee written by George W. Pierson, with
whom he had served on the Course of Study Committee
and who was then hard at work on Volume II of his
Yale history. Writing on October 19, 1953 to A.
S. Foord, a member of the President's Committee,
Pierson said,
    "Sympathizing with the analysis and essential
    purpose of the President's Committee, one casts
    about trying to see how the difficulties can
    be met. This has led me to wonder whether it
    might not be useful to consider adapting the
    reforms, and in particular Plan B, for more
    limited application.
    Roughly, how would it be to consider Plan
    B for the abler and more ambitious students
    and the present distribution plan (perhaps with
    some elements of Plan A) for the great majority?
    . . .
    This would not be ideal. But study of past
    efforts leads me to believe that trying to lift
    the standards of everyone almost inevitably
    means, first the sacrifice of opportunities
    and special attention for the able. Next it
    turns out that not all of the poorer students
    can handle the new requirements. And so retreat
    becomes necessary.
    . . . At Yale once we have discovered a pro-
    gram that is good for the few, the temptation
    is to generalize it for the many, without enough
    consideration of what happens both to the program
    and to the few." (Attached to CSC Minutes,
    12 November 1953)

efforts for consideration, Profesor Dahl, a member
of the Committee, suggested

> that there were areas other than the revision
> of the curriculum to which the Committee should
> still address itself. Can any change in the
> fundamental social structure of undergraduate
> Yale be made to improve the intellectual climate?
> . . . Should the Committee strive for longer
> and more comprehensive final examinations?
> What improvements could be made through adoption
> of a new grading system?

The Committee debated these and other issues and
finally decided "to support a policy of concentrating
on the curriculum itself as the most effective way
of engaging the student's interest and improving
the quality of his performance." This was a pretty
basic issue to be debating while a final report was
being drafted, but the Committee pressed on, holding
on March 24, its last meeting which the Committee's
Secretary, perhaps jocularly, referred to as the
"47th meeting devoted to the Report of the President's
[Committee] on General Education."[1]

The purely curricular changes which the Course
of Study Committee recommended established a "program
of distribution and concentration," which was a compromise between the advocates of the two opposite
views of the purposes of breadth. Every student
was required to complete by the end of Sophomore
year a full-year course in each of six fields, unless
the course work had been satisfactorily anticipated
in secondary school. Further, in the process of
satisyfing the requirements of distribution, every
student had to achieve a degree of concentration
in preparation for the major by completing, during
his first two years, three courses in one of the
three "areas of concentration," and two courses in
a second "area." A course used to satisfy the requirements of distribution, if qualified, could also be

---

[1]CSC Minutes, 3 February 1954, 24 March 1955.

used to satisfy the requirements of concentration.[1]
The Course of Study Committee's second recommendation
contemplated transforming the four existing Divisional
Majors into a single honors program "operated in
the general design of Plan B, for sophomores, juniors
and seniors." A sophomore enrolled in this program
was to join a seminar in his "area of concentration,"
was responsible for a reading list in addition to
the normal requirements of distribution and concentration, and was expected to pass an oral as well
as a written examination at the end of sophomore
year. Junior and senior years were characterized
by discussion courses with syllabi, reading lists,
Senior Essays, and final examinations before outside
examiners--in short, the instructional methodology
of Plan B. The Faculty adopted this recommendation
only in principle, and in fact, the concept was never
tried in practice.[2]

The Reforms of 1955 ended up rejecting most
of the fundamental premises underlying the Report
of the President's Committee. The faculty were not
willing to confine their attention to grades 13 and
14, as the compromise which limited the concept of

---

[1]Faculty Record, 14 April 1955, 21 April 1955.
Report of the Committee on the Course of Study
to the General Faculty of Yale College, April 1955,
pp. 1-5; attached to CSC Minutes, 31 March 1955.
The six distributional areas were (1) English; (2)
a foreign language--ancient or modern; (3) history--
ancient or modern, or history of art, or history
of music; (4) the social sciences; (5) the natural
sciences or mathematics; (6) classical civilization
or philosophy or religion. Courses in 6 could be
postponed to junior or senior year and might not
be anticipated in secondary school.
The three Areas of Concentration were (1) the
Humanities and the Arts; (2) History and the Social
Sciences and (3) the Natural Sciences and Mathematics.

[2]Faculty Record, 14 April 1955, 21 April 1955;
1955 Report of the Committee on the Course of Study
to the General Faculty of Yale College, pp. 6-7.
When the Faculty did adopt the honors program,
it was actually adopted in the shape of the existing
four Divisional Majors, each infused with Plan B
methodology. See CSC Minutes 19 January 1956 and
attachments.

"progress in strength" to the "area of concentration"
shows. And the concept as a whole was rejected except
as it conformed to the needs of the student's eventual
major. For similar reasons, among them the habit
of departmentalized thought, the faculty was wary
of the President's Committee's recommendations, particularly Plan B. They were well aware of the difficulties of developing interdisciplinary courses,
because Directed Studies, which was the clear model
for Plan B, had provided sound experience. The Course
of Study Committee explained it excellently, listing

> the essential concomitants of successful col-
> laboration in such ventures: individuals com-
> petent in their own disciplines, intellectually
> and personally committed to working with men
> from related fields, supported and protected
> by their departments and the administration,
> and operating with students in manageable, quali-
> fied groups.

The Committee then pointed out that

> . . . although such efforts in intellectual
> cooperation require assistance from above, they
> cannot be developed by fiat but rather must
> be encouraged to grow out of whatever favorable
> combination of research activity, natural develop-
> ment of interdisciplinary interest, personal
> friendship, and common concern for teaching
> may happen to bring two members of the faculty
> together into a classroom.[1]

Nor was the faculty willing to accept the
Report's suggestion that they reorganize themselves
into a Faculty in General Education at the expense
of the existing departmental structure. Individual
professors were only too aware of the need for "support and protection" by their Departments. DeVane
commented that "the intense departmentalization which
has flourished at Yale since the reform of 1919 was
never stronger than it is now." To make matters

---

[1]1955 Report of the Committee on the Course
of Study to the General Faculty of Yale College,
p. 23.

130

worse, the Provost, as chief educational officer, had recently issued a new policy with regard to appointment and tenure. This policy stabilized the number of tenured professors (because of financial limitations) and permitted appointments only as vacancies occurred. To be appointed "the individual must have a record of research achievement represented by publication." To hammer home the point, the policy specifically asserted that time of service at Yale alone (presumably largely teaching time) does not count for tenure consideration. The Fellows of Berkeley College regarded this tenure policy as "inconsistent" with the "time to be devoted to teaching duties in the new curriculum proposal."[1] When talk of this nature reached Griswold, he claimed that the President's Committee "had no inclination whatsoever to undermine either time for research or time for teaching." But the faculty was not so easily reassured, feeling (1) that the instructors in general education at Chicago had been deceived about their futures; wondering (2) if the same were true at Harvard; asking (3) if recent departures from Directed Studies had had the same cause; pointing out (4) that the new programs were doomed if teaching in them cut individual faculty members off from their Departments; and concluding (5) that "the issue of promotion was so closely related to the educational changes suggested . . . that both must be considered together." They were not so considered, and that lack of coordination helped destroy the faculty's willingness to accept the revisions recommended by the President's Committee's Report.[2]

---

[1]DeVane quotation in Dean's Report, 1952-53, pp. 6-7. He went on to say "These Departments are prone to regard their own interests so closely that they forget they are but parts of a larger purpose and a more comprehensive enterprise in which they should participate."

The tenure and promotion policy is attached to Educational Policy Committee Records, 10 April 1953.

The Fellows of Berkeley College are quoted in CSC Minutes, 22 October 1953.

[2]CSC Minutes, 29 October 1953. The same matter was raised, but without suggesting conclusions, in the April 1955 Report of the Course of Study Committee, p. 31.

In reporting to the alumni concerning the "action taken by the Faculty of Yale College on the recommendation of the President's Committee on General Education," President Griswold put the best face on the result that he could:

As we review the entire program from start to finish, it becomes evident that it does not constitute a curricular revolution. It is selective and optional rather than uniform and obligatory. It rests on opportunity rather than compulsion. . . . Educational dictatorships are no more successful than political ones . . . just as democracy puts the fulfillment of opportunity up to its citizens, the new Yale College program puts the fulfillment of opportunity up to its students. . . . Yale College has, I think, gone about as far as it can go to meet the demands of its best students and to serve the needs and best interests of all of them. The other half of the way is up to the students.[1]

Griswold claimed that by means of the distribution and concentration program, "the ancient liberal concept of the unity of knowledge is preserved and at

---

[1]Pres. Report, 1954-55, pp. 1-15; quotation, p. 8. Much later Griswold told members of the Corporation that "While neither Plan A nor Plan B of the President's Committee on General Education seemed to commend itself in its entirety to the Yale College Faculty, many of the recommendations (e.g., with respect to seminars, advanced credits and admission, refinements in the requirements for standard and honors programs, etc.) had been adopted and that the report had stimulated a thorough restudy of the entire curriculum." Education Policy Committee Records, 10 January 1958. Earlier Griswold had said "[We are] examining means in the light of clearly defined ends and objectives. . . . We could take present means for granted and reject any ends that might cause us to revise or even reexamine them. . . . If we confuse existing ways and means with ends, or think of them as sacred and untouchable, the chief academic activity of 1953-54 will have been shaking, not moving." Pres. Report, 1953-54, pp. 11-12.

the same time individual aptitudes and special interests are provided substantial incentives."

One could argue, however, that "individual aptitudes and special interests" as reflected in possibilities for specialization, concentration, and majoring had in fact been the beneficiaries of the curricular turmoil created by the Report of the President's
Committee which had been specifically aimed at foster-
ing "non-specialized" education. There was considerable evidence. For example, while the Course of
Study Committee was considering the Report, the
Faculty, in an almost unnoticed action, increased
the number of courses available to the major in junior
and senior year from five to six. In addition,
despite the Faculty's one-course limitation on prerequisites, after 1955 specialization was possible,
even encouraged, in freshmen and sophomore year by
means of the required "progress in strength" in the
"area of concentration," chosen before the student
spent an hour in a Yale classroom. The whole reversal
from the original purpose is perhaps seen most clearly
in the transformation of Plan B from a series of
interdisciplinary general education courses into
an honors program which included a sophomore seminar
in a major field and comprehensive examinations at
the end of the same year. Before the fact, President
Griswold and the President's Committee on General
Education would have identified the Divisional Honors
Program not as "the climax" of a whole program of
general education, but as proof that "the major looms
large in all eyes."[1]

Why had this ironic result come about? There
are several reasons. To begin with, the administrative reforms inducing intellectual rigor, such as
the introduction of more seminars, comprehensive

---

[1]Griswold quotation from Pres. Report, 1954-
55, p. 7.
For faculty vote to change major requirements,
see Faculty Record, 18 November 1954. One prerequisite was still permitted.
"Climax" appears in Pres. Report, 1954-55, p.
7, and "Major looms large in all eyes," in Report
of the President's Committee on General Education,
p. 9; Yale Archives.

exams and closer articulation of entrance requirements and advanced placement, were not logically or organically tied to the content of the President's Committee's curriculum--as we have seen. Thus, these procedural reforms could be separated from general education subject matter, as indeed they were, only to be joined to specialized study. The transformation of Plan B into a Divisional Honors Program is the representative case. Another reason for the Faculty's unwillingness to follow the President's Committee's leadership was its awareness that Yale alone could not reform the shortcomings of secondary education, nor the imperfect coordination between it and the colleges. Often this concern was expressed in terms of foreign language preparation, which many high schools, for example, chose not to undertake. The Course of Study Committee made several fruitless attempts to make contact with Harvard and Princeton relative to this concern.[1]

Yet another fact which militated against the proposed curricular reform was that peculiar Yale tendency already traced to look at the matter of dividing the unity of knowledge through a prism which had itself already divided the humanities from the sciences. The sciences had been separated from Yale College historically, and, as DeVane never tired of pointing out, they continued to be separated geographically upon the campus. Yale College continued to award both BA and BS degrees. Perhaps for these or for whatever reasons, Yale professors were unable to think of the problem of special courses for nonspecialists without meaning science courses for nonscientists. Never was it classical courses for nonclassicists or language courses for non-linguists. This tendency turned the matter of specialized versus non-specialized education into an interdepartmental negotiation: In the current instance, were the sciences to "get" one distributional requirement or

---

[1]See letter from George W. Pierson to A. S. Foord, 19 October 1953; Carroll Mss., Box 2, folder marked Course of Study Minutes, 1953-54, after Minutes dated 12 November 1953.
See also CSC Minutes, 15 March 1954, p. 2. Bellinger did write to Dean Bundy at Harvard and the Dean at Princeton, but their replies are not noted.

two? Arousing departmental concern was surely not
conducive to achieving an interdisciplinary curriculum.[1]

Still another reason for the fate of Griswold's
initiative was the changed nature of Yale College
Faculty. Since the days of the 1945 Reforms, it
had grown enormously, by the addition of the Sheffield
Scientific School Faculty and the Freshman Faculty,
as well as by the normal increase that the Provost's
tenure policy was designed to halt. The diminishing
of its corporate sense was noted by all, the President's Committee in particular, and regretted by
many. Dean Bellinger, for example, said that "the
Faculty has been so useful and so influential that
it would be a great pity to have it subside into
a body which operates by Committees only and regards
life through Departmental eyes." There is evidence
that that point had been reached: Mendenhall told
Griswold several times that he had been unable to
provoke a Faculty discussion of the President's Committee's Report despite the efforts made to involve
a great many of them in the process of considering
the Report. And the Faculty as a whole never disputed
the Provost's new tenure policy as possibly not in
the best interest of the "larger purpose and more
comprehensive enterprise" that DeVane felt was, or
should have been, at the heart of the Yale College
Faculty's function and existence. Things had changed
in the decade between 1943 and 1953, between Gabriel's
report to the Educational Policy Committee and the
Report of Griswold's Committee on General Education.
Gabriel's committee came from a small Faculty that

---

[1]Griswold himself was not free from this prism
effect. As spokesman for the liberal arts, he was
well aware, and often stated publicly that the original liberal arts included the sciences, specifically
mathematics, geometry, and astronomy. Yet upon occasion he referred to "the Liberal Arts and Sciences,"
which epitomizes the mind-set I am describing. For
an example, see the Pres. Report, 1954-55, p. 4.
More substantially, in establishing seven Aims for
Yale, Griswold listed as no. 2 "To strive
for a balance between the arts and sciences in which
each becomes instructive and useful to the other,
as an object lesson to the country that such a thing
is possible." Ibid., p. 19.

was socially compatible, if academically argumentative, thoroughly Yale in background and training. They met frequently and accomplished things in their meetings. The Course of Study Committee could and did represent their views, and knew that they were doing so. Ten years later, when the President's Committee did not represent the Faculty, the situation had been altered so markedly that it might be fair to conclude that no committee, however chosen, would ever speak for the Faculty as a whole, since there was, in fact, no whole Faculty.[1]

Put another way, at the very least there was no longer a faculty consensus, either assumed or articulated, on the definition or curiculum of liberal education. As we have seen, the President's Committee did not distinguish between a two year "non-specialized" general education program and the traditional liberal education which was Yale's ideal. In the President's Committee's unexamining eyes, the first was an appropriate and integral part of the second. That assumption might have been agreed to by many of the humanists of generalist persuasion who dominated the Yale College Faculty and the Course of Study Committee in the 1940s. But now, though the ideal of liberal education was as cherished as ever, its definition had gotten so blurred and its adherents so widely diverse that in the majority they would not accept the President's Committee's truncated definition in lieu of the real thing, though they were often unsure what exactly that was. And since the President's Committee had done nothing to help clarify the confusion, in fact had unwittingly added to it, the Faculty simply voted no and conservatively elected merely to reform the familiar curriculum without altering its conceptual bases.

In the last analysis, the question arises whether Griswold and all the others who were interested in intellectual vigor and liberal education were, in fact, asking more of the course of study than even a thoroughly and well reformed curriculum could deliver. In other words, was the Course of Study Committee correct in its assumption that the

---

[1]Bellinger quotation in Dean's Report, 1953-54, p. 10.

curriculum was "the most effective way of engaging the student's interest and improving the quality of his performance?" By the time it actually reported to the general Faculty, even the Course of Study Committee seemed to be having second thoughts, for at the very end it suggested a willingnes to consider other alternatives:

> [there] remain two very fundamental questions which it would be false to pretend we have answered. First, how far can any manipulation of the curriculum make intellectual achievement more attractive than these [sic] outside activities in the context in which the educational process now operates? Second, how far does the faculty wish to go beyond the curriculum to explore the conditions that foster or impede the achievement of the educational goals which it sets?[1]

The Faculty had no immediate response, but the Course of Study Committee began to discuss these concepts in an informal way. Several years later, the faculty itself would take interest and suggest experiment. But for the moment, enough was enough. On April 22, 1956, the Course of Study Committee concurred "with a sentiment which is widely held throughout the Faculty, namely, that the curriculum should be left alone for a while . . . ," and even Whitney Griswold agreed.[2]

---

[1]1955 Report of the Committee on the Course of Study to the General Faculty of Yale College, p. 34.

[2]Report of the Committee on the Course of Study, 26 April 1956, Griswold Mss., Box 20, folder marked Yale College, Courses of Study, together with Griswold's handwritten note "Cooling Off Period! O.K. AWG." Faculty Record, 26 April 1956.

Chapter VI

DIRECTED STUDIES

By the mid-1950s, the Directed Studies program
had accomplished much to be proud of. Following
Mellon's magnificent gift in 1952, the program had
been expanded and had had good years. Applicants
for admission to the program were increasing, and
it was generally thought that those accepted were
"clearly superior to a cross-section of the Freshman."
Dean DeVane believed that "the word has spread to
the better schools and the better students entering
Yale that the Directed Studies program is the one
to take if the student is willing to work at his
studies." Many of the recommendations of the President's Committee on General Education had been rooted
in Directed Studies, and in many ways, the whole
of Griswold's initiative had been an attempt to adapt
what was perceived as a successful experiment to
general usage throughout Yale College.[1]

When the Faculty disposed of the recommendations
of the President's Committee, Directed Studies was
left in an awkward position. Shorn of the accepted
and clearly understood function of an experiment,
it desperately needed to define another goal and
identify a new purpose, particularly since President
Griswold's attention had been turned toward the residential colleges and their potential for the liberal
education of undergraduates.[2] Several new rationales

---

[1]CSC Minutes, 27 January 1955; Dean's Report,
1952-53, p. 8; Dean's Report, 1954-55, p. 14. In
1954-55 there were 148 applicants for 90 places in
Directed Studies. In 1955-56, there were 170 applicants for 110 places.

[2]The faculty had clearly realized that it was
not possible for Directed Studies and Plan B as proposed to co-exist:
"The factors of diversity and motivation were
clearly present in the Directed Studies group
of students. The program was no longer experimental, but had reached the status of a special
program. Instructors in the programs believed
that the better-than-average student seemed
to benefit more than his classmate of less than
average abilities. While some expansion of

for Directed Studies were tried, among them the conception of the program as a testing ground for new courses, as a bellweather for good teaching, and as a highly visible public relations effort which attracted exceptionally capable admissions applicants. None were successful, and Directed Studies was soon in great difficulty. The program could not sustain its contention that it was generally available nor defend its adequacy as broad preparation for any major. Nor could Directed Studies maintain its prescribed curriculum and the corollary concept of a common intellectual experience. And finally, Directed Studies could not accurately assert that its curriculum was philosophically coordinated and integrated. When, at the end of the decade, financing became a serious problem once again, Directed Studies was indefensible. Just as the whole of Griswold's initiative, which started out as a signal effort to promote broad-based liberal education, ended up permitting earlier specialization, so Yale's planned experiment in liberal education ended up as a small honors seminar specializing in the humanities as early as freshman year.

The story is another instance of the purposes of specialization necessarily controlling the non-specialized education for which it has become the referant. In the case of Directed Studies, this occurred because the needs and prerequisites of the various majors had to be reflected in the program, and as these needs differentiated, so did the program fracture and fragment, until it could no longer be considered liberal education in any traditional sense. This result was probably inevitable from that moment in the 1940s when the decision was made that turned a four year planned experiment into a two year preparatory program.

Directed Studies had been initiated as a program for a cross-section of Yale College students for the obvious reason that any experiment in general education would have to be of general rather than

---

the program might be contemplated, the consensus was that it should never be greatly expanded. It was the general opinion that there would not be room for Plan B and Directed Studies, and that preference for retaining Directed Studies was clearly marked among the instructors in that program." See CSC Minutes, 6 May 1954.

limited accessibility. This tenet was not strictly
adhered to from the beginning: The Course of Study
Bulletin annually stated that Directed Studies was
suitable preparation only for the BA degree (the
BS degree was pointedly omitted in the statement).
Nevertheless, the principle was honored, if in the
breach, though the breach did widen when <u>Science</u>
<u>I</u> was removed from the prescribed curriculum and
when ROTC had to be accommodated in the early fifties.
The principle was also slighted by the program's
drop-outs, a problem which began in the late forties
and accelerated in the mid-fifties. In 1954-55,
more freshmen than usual resigned, most of them pre-
med or engineering students "who had been admitted
in numbers for the first time." DeVane believed
that the combination of Directed Studies and the
pre-professional programs was "too much to take."[1]
Directed Studies had never been considered suitable
preparation for the BA major in music, and in 1956,
a Directed Studies student intent on majoring in
math had to make special arrangements with the Mathematics Department. More insidiously, there is some
evidence that applicants to Directed Studies had
been screened since the early 1950s and that freshmen
who intended to major in subjects like math or industrial engineering--even economics--were simply not
admitted to begin with. This bias in favor of the
traditional humanities was formalized in the academic
year 1957-58 when students interested in majoring
in scientific fields were advised in the Course of
Study Bulletin not to enroll in Directed Studies
without consulting the Dean. This statement was
probably inserted because 1957-58 was the first year
that the Yale Faculty permitted the science Departments to offer the BA degree, but whatever the reason
for its inclusion, Directed Studies was now formally

---

[1]Dean's Report, 1954-55; see particularly Appendix C. It is interesting to note in this document,
a positive commentary on Directed Studies, that DeVane
justified the program on some new bases: First,
that Yale had received excellent publicity for its
high quality hard work; second, that a diversity
of course offerings was an excellent way to fight
the growing standardization of American life. This
latter argument, pushed to its limit, will destroy
any prescription of any kind within the curriculum.

and officially a program for non-scientists. Directed
Studies in the Liberal Arts and Sciences had become
Directed Studies in the Liberal Arts, indicating
yet again the strangely one-sided definition Yale
often gives to that nomenclature.[1]

From the beginning, the first two years of
Directed Studies had been conceived as a prescribed
set of courses designed to promote a common intellectual experience. This concept was as fundamental
as general availability to all kinds of students,
though this principle too had not been strictly
adhered to. Since it was nonsensical to ignore the
variety of foreign languages studied or not studied
by all Yale applicants to Directed Studies, the
original intention, as we have seen, was that all
students should share the experience of studying
some foreign language for the first time. In practice,
this ambition was immediately reduced to the new
or continued study of some language at any level
appropriate to the individual. In effect, this meant
that even initially only four-fifths of the student's
courses were prescribed, therefore shared and therefore part of the common intellectual experience.[2]
The substitution of history of art for the required
freshman science course in 1950-51 did not alter
the amount of the student's work which was prescribed,
though it necessarily opened to question the basis
upon which the prescribed courses were integrated
and consequently cast doubt upon the central function
of the philosophy course. In 1951-52, the program
was adapted for ROTC students, and the next year,
the first acknowledged options appeared in the freshman year: The Directed Studies applicant could choose
betwen Math and Elementary Atomic Physics (or substitute ROTC). Now only three-fifths of the work was

---

[1]Course of Study Bulletin, 1956-57, 1957-58.
For applicant screening see "Directed Studies Candidates: Class of 1956," 18 July 1952 and handwritten
notes thereon in Carroll Mss., Box 8, folder marked
Directed Studies Program.

[2]Course of Study Bulletin, 1946-47; 1945 Report
of the Committee on the Course of Study to the Yale
Faculty, Yale Archives.

prescribed in either year, though that work was,
to be sure, common to all students. In 1956-57,
a freshman could elect, as always, his language (or
substitute ROTC); and choose among math and science
and physics. Philosophy, literature and the history
of art alone remained prescribed. In sophomore year,
only philosophy and history were mandated. Studies
in Society I, which included the Spring Project,
DeVane had once described as the "capstone" of the
whole program, could be replaced by Studies in Society
A and Studies in Society B. In short, options had
appeared once more, and the common prescribed work
of sophomore year was now reduced to 40 percent.[1]
The detail of the changes is unimportant; it simply
documents a clear trend toward the proliferation
of alternatives. This tendency, rooted in language
preparation and ROTC requirements, aided and abetted
by advanced placement and the increased numbers applying to the program, helped destroy the notion of
Directed Studies as a prescribed set of courses leading to a common intellectual experience for a significant number of students. The propensity of sophomores
to drop out after the first year also damaged the
concept of a community of common understanding.
    Although the rhetoric of philosophy's role as
a central coordinating element survived, such coordination could not be achieved. It had been difficult
enough at any time, even in the heady early years.
When the various configurations of courses open to
Directed Studies students exploded as they did, it
simply became impossible. Consequently, with the
tenet of accessibility, the tenet of prescription
and common experience, and the tenet of philosophical
coordination removed from the articles of faith of
Directed Studies, one can surely conclude that the
program had been basically reduced to a philosophically foundationless collection of courses, some
of which happened to be very good and very challenging
to able students. They also tended to be excellent
preparation for humanities majors. This being the

---

[1]Course of Study Bulletin, 1950-51, 1951-52,
1952-53, 1956-57. The ROTC adjustment of 1950-51
and the Spring Project of Studies in Society I are
covered in Chapter III. In 1957-58, a new Sophomore
elective called Art and Literature was added.

case, it was only a matter of time before some non-humanities department which felt it could offer courses of equal breadth and value to its potential majors, and which was having trouble doing so in the Standard Program, would propose such an undertaking under the Directed Studies rubric. As it turned out, it was the science Departments who seized the opportunity, assisted by the Directed Studies "faculty" and the Russians' sputnik.

In 1956 Yale awarded 75 BS degrees and 696 BA degrees. This disparity troubled even the humanists. Yale's pride as a bastion of the liberal arts was hurt, DeVane claimed, because Yale did indeed understand that the pure sciences were part of the liberal arts. Nevertheless, the 1955 Report of the Course of Study Committee combined the natural sciences and mathematics for distributional credit purposes, thereby making it possible for a student to obtain a Yale degree without completing a science course of any kind. And this at the very time the University was making great efforts to build up the science Departments and provide them with new facilities and laboratories. This particular nadir for the natural sciences in Yale College was particularly unfair because these Departments had cooperated with the President's Committee on General Education and had assisted the Course of Study Committee in its deliberations leading to the 1955 reforms. The Special Subcommittee on the Natural Sciences had submitted a long and thoughtful report, which among other things, outlined a two year sequence of courses for "non-concentrators" in the natural sciences.[1]

---

[1]This report claimed that it was impossible in the sciences to offer introductory courses that would satisfy both specialists and non-specialists. However, it admitted the validity of courses of the second type, which, from the point of view of Yale College and the Course of Study Committee, was a marked improvement. Interestingly, the report also suggested a senior year course "on the impact of the natural sciences upon the political, psychological and artistic aspects of modern civilization which would serve as an extremely valuable background for students concentrating in literature, history or the social sciences." This concept became intertwined

Dean DeVane continued to believe that large numbers of students came to Yale intending to major in science, were turned off by the initial teaching that was proffered, and ended up in other majors instead. The scientists, on the other hand, still wondered about admissions policies and the counselling of freshmen. Neither wrestled with the problem of how one entices a "non-concentrator" into a science major with a course which will not serve him later as a specialist. However, this problem could be minimized and a lot of departmental hard feelings avoided if one of the courses developed by the Sub-committee on the Natural Sciences could be utilized in the Directed Studies program. This approach also appealed to DeVane, because it conformed to his newly asserted notion of Directed Studies as a testing ground for course improvements, which if successful could be generally applied later. Accordingly, a new Science I, Concepts of the Physical Sciences, replaced physics in the freshman year of Directed Studies.[1]

At about this time, the Yale School of Engineering under the influence of the President's Committee on General Education was participating in a study, funded by the Carnegie Corporation, of the proper amount and type of humanities courses suitable to engineering education. A joint committee of Yale

---

with the Divisional Major in General Science, which never came into being. Report of the Special Committee on the Natural Sciences, p. 9, Carroll Mss., Box 2, folder marked Course of Study Committee, 1954-55; Dean's Report, 1955-56, pp. 2-5.

[1]DeVane justified the dismembering of Studies in Society I on the same bases, i.e., giving the sciences a chance and experimenting in Directed Studies. DeVane believed with Mendenhall that it was a mistake not to have tested the original Science I and Science III in Directed Studies in the 40s before requiring them in the Standard Program. DeVane was genuinely concerned about the sciences and was convinced that teaching was responsible for their unpopularity. He was, therefore, receptive to the sciences' new initiative. Dean's Report, 1955-56. The appendix to this Report is DeVane's status report on Directed Studies.

College and the School of Engineering designed an integrated humanities program consisting of four courses: literature and history in the first year, social science and philosophy in the second. These courses, which were to be electives, were "planned to be a coordinated unit as in the present Directed Studies program," a not-surprising conclusion, since members of the Directed Studies "faculty" had been involved in their design. DeVane and Mendenhall then got the Carnegie Corporation to allocate $75,000 to fund a three year experiment for 60 students in the Engineering School. Although favorably received, the program ran out of funds after two years, which meant either that the University had to make up the difference, or that the program had to be reduced in scale, which it was. Priorities in the Engineering School were such that it was then decided not to try to raise funds to extend the program beyond 1961.[1]

In February 1958, Professor Harold G. Cassidy, a chemist who had served briefly as the first executive secretary of the President's Committee on General Education, was chairman of a Committee on Teaching Science, set up by the University-wide Division of Sciences. Cassidy recommended to the Course of Study Committee a Directed Studies Program in Science which would enroll twenty men who would go through the two-year program as a group, although they would be sharing several courses with "ordinary" Directed Studies students. Two new courses would be created for the program: Math II (to follow Math I) and Science IV: Life and Its Enrivonment (also to be offered in sophomore year). The introduction of these courses created two-year sequences in math and in science along the lines previously recommended to the Course of Study Committee by the earlier Subcommittee on the Natural Sciences. Until foundation

---

[1]Dean of the Engineering School Report, 1955-56, p. 6; Dean of the Engineering School Report, 1956-57, pp. 1-2; Dean of the Engineering School Report, 1958-59, pp. 4-5; Dean of the Engineering School Report, 1959-60, pp. 1-2; "Carnegie Studies in Engineering: A Report on the Year 1958-59," Griswold Mss., Box 17, folder marked Carnegie Corporation of New York (1959-63).

support could be achieved, the new science program
would be funded from the regular Directed Studies
budget, since "the program was designed to be a satisfactory preparation for almost all majors in Yale
College, both science and non-science." In approving
this proposal, which had the full support of DeVane,
one wonders if the Course of Study Committee realized
that it had certified two different Directed Studies
programs supposedly directed to exactly the same
end. More probably, the Committee was reacting to
the national crisis created by the launching of sputnik and the oft-noted need for Yale College to be
dealing effectively with scientific instruction.[1]

The new, that is, the second, Directed Studies
program was conceived with such speed that there
was no time to include it in the Course of Study
Bulletin for 1958-59. Nevertheless, thirty-three
students with relatively high mathematics aptitude
and achievement scores applied. None had decided
to major in a science Department, and most were still
undecided and neutral. As had been true in the first
years of Directed Studies, this year was characterized
by much enthusiasm, among both students and faculty.
The program rapidly developed an honors flavor, as

---

[1]CSC Minutes, 20 February 1958; Dean's Report,
1957-58, p. 14. DeVane made it clear that the sciences were in better graces than ever. Since 1956
they had been allowed to award the BA as well as
the BS degree, and Science I, II and III which were
aimed at "scientific literacy" were doing well.
Ibid., p. 11.
    Science IV bore a direct "family resemblance"
to the second course of the science sequence proposed
by the Subcommittee on the Natural Sciences in 1955.
    A year later the Course of Study Committee
strengthened the distributional requirement for science
in the Standard Program.
    For the inadequacies of instruction, see letter
from Brand Blanshard, Chairman of the Committee on
the Yale College Deanship, to Griswold, 15 January
1958, which mentions the prevalent concern that the
sciences were not as strong as the humanities, and
that the disparity was growing. Griswold Mss., Box
20, folder marked Yale College: Deanship Committee,
(1957, 1958).

might have been expected, and if there were any problems, they lay in the students' response to the prescribed literature course. Most happily, in late 1959, the Carnegie Corporation, which had been involved in Directed Studies in one way or another for a decade, appropriated $100,000 to fund the new program. Now Yale had a second, philosophically foundationless collection of courses, some of which happened to be very good and very challenging to a second group of able students.[1]

The problems facing Directed Studies were not limited to finding new conceptual foundations for the program, or programs, as they now were. It emerged that the creation of <u>Studies in Society A</u> and <u>Studies in Society B</u> in the regular program was a "drastic overhauling" of the second, less successful year of Directed Studies as well as an opportunity for the social sciences to make a more visible display of their offerings to students who might major in these subjects. The Carnegie interns urged a long look at the sophomore curriculum and reported that the program was no longer a strong attraction to the teaching staff. Since many professors were hesitant to undertake the assignment, the temporary instructors also suggested asking the Departments involved to assign at least one tenured faculty member to the program. The Carnegie interns, who were not members of the Yale Faculty, had heard much criticism of Directed Studies as a "training ground" with a large turnover in personnel.[2]

---

[1]Course of Study Bulletin, 1958-59. The Directed Studies Program in Science was listed in 1959-60.
See Harold G. Cassidy, "Directed Studies in Science," <u>Newsletter of the Inter-University Committee on the Superior Student</u> 2 (November 1959), in Griswold Mss., Box 32, folder marked Directed Studies (1950-1963).
One hundred thousand dollars was payable at the rate of $20,000 annually for five years, the last payment being due December 1, 1963. Letter, from Florence Anderson to Griswold, 18 November 1959, Griswold Mss., Box 32, folder marked Directed Studies (1950-1963).

[2]Dean's Report, 1956-57, p. 2; CSC Minutes, 18 April 1957.

Most ominously, Directed Studies was again running out of money. By 1956, expenditures on the four programs supported by the Mellon gift--that is, Directed Studies, the Divisional Majors, Scholars of the House, and the sophomore seminars--exceeded revenues from their endowment; and reserved surpluses from the preceding years were being rapidly eaten away. The cost of buying teaching time from the Departments had gone up, and the funding of the Carnegie interns was to end in 1957. By 1958, the surpluses had been exhausted. DeVane, who administered the budget for Directed Studies, was then forced to ask the University for further assistance. The only alternative, said DeVane, was to curtail the program drastically, beginning in 1959-60.[1]

Since the 1955 Reforms DeVane had, as we have seen, begun to justify the Directed Studies program first, as a testing ground for new, experimental courses; second as an exemplar of fine teaching in seminar format which he felt needed stressing; third, as a powerful attraction in recruiting top students; and fourth, as excellent public relations. None of these rationales were related to the content of the curriculum in Directed Studies; none were related to the original general education purposes of the program; and all could be or were equally true of the sophomore or college seminars. In addition, there is some doubt that the teaching in Directed Studies was as good as it had once been or as DeVane claimed. For all these reasons, Norman S. Buck, who had been Dean of the Freshman Year and who was now Provost, was properly suspicious of investing University funds to maintain the program in its present size and scope. His position was appropriate in view of the fact that the Yale College Faculty had, in 1955, determined that Directed Studies was not an experiment which merited wider adoption in the standard college curriculum. On what sound basis could Provost Buck increase support for a "failed" experiment which was now searching, rather

---

[1]Dean's Report, 1955-56, p. 8; letter from DeVane to Norman S. Buck, 3 October 1958, Griswold Mss., Box 60, folder marked Old Dominion Foundation (Paul Mellon) (1951-63).

unsuccessfully, for a new role as a "special" program, apparently dedicated to offering a sort of better duplicate, or duplicates, of what was already offered in the Standard Program? Thus, when DeVane suggested to Buck that he credit Directed Studies with an amount equalling the estimated cost of educating its students in the Standard Program, the Provost refused to do so despite DeVane's strong recommendation that Directed Studies be continued as "the University's conscience in the matter of good and careful teaching in the first two years of college."[1]

Buck was no doubt also influenced by the fact that President Griswold had found a new vehicle to promote liberal education which did not involve either the course of study or Directed Studies. When the Yale College Faculty had taught the President the limits of his power to reform the curriculum of the College, Griswold's enthusiasm for liberal education had not been destroyed but redirected, in this case toward the residential colleges and the sophomore (or college) seminars (or discussion groups). In the summer of 1955, Griswold and his friend Mendenhall had gone to England to study the residential colleges at the principal British universities, and particularly those at Oxford and Cambridge, which had, in the 1930s, been the models for the ones built at Yale. Their trip was prompted by two concerns about the situation at home. The first, the most pressing though the least fundamental, was that the overcrowding of the residential colleges in New Haven was threatening the purposes for which they had been built, namely to build a sense of community among the students and a shared life between faculty and undergraduates. The second concern, a deeply philosophic one, was that the colleges had not yet found an entirely appropriate educational purpose, perhaps

---

[1]CSC Minutes, 19 November 1959; letter from DeVane to Buck, 3 October 1958. DeVane calculated that Directed Studies accounted for three fifths of the instruction of 10 percent of both the sophomore and freshman classes. These 210 students paid $1200 each in tuition, so that the credit DeVane was requesting totaled $151,200, which would have solved the financial problem handsomely.

because that had not been a priority intention of
the donor.[1]

The overcrowding at Yale had come about during
World War II and after the war when the University
felt morally obligated to accommodate the returning
veterans. When that immediate crisis passed in the
early fifties, Yale had found itself unable to reduce
the number of undergraduates to pre-war levels,
because everyone had gotten used to the extra income
the extra tuitions provided, and even they, in fact,
did not provide sufficient revenues. Thus, the residential colleges were housing 52 percent greater
populations than they had been designed for. The
obvious solutions to this overcrowding, which
afflicted virtually every college dormitory in the country, were to move students off-campus or to build
more housing. The first was counter to every historic
tradition at Yale, which had been a residential college from its beginning; the second was enormously
costly. Griswold did not wish to incur that huge
expense, unless he were convinced of the educational
validity of the residential college, which necessarily
meant a reexamination of its present educational
functions and an analysis of future objectives.[2]

---

[1]Griswold and Mendenhall's trip was financed
by a grant from the Commonwealth Fund, the foundation
which had received the estate of the donor of the
colleges, Edward S. Harkness. See Griswold Mss.,
Box 62, folder marked Trip Abroad, 1955. For the
definitive account of the establishing of the residential colleges at Yale see Pierson, Yale: The
University College 1921-1937, chaps. 10, 11.

[2]A. W. Griswold, "A Proposal for Strengthening
the Residential College System in Yale University,"
29 April 1958, p. 9; Griswold Mss., Box 74, folder
marked Undergraduate College: New Colleges: Morse
and Stiles: Final Proposal to Mellon--Old Dominion
Fund: Copies dated 29 April 1958. A. W. Griswold
and T. C. Mendenhall, "Yale's Stake in the Residential
Principle: Evidence from the British Experience,"
pp. 1-4, 13-16; Griswold Mss., Box 94, folder marked
Yale's Stake in the Residential Principle.

If the original connections between Yale's colleges and those in England and the prospect of a pleasant sojourn enticed Griswold and Mendenhall across the ocean, there was also something happening abroad which was truly significant. War-torn Britain was investing money in the residential hall principle, not only at Oxford and Cambridge but at the Scottish universities and the new provincial universities. This expensive policy, which was financial nonsense, was fully supported by the University Grants Committee, the government agency which was the source of two-thirds of the total income of all British universities. It was also supported by the Ministry of Education. Two main arguments supported the practice: first, the belief "that undergraduates educate each other fully as much as they are educated by the faculty and that the residential collegiate unit represents the most perfect setting for this process"; second, the democratization and increased accessibility of higher education, the influx of many "who came from homes with little or no tradition of culture" necessitated residential halls to "enrich" the lives of the new undergraduates. Everywhere the Yale visitors found "a widespread public conviction in the value and importance of the residential principle in higher education," and they were quick to conclude that Yale must and should build new colleges and eliminate overcrowding: "the Yale residential college now looms up as the means whereby the university may fulfill that historic obligation" to prepare students "for life" as well as educating them "in specific fields of learning."[1]

---

[1]Griswold and Mendenhall, "Yale's Stake in the Residential Principle: Evidence from the British Experience," pp. 5-13. See also University Grants Committee, "Report of the Subcommittee on Halls of Residence," Her Majesty's Stationery Office, London, 1957, in Griswold Mss., Box 74, folder marked Undergraduate College: New Colleges: Morse and Stiles: Mellon-Old Dominion Proposal: Working Papers (File B). This report was attached to Griswold's April 29 proposal when it was forwarded to Paul Mellon, who had himself done some graduate study at Clare College, Cambridge. Quotation from "A Proposal for Strengthening the Residential College System in Yale University," 29 April 1958, pp. 7-8.

During the boat trip home, Griswold and
Mendenhall wrote a report on their visit, which
Griswold gave to his supportive friend Paul Mellon.
Shortly afterwards, Yale had an opportunity to buy
land suitable for the construction of two new colleges,
once the city high schools on the site could be
vacated and demolished. Meanwhile the priority of
building new residential colleges escalated until
the Corporation declared it to be first among all
Yale's needs. Intrigued, Mellon apparently vacillated
anonymously because a year and a half later, in
January 1958, Griswold wrote his classmate that the
Corporation was forcing him to consider the unpalat-
able alternative of government-financed sophomore
dormitories: Time was moving on, and something had
to be done. In the nicest possible way Griswold
was demanding a decision from his potential donor,
and when it came, it was favorable. That spring
Mellon and Griswold worked out the details of a
$15,000,000 gift. Only half of Mellon's contribution
was intended for the bricks and mortar of the two
new colleges. The remaining $7 plus million went
to endow the educational purposes of the residential
college--to create college libraries and college
book purchase funds, to sponsor 47 new sophomore
seminars, and to create 11 new upper-class seminars
which, like the sophomore seminars, were to be given
in the colleges. Mellon's generosity was specifically
designed to further the "educational aims" of the
"Residential College Plan," among them "the educational functions of the Fellows in the Colleges,
with particular emphasis on College teaching and
counseling duties." Griswold had already equated
these aims with the traditional purpose of liberal
education, to prepare undergraduates "for life."[1]

---

[1] Griswold, "A Proposal for Strengthening the
Residential College System in Yale University," passim;
letter from Griswold to Mellon, 23 January 1958;
also letter from Mellon to Griswold, 5 June 1958;
Griswold Mss., Box 74, folder marked Undergraduate
Colleges: New Colleges: Morse and Stiles: Proposal
Made to Mellon-Old Dominion Fund: Correspondence
(1958, 1959, 1962). Other folders relevant to this
subject are located in Griswold Mss., Box 74. A
further educational purpose of the residential college
cited to Mellon was the opportunity for a reintegration of knowledge: Communication among professors

Although Mellon had mentioned Directed Studies
as a sort of contingent beneficiary of any excess
income from the new endowment, he had also pointed
out that program's close relation, "in spirit and
purpose" to the college seminars. Indeed, the Course
of Study Committee briefly considered whether the
second year of Directed Studies might be merged with
the sophomore seminars (which would have solved
Directed Studies financial problem). This concept
was not pursued, since there were enough problems
involved in expanding the college seminars and extending their benefits to upperclassmen. These benefits
were intended to include fine teaching in the same
small seminar format which had once characterized
Directed Studies and only Directed Studies. And
once more, one rationale for the continuance of the
Directed Studies program went by the boards. Any
perspicacious observer could have extended the argument: The college seminars could, as easily as
Directed Studies, serve as a testing ground for new
courses, attract top students, and make for good
public relations. In other words, the rationales
DeVane had used to defend Directed Studies to the
Provost were equally applicable to the college seminars and hence were not, in the last analysis, valid
at all. Thus, seeing the direction in which Griswold
was moving, and considering the fact that the President could have, but did not, ask Mellon to increase
the endowment of Directed Studies, the Provost must
have found it relatively easy to decline to support
Directed Studies with scarce University funds.[1]

---

of the various disciplines was both desirable and
possible within the residential college. Cardinal
Newman would have enjoyed this particular argument.

[1]See letter from Mellon to Griswold, 5 June
1958, and letter from DeVane to Buck, 30 October
1958. There is also some reason to believe that
later on the Old Dominion Fund began to question
the allocation of funds from the 1952 gift to Directed
Studies. See Memo from Griswold to DeVane, 30 October
1962, Griswold Mss., Box 32, folder marked Directed
Studies.
CSC Minutes, 5 February 1959. Mendenhall
attended this meeting as a guest. Although still on

Short of money, confused of purpose, and lacking the classroom vitality which had characterized its early years, Directed Studies was in terminal trouble, though the $100,000 Carnegie Corporation grant for Directed Studies in Science eventually enabled both programs to go forward in 1958-59. During the academic year 1959-60, the situation became critical and was much discussed by the Course of Study Committee, after DeVane advised them of the unavoidable need to trim the financially over-extended program. There were two alternatives: Reduce the number of students involved or reduce the number of courses offered. Complications emerged immediately. The Admissions Office was anxious to preserve Directed Studies as an attraction for top quality applicants, particularly in view of Harvard's new program of freshman seminars. On the other hand, there was confusion whether or not Directed Studies in Science was or was not for prospective science majors. No consensus had been reached on this question, and apparently even the Departments involved were confused. Still another survey analyzing the effects of the program on Directed Studies students was authorized, and possible new sources of funds were fruitlessly discussed. DeVane summarized the situation by stating that it was time, even without regard to the financial situation, for a sweeping reevaluation of Directed Studies, though that major reorganization, not being

---

the Faculty, he had recently been elected President of Smith College and would leave Yale at the end of the academic year. In 1956, DeVane had told Griswold, "the secret of the success of [Directed Studies] seems to lie in the small classes, taught by excellent teachers around a table, and students deeply engaged in a common enterprise." Dean's Report, 1955-56, p. 8. This concept was exactly what Griswold wanted within the residential colleges and not in a "special program."
For the Faculty's disinterest in combining Directed Studies with the College Seminars, see CSC Minutes, 29 October 1959.

as pressing as the financial crisis, could be postponed for a year.[1]

The student survey, though it solved none of the Committee's confusions, made some interesting observations. As expected, Directed Studies students were initially very able, but when compared to equally able counterparts in the Standard Program, their upper-class records were strikingly similar. To a man Directed Studies students liked their program, but many of them believed that the hoped-for integration of knowledge did not operate effectively, and that it should not be emphasized, as it was, in the pamphlet describing Directed Studies. Nothing else the students had to say about their program was new to the Committee, and nothing in their comments obviated the need for a shakeup. "Experiments," said DeVane, "lose their luster after a time," and he told Griswold he would make "a drastic revision" over the summer. The Dean attributed the decline of Directed Studies partly to financial pressure and partly to the increasing number of freshmen who achieved advanced placement. This was an oversimplification.[2]

DeVane chaired the special committee, which, after some minor modification to his suggestions, developed a specific recommendation covering the

---

[1]CSC Minutes, 29 October 1959, 10 November 1959, 14 January 1960. For an example of an unclear clarification of the purposes of Directed Studies in Science, see remarks of Harold G. Cassidy, in CSC Minutes of 14 January 1960.

The Harvard Freshman Seminars, supported by an anonymous donor, later revealed to be Edwin H. Land of Polaroid, were a one year experiment involving approximately 200 Harvard and Radcliff freshmen engaged in supervised independent study organized into 18 projects in fields ranging from astronomy to drama, metallurgy to behavioral science. "All [were] concerned basically with general education and with invigorating the Freshman Year." CSC Minutes, 29 October 1959.

[2]CSC Minutes, 26 April 1960; Dean's Report, 1959-60, p. 4.

freshman year of Directed Studies. The two Directed Studies programs, in the sciences and in the humanities, were to be combined into one honors program limited to 50-60 freshmen. Sophomore year was to be optional for the student and selective for the faculty, with the result that second-year enrollment would be reduced by at least ten students. Although all students in the program were to meet the distributional requirements of Yale College, at least two of these requirements, hopefully one of them in language, were to have been satisfied before admission to Yale. Six courses would be offered: Literature I, Philosophy I (Revised), History I, History of Art I, Mathematics I and Science I. "Students with an aptitude" for the humanities could choose between Math I or Science I. Students "with an aptitude" for science could choose between History I and History of Art I. "Science I," the special committee on Directed Studies noted, "would necessarily have to be taught under two rubrics: (1) for science concentrators . . . as a demanding professional course, and (2) less stringently and more interpretatively for humanities concentrators."[1]

This "drastic revision" was basically a restructuring of Directed Studies which on paper limited access to the program to those who were already taking advantage of it. The program now officially emphasized freshman year, a characteristic which those who dropped out before sophomore year had already given it. The urge to compete with Harvard's freshman seminars influenced the decision that Directed Studies would be openly acknowledged as an honors program, and indeed DeVane, who always championed honors programs, had been making this point with regard to Directed Studies since 1958. Internal developments already cited within the program's curriculum and

---

[1]The members of the Special Committee on Directed Studies were V. H. Brombert, J. C. Haden, L. Krieger, M. Mack, C. Seymour Jr., H. J. Smith, H. B. Whiteman. Faculty Record, 29 September 1960. DeVane, "Directed Studies, Humanities and Sciences," 28 December 1960, and Minutes, the Committee on Directed Studies, 10 January 1961, both appended to CSC Minutes, 12 January 1961. Also CSC Minutes, 29 May 1961; Faculty Record, 23 February 1961, 9 June 1961.

external developments particularly in regard to the residential colleges really left no other direction to take.[1] Once in motion, the Course of Study Committee was not to be held back: The "Planned Experiment" of 1945 bred a further experiment in 1961. Ten to twelve students would be admitted to the Directed Studies honors program, those of truly exceptional ability and motivation who were, as a group, to take all six of the special courses in the freshman year, taught in three paired groups. A record of significant advanced placement was a prerequisite for admission to this favored unit, the so-called Intensive Program, and its students were generally expected to move from freshman to junior year. The interdisciplinary nature of their experience was to be stressed. DeVane commented that their "course [of study] would integrate knowledge and disciplines without letting the student know." The Dean intended to refer to the program's publicity in various catalogues, but the irony of his remark is entirely suitable.[2]

In the early fifties when the Ford Foundation saw Directed Studies as a vehicle for promoting general education in the face of the Korean emergency, the Dean of Freshman Year, into whose bailiwick Directed Studies intruded, had said that the program "has never been known as 'General Education' at Yale, but its purposes are roughly equivalent." In 1961, the Course of Study Bulletin made a far-different claim:

> The purpose of the Directed Studies programs
> is twofold. First, to introduce the student
> to an advanced level of study in his first year,
> and so prepare him as speedily as possible for

---

[1] DeVane told Griswold, "The Directed Studies Program provides a base for later honors work." Dean's Report, 1957-58, p. 14. In fact, the program had, from the beginning, an honors bias, because applicants were always selected from the top half of the freshman class.

[2] CSC Minutes, 12 January 1961 and attachments; Course of Study Bulletin, 1961-62; CSC Minutes, 29 May 1961.

independent work in upper-class Major and Honors programs. Second, to take full advantage of the opportunities for understanding relationships among fields of study which arise from a carefully organized combination of specially designed courses. Implicit in both purposes is the goal of providing a broad and firm basis for later specialization.[1]

For a few more years, the specialization for which the Directed Studies program was "a broad and firm basis" remained unspecified. Eventually, the program's bias toward the humanities was officially recognized.[2]

---

[1]Course of Study Bulletin, 1961-62, p. 9.

[2]It is intriguing to trace the descriptions of the Directed Studies program between 1961 and 1978 in the sequential Course of Study Bulletins. In 1962-63, the sophomore year was revised so that students who continued in the program were required to elect three of six largely new Directed Studies courses, a varied set of departmental studies arranged with special reference to the twentieth century (see also CSC Minutes, 8 March 1962). The balance of the program was elective. In 1963-64, Science I became Science I(A) and (B), and the intensive program was reduced to four special courses, Science I(A) and Math I being regular Directed Studies courses. In 1964-65, Directed Studies became one of two Special Programs for Freshmen and Sophomores, the other being the Early Concentration Program, basically, the old Intensive Program expanded to accommodate 60-70 freshmen, concentrating without delay within their fields of interest in semi-tutorial seminars, one of which was taught by William C. DeVane. In 1967-68, once again Physics I replaced Science I. In 1968-69, students "already certain of their intention to major in a science" were urged to consult with the authorities before entering the program. In 1972-73, Directed Studies applicants were told to expect (1) seminars limited to small groups; (2) stimulating fellow students; (3) "a curriculum in which courses are designed to enrich and roughly relate to each other"; (4) assignments involving unabbreviated, original texts; and (5) hard work, substantial reading and frequent papers. All freshmen core courses started with Greek civilization and moved at different

The label liberal education has a tendency to
be applied as desired, and, according to this rule,
Directed Studies in its new honors format could be

---

rates over different territory to the threshold of
the twentieth century. The sophomore year became
completely voluntary, though Directed Studies courses
were not open to those not enrolled in the program.
In this year, the Freshman Seminar in HAL joined
Directed Studies and the Early Concentration Program
as a Special Program for Freshmen and Sophomores.
    In 1973-74, the freshman year of Directed Studies
was renamed The Special Courses in the Humanities,
and sophomore year became the Sophomore Seminar in
the Humanities. These two programs, when combined
with the Divisional Major in the Humanities (which
included the HAL Major), were designed "to contribute
to an integrated understanding of the Western Cultural
tradition." Freshmen in this program were required
to take but three of the offerings of five interdisciplinary special courses; the sophomore seminar
was optional to those who completed the freshman
courses, and it was open to students who had not
been in the freshman year of the program. All who
applied had to be accepted into the seminar.
    In 1976-77, Directed Studies reemerged under
the rubric of a Special Course in the Humanities
as a two-year program limited to forty-five applicants
(half the previous number), the second year remaining
optional. Three Directed Studies courses were
required in freshman year, two in sophomore year.
In addition, a Freshman Seminar in the Humanities
joined the Sophomore Seminar as a special program,
aimed at but not limited to those who intended to
pursue the HAL major.
    In 1977-78 a monthly colloquium was added to
the Directed Studies curriculum, and no mention was
made of the sophomore year introduced the preceding
year (when, of course, there were no sophomores available to enter the program and hence no courses
offered).
    In 1978-79, the Directed Studies program was
unchanged. The description of the Freshman Seminar
in the Humanities was unchanged, but it was not in
fact being offered until the following year.
    In 1979-80, there were but two Special Programs
in the Humanities: Directed Studies, unchanged except

and was called liberal education. But it was not
the traditional liberal education which is generally
accessible to all and has its own humanistic end.
The original, laudable goal was, in the case of
Directed Studies, slowly but surely subverted to the
ends of specialized study, and that subversion had
been accomplished by making generalized study instrumental to more limited purposes, in this instance
yet again, to the requirements of the majors, particularly the humanities majors. The anxiousness of
the science Departments to use the Directed Studies
format to their own ends shows the excellent quality
of preparation which the program provided, but it
also makes clear that Directed Studies' claim to
be a valid general preparation was not accepted.
There were, as DeVane suggested, many practical,
programmatic, and fiscal reasons for the decline
of Directed Studies. But the fundamental reason
remains the equation of general education with the
first two years' work, which was then seen as preparation for the major, which had already been acknowledged as the dominant influence on undergraduate
education. The major, or really majors, came to
dominate Directed Studies, and their differing prerequisites came to destroy it as a unified concept.
There were really only two possibilities for the
future: The Faculty could create as many Directed
Studies programs as there were majors or groups of
majors; or the Faculty could reduce Directed Studies
to one program and overtly acknowledge which set
of majors it was preparation for. Finances, as well
as Yale's propensity to equate the liberal arts with
the humanities, made the latter choice the only choice.
A short while afterward, much the same mind set began
to affect the viability of the system of distributional requirements, since no one was apparently
willing to question the purpose of the current majoring system to determine if it were a valid instrument
of liberal education.

---

for teaching staff; and the Program in HAL, which
included the absorbed and renamed Freshman Seminar
in the Humanities, the Sophomore Seminar, the HAL
Major, and several random seminars, including one
taught by the President of the University.

In the Fall of 1980, the Faculty voted to end
the HAL program.

161

Chapter VII

THE GUIDELINES OF 1966

In Yale College, liberal education had been
protected in the Standard Program largely by means
of the system of distribution. The concept, as we
have seen, was that the depth of the specialized
major would be combined with the breadth enforced
by the distributional requirements. For nearly twenty
years, since the Reforms of 1945, a student's education had been organized with reference to these
crossed criteria or opposed axes, with the Course
of Study Committee adjusting the delicate balance
between them. This approach had been reaffirmed
by the Reforms of 1955. But over the years, the
balance had begun to favor the claims of the major,
though never exclusively and never consistently.
By 1966, it would become apparent that the claims
of specialization were to have virtually complete
preference, that the distribution system would be
harnessed to the major, that university interests
would take precedence over college interests. There
are two main reasons: First, the whole tenor of
this trend was codified, rather ironically, in the
1962 Report of the President's Committee on the Freshman Year, whose recommendations, with varying degrees
of speed became plans of action for reforms; second,
the distribution system itself became increasingly
unwieldy, less adept than it once had been at handling
what was demanded of it, namely, that it keep liberal
education from the perils, on the one hand, of the
free elective system, and on the other, of the spe-
cialization-oriented, service station approach.
Confusion about what exactly constituted a major
and how the majoring system was itself to be regulated
simply compounded the difficulty.

The key to understanding the transformation
of the venerable distribution system into the Guidelines of 1966 is an examination of the purposes of
distribution. Originally, the purpose of the distribution system was to acquaint the student with all
the various segments of the body of knowledge which
it was encumbent upon the educated individual to
know. Knowledge for its own sake meant all of knowledge, or at least as much of it as possible, and
not some specialized fragment. This purpose had

been subtly but significantly altered at Yale in the mid-fifties when liberal education (and general education) were equated with non-specialized education, with the breadth criteria alone. The change implied that non-specialized education was preparatory to specialized education. Therefore, its purpose was necessarily changed. Distribution was no longer to be achieved for its own sake, but for the sake of specialized education, of the major to which it was preparatory. And since each major was obviously the ultimate authority on what constituted the best preparation for its specialized demands, the majors inevitably began to control the distribution system. Because each major's requirements were a little different, and for that matter a bit ill-defined as well, the distribution system had to be adapted bit by bit until it basically fragmented uncontrollably, in much the same way as the Directed Studies program had. Finally, it became clear that the only concept upon which the departmental specialists could agree was that overspecialization, particularly premature overspecialization, was bad, even for the future specialist qua specialist. Thus, the distributional requirements came to be expressed negatively: So many courses outside the major or the Division of the major, before sophomore year or before graduation. Because the real, if unacknowledged purpose of the distributional system, was to effect better preparation for the major, this negative tone was entirely appropriate. The new regulations, however, provided no broad guidance to the student toward the traditional, liberal ideal and thus, at the last moment, Guidelines were developed to assist the undergraduate in following an essentially negative regulation of the curriculum. To the historical observer, the change of purpose makes clear what happened, though it was not at all apparent to the Course of Study Committee and the Faculty engaged in the immediacy of life at rapidly changing Yale.

When the Faculty agreed, after the Reforms of 1955, "that the curriculum should be left alone for a while," it also left unanswered its own questions about the problem of the curriculum as a whole. Specifically, could the curriculum be organized in any way so as to make intellectual achievement the most prestigious student activity? Or, opposite face of the same coin, did the Faculty wish to

regulate college life beyond the curriculum in order
to foster Yale's educational goals? Into this vacuum
moved A. Whitney Griswold, as it were, sideways and
perhaps a bit inadvertantly. The President had been
concentrating, as we have seen, on the residential
colleges. The two new residential colleges had obviated the need to build separate sophomore housing,
and the residential colleges, by means of the sophomore seminars, had done much to cure the so-called
"sophomore slump." All of this had been accomplished
to the supposed benefit of liberal education. What
could be more natural now than to address the problem
of the Freshman Year? Griswold originally intended
to focus on the curriculum, but the Report of the
Committee on the Freshman Year ended up going far
beyond the course of study.

The Freshman Year, it will be remembered, had
been established in 1920 in part to deal with the
divisive problem of competition between Yale College
and the Sheffield Scientific School. As a separately
administered entity, it had developed its own interests: a safe school-to-college transition, a limited
curriculum imposed on all freshmen, personal methods
of instruction. An emphasis upon good teaching permeated the Faculty of the Freshman Year. By 1954,
the "Ac"-"Sheff" rivalry had been forgotten, the
core curriculum had become unstrung, and the Freshman
Faculty was as engaged in research and graduate teaching as the Yale College Faculty. Numerous freshmen
were taking courses, some of them advanced, in Yale
College; and for nearly ten years Directed Studies
had been undercutting the notion of an integral,
homogeneous Freshman Year. Thus, in 1954, as we
have seen, the Faculties were combined, and responsibility for educational policy was transferred in
toto to Yale College. What indeed was the remaining
purpose of the Freshman Year, or, as Griswold first
put it in a memo to himself, "How can the Freshman
Year best serve the entire purpose of the whole
University--including Yale College and the Graduate
and Professional Schools--."[1]

---

[1]The Report of the President's Committee on
the Freshman Year, 13 April 1962, pp. 6-7, and handwritten undated memo, Griswold Mss., Box 38, folder
marked Freshman Year Committee (special) to study

Griswold outlined his purposes more formally
to the alumni:

> Throughout our colleges and universities voca-
> tionalism was browning the edges of liberal
> education, and even at Yale, where the blight
> was stoutly resisted, graduates were pouring
> into the professions, into business and govern-
> ment who, though of obvious intelligence and
> great potential ability, were not as well edu-
> cated as they were highly trained. [These stu-
> dents] seemed to move from one phase of education
> to another as if on a conveyor belt without
> ever stopping to ask what it was all about and
> why they were doing it. If at the beginning
> rather than the end they could see the purpose
> of higher education and see it whole, with them-
> selves as part of it, the magic word "motivation"
> could be given greater meaning. . . .[1]

The President took great care in forming his Committee
on the Freshman Year, selecting representatives from
the graduate schools as well as Yale College, and
gave it directions in the form of two questions:

> 1. Can our students be given a more lively
> sense of the educational process in which they
> are engaged at the beginning of that process,
> i.e., in the Freshman Year?
> 2. Can the Freshman Year, both in its cur-
> ricular and in its institutional arrangements
> be brought into a more integral and more profit-
> able relationship to the upper-class graduate
> and post-graduate years?

Curricular and Extra-Curricular Activities (1961,
1962). Report was also printed in Yale Alumni Maga-
zine, June 1962, pp. 8-13, where it was headlined
"Education of First Year Students in Yale College."
For 1954 reorganization, see also Griswold Mss.,
Box 20, folder marked Committee on Common Freshman
Year.

[1]Pres. Report, 1961-62, pp. 29-30.

In short, can the beginning of the educational process at Yale be more significant to its conclusion?[1]

President Griswold's overriding purpose had been, as one might expect, to advance the interests of liberal education, and he had first intended that the curriculum be the vehicle of reform, a point made clear by the early drafts of his instructions to the Committee. But his Committee finally chose to concentrate elsewhere, that is, outside the curriculum, on "institutional arrangements." And despite the continuing presence of DeVane, and on occasion of Griswold himself, the Committee did not accept the President's intentions. Their views were narrowly focused:

> More of the graduates of Yale College, we think, must become professional scholars and teachers. It is incumbent upon Yale and similar institutions consciously to increase the number and proportion of learned men in our society.

DeVane's reminder that "there are many important people in the world who are not professors" went unheeded by the Committee of which he was a member. So did Griswold's concerns about the "browning" of liberal education and the confusion of advanced training with higher education, concerns, incidentally, which were not made explicitly clear even in the President's charge to his own Committee.[2]

_____

[1]Ibid., p. 31. Members of the Committee were Leonard W. Doob (Professor of Psychology and former Chairman of the Course of Study Committee), Dean DeVane, G. Evelyn Hutchinson (Profesor of Zoology), John Perry Miller (Dean of the Graduate School), Frederick A. Pottle (Professor of English), Eugene V. Rostow (Dean of the Law School) and George A. Schrader, Jr. (a philosopher who was Master of Branford College).

[2]Report of the Committee on the Freshman Year, p. 5; DeVane quotation in CSC Minutes, 17 April 1962. Griswold's May 1961 draft of his instructions to

The Committee's deliberations resulted in both
ultimate and immediate recommendations, goals to
be clearly envisioned and changes presently feasible.
The ultimate objectives, which would require major
funding that was simply unavailable at the moment,
were the inclusion of all freshmen into the residential college system upon arrival in New Haven, and
the admission of women on an equal standing with
men. The immediate recommendations were five: First,
the remaining administration of the Freshman Year
was to be absorbed by the Office of the Dean of Yale
College; second, the Yale College Faculty was to
become actively involved in the admissions process,
which was to be redirected "to attract students of
intellectual distinction" while giving special consideration to candidates "whose records show exceptionally high promise of continuing intellectual
achievement"; third, financial assistance was to
be reorganized so that bursary work was voluntary,
a change which lessened the possibility of its detract-
ing from intellectual achievement; fourth, freshman
access to the college seminars and immediate affilia-
tion of the freshmen with the residential colleges,
where the counselling system was to be relocated,
were suggested; and fifth, the undergraduate curriculum was to be changed to permit greater flexibility
of pace and specialization. In other words, the
Committee was largely looking beyond the course of
study for ways to develop "professional scholars
and teachers" and increase the number of "learned
men" in the society. Selective admissions which
would sort out the unqualified in advance would certainly help. So would the attractions of immediate
treatment as upper-classmen in the colleges. And
none would be deterred by the public opprobrium of
onerous bursary work. Intellectual rigor was to
be achieved, and the function of the curriculum was
to keep out of the way. If sacrificing the individual

---

the Committee read:
    "the task of the Committee will be to re-examine
    the curricular policies of Yale College, includ-
    ing the Freshman Year, with a view to clarifying
    and strengthening the ideals and purposes of
    liberal education and with particular attention
    to the opportunity for beginning this process
    in the Freshman Year."

with a well-rounded diversity of interests was the cost, well so be it.[1]

The Committee's conclusions with regard to the curriculum were not encouraging to those who hoped to emphasize a broad liberal education. "The fact and the reputation of toughness" in the Yale College curriculum were both "highly desirable." So was the policy of granting advanced placement and college credit for excellent work in secondary school. The Committee emphasized the need for flexibility in the environment of Yale's "rich resources," particularly for the talented: "Gifted students who arrive at the University with a passionate interest in a particular field or subject already developed should be able to pursue their interests without delay. Such students . . . should be allowed to go far with their specialization or major before they have completed their general education." The Committee hoped "that every student could have what we can only call a creative experience." Beginning the study of a new subject was one measure to this end, but so was extra work or a "stretching" essay in a familiar discipline. And the same result might be achieved in bursary work, a summer's worthwhile activity, or an observant journey abroad. The end in view was somehow, anyhow, to "quicken the intellectual interests of all freshmen."[2]

The Committee did not intend, however, to abandon the nomenclature and beneficent cloak of liberal education. Though its report made no provision for its advancement or preservation, the concept was briefly endorsed:

> Without question, the experience of a liberal arts education at the undergraduate stage should be carefully preserved. A college education should not be a transitional four years between expanding secondary schools and demanding

---

[1]Pres. Report, 1961-62, pp. 32-35; Report of the President's Committee on the Freshman Year, passim.

[2]Report of the President's Committee on the Freshman Year, pp. 13-14.

graduate or professional schools. It provides
an almost unique opportunity for the individual
to acquire a breadth of knowledge, a degree
of mastery in one subject or field, and the
attitudes and habits of mind which will enable
him to see things in perspective, to understand
and evaluate, and often to solve a wide variety
of elusive intellectual, social and emotional
problems.

Following this genuflexion to the traditional ideal,
the Committee passed on to its final recommendation
and revealed its real intention:

At the same time, we can improve undergraduate
education by the careful introduction of more
graduate training, in all its seriousness and
rigor, into the undergraduate curriculum. . . .
[It should be possible] for the thoroughly well
qualified student to obtain the bachelor's degree
and the master's degree at the end of four years.

Like most of its predecessors, this committee was
unable to separate "seriousnes and rigor" from "a
passionate interest in a particular field or subject"
and it could not link the former with that "unique
opportunity to acquire a breadth of knowledge."[1]

Upon honest reflection, Griswold--and DeVane
too--should not have expected it to. For one thing,
the make-up of the Committee itself was "university
minded." Three of the seven members were graduate
school Deans. Two more were highly regarded full
professors, one of them a scientist. Doob, the Chairman, had, as a member of the Course of Study Committee
nearly a decade before, insightfully questioned the
basic analysis of the Report of Griswold's Committee
on General Education. That left only DeVane and
the Master of Branford College to champion the cause
of liberal education. They were too few. However,
it was more than a matter of personalities. When
DeVane proposed that the entire first term of freshman
year be devoted to a series of courses organized
into a liberal arts orientation, the proposal was

------

[1]Ibid., pp. 15-16.

"flatly" not endorsed.[1] University intrusion into
the atmosphere of the College had increased in recent
years. DeVane commented on it as early as 1957.
During the academic year 1959-60, the Yale College
Faculty Appointments Committee had been merged with
that of the Graduate School into a joint committee,
though for a couple of years DeVane continued to
preside. And the fact was that a number of graduate
level courses were already being offered in the
College.[2] Most significant of all, specialized depth
was increasingly deemed the purpose of the major,
and because general education was perceived in the
Committee and elsewhere as preparatory to the major,
increasingly the major was deemed the essential purpose of a college education. And a college education
began more and more to resemble graduate work, particularly for honors students. DeVane identified
the trend accurately. In 1956, he suggested to the
Course of Study Committee a careful examination of
the function and purpose of the major in a liberal
arts college. Nothing happened. Three years later,
even the Dean's position had altered, and he said,
"we are at the point where we may expect the secondary
schools to take over a much greater share of the
work of general education . . . leaving to institutions like Yale more time and resources for work
of a collegiate or university level." No longer
did DeVane, apparently, clearly distinguish between
the two, and many distinguished even less than he.[3]

Like the 1953 Report of the President's Committee
on General Education, the Report of the President's
Committee on the Freshman Year was submitted to the
Yale College Faculty for discussion. Unlike the

[1]CSC Minutes, 17 April 1962.

[2]Dean's Report, 1956-57, p. 3; Dean's Report,
1959-60, p. 1; CSC Minutes, 7 May 1963. The number
of undergraduates taking graduate courses jumped
from 41 in 1950-51 to 405 in 1961-62.

[3]Dean's Report, 1955-56, p. 7; DeVane,"A Plan
of Study for Yale College," attached to CSC Minutes,
12 March 1959.

earlier document, it was discussed at one meeting,
attended by President Griswold and the new Provost
Kingman Brewster, and promptly adopted "in principle
. . . with respect to those [proposals] which can
be put into effect without waiting for sizable new
capital resources." This speedy action resulted
in part from the fact that the Report's general recommendations were left, where appropriate, to the
Faculty for interpretation in detail by its standing
committees (both Griswold and DeVane had committed
themselves openly to this approach). But in part
it also resulted from the fact that the tenor of
the Report, again unlike the earlier report, was
entirely in accord with the tenor of the faculty.
There was considerable truth in the statement of
one member of the Course of Study Committee that
the Report was "not revolutionary but simply asked
that more be done in a certain direction."[1]

The job of implementing the combined BA-MA program, the entrance of freshmen into sophomore seminars,
early entrance into the major, and the provision
of a "creative" educational experience--all recommended by the Committee on the Freshman Year--clearly
fell to the Course of Study Committee. This particular Committee was, in addition to its routine business
of approving course changes, already at work on a
reexamination of the major and the distributional
requirements. That is, the Committee was yet again
adjusting the "delicate balance" between the demands
of mastery and the requirements of breadth. Inevitably, the two tasks became intertwined in the details
of administering the curriculum. As it turned out,
the emphatic thrust of the Report on the Freshman
Year could not be effectively countered by the weak-
ened philosophy underlying the Reforms of 1945, particularly when the distributional requirements were
becoming increasingly inefficient to administer and
increasingly ineffective in accomplishing the ends
for which they had been designed. The stress was
produced, in large part, by the explosion in the
number of courses offered in Yale College, by the

---

[1]Faculty Record, 19 April 1962; CSC Minutes,
17 April 1962.

merger of the Engineering School into the College, and by the requirements of the various Honors and Divisional Majors. The manifested symptoms of stress were the expressed need to compete with Harvard, the difficulty of categorizing courses within the distributional scheme, and the question of whether electives were to be included or excluded from the major field.

In 1961, the Ford Foundation gave $3,000,000 to support international and foreign area studies at Yale, where this challenge to "revise the intellectual map of the world to coincide with the physical map" was readily accepted. Reporting this latest explosion in that subject matter which the educated man ought to know, President Griswold documented for the alumni the extent of the increase: In 1931, excluding languages, there were four courses dealing with the non-western world; in four years, 102 students of the class of '31 elected them; in 1961, there were 34 courses, with an average student enrollment of 2363. Something similar occurred in the more traditional areas of study, a trend aided by the tenured faculty's concern that junior members should be identified with some curricular specialty in the not unlikely event that they should eventually have to seek employment elsewhere.[1]

Then, a large number of unfamiliar engineering courses were suddenly added to the curriculum when the College "merged" with the Engineering School. Griswold had been concerned about the purpose and function of the Engineering School at least since the time of the President's Committee on General Education. His concern was based on his belief that "it is a matter of the greatest practical importance to society to prevent the fragmentation of knowledge through overspecialization or the emergence of

---

[1]Pres. Report, 1961-62, pp. 16, 21; personal conversation with George W. Pierson, 10 June 1980. The older faculty, aware of the freeze on tenured positions and knowing that teaching a course was an excellent way to master a subject, were reluctant to deny this opportunity to younger colleagues who needed something to peddle to the academic world. On February 11, 1964, for example, the Course of Study Committee approved forty new courses.

mutually uncomprehending and uncommunicative castes of managers dealing with things on the one hand and people on the other." The inevitable committee, pointing to the "vital relevancy between engineering . . . and the humanities and social sciences," recommended the creation of a Department of Engineering and Applied Science offering undergraduate majors within Yale College and a graduate PhD program within the Graduate School. There was also to be a separate, overtly professional School which would award the Master of Engineering and Doctor of Engineering degrees. Griswold may have seen this development as allowing the engineering curriculum to become a "truly integral [part] of the arts and sciences curriculum and as such direct beneficiaries of its resources," and the whole effort may have been a valient attempt to subjugate the "fragmentation of knowledge," but to the Course of Study Committee, it was one more difficult problem involving the distributional requirements; for the traditional requirements of the engineering curriculum were simply not always compatible with the existing distribution system. Although the Committee wondered at first whether some engineering instruction, particularly the Industrial Administration Major, belonged in a liberal arts college at all, it was confronted with a _fait accompli_ which had to be dealt with, and which was dealt with by means of various compromises, before the 1961-62 academic year was over.[1]

The distributional requirements were being stresed in other, less apparent ways. Freshman advisors often recommended that their counsellees undertake courses in new and hopefully stimulating areas of study, but at the same time the advisors were generally hesitant to suggest that a student abandon a field of acknowledged interest. Thus, the fulfilling of the "less-relevant" distributional requirements tended to get delayed. Those students, usually among the better ones, who then went on to Honors or Divisional Majors found that the stringent requirements of those majors did not allow them sufficient time to satisfy their unsatisfied distributional requirements. The same problem occurred with those who

[1]Pres. Report, 1961-62, pp. 21-26; CSC Minutes, 16 November 1961, 8 March 1962.

changed their minds about their majors in sophomore year, which was ironic since one of the original purposes of the distribution system had been to expose students to a new, broader range of intellectual concerns. Quietly, the Course of Study Committee permitted the Dean to excuse Honors and Divisional majors from the distributional requirements, and once again intellectual capability was severed from breadth of curricular interest.[1]

The fact was that there was no longer an agreed conceptual basis either to the system of distribution or to the system of majoring. The confusion had been inherent since the 1955 Reforms had appended the concept of "areas of concentration" to the original purposes of the distribution system. In 1958, the Course of Study Committee had added a comprehensive distribution requirement which effectively forced students either to go further into a foreign language or to accomplish a wider or deeper acquaintance with the sciences. The student's choice would be determined by his intended major, a situation which, like the "areas of concentration" that it resembled, was not at all compatible with the 1945 purpose of the distribution system. This bastardized distributional requirement indicated the extent to which the whole system had come to be thought of as preparatory to the major. So did the Course of Study Committee's discussion of the relationship between the language requirement and the requirements of the Graduate School for the PhD. In fact, one member of the Committee recalled frequent, inconclusive discussions whether the distributional requirements should be the same for the humanities and the sciences. Then, in 1961, the Course of Study Committee voted to abandon the concept of "areas of concentration," which in theory permitted the distribution system to operate as conceived in 1945, that is, to promote broad exposure and to maximize the scope of a student's course of study.[2]

---

[1]CSC Minutes, 11 October 1961, 26 October 1961.

[2]CSC Minutes, 7 December 1961; Dean's Report, 1958-59, p. 2; CSC Minutes, 14 December 1961.

The situation involving the system of majoring was equally unbalanced. If there had once been a consensus about the major, it had disappeared. At the extreme, there were the huge humanities majors, with literally hundreds of students enrolled; and there were those, like microbiology, in which no one was enrolled. Several dozen courses might be offered by a big Department like English, and only a handful in, say, Slavic Languages. Thus, to major in a small Department with limited course selection was a confining intellectual experience compared with taking all one's courses in the History Department, where a student could move from Ancient Greece, to the Orient, to British intellectual history, to twentieth century America. The profusion of course offerings in the popular majors was made possible by the very popularity they enjoyed, but the problems of classification for purposes of distribution immediately arose. Was Greek and Roman art, for example, an art or a classics course? or both? Was a history of Marxian economics social science or political history? In other words, were not some, though not all, of the majors in their own right broad enough in subject matter also to satisfy the present aims of the distribution system?[1]

The specific question at hand was whether the electives of junior and senior years could be selected within the major Department. Or were electives to be limited by definition to selections of non-major courses, an unnecessary restriction, it would seem, if the distribution system were effectively accomplishing its preparatory and general education tasks. This problem merged with a debate over the virtues, particularly in junior and senior years, of a four-course program, like the traditional one at Harvard which was attracting many talented applicants. The faculty's interest in the four-course schedule was to reduce its teaching load in exchange for more time for research, and the faculty was also disinterested in the concept of exposure or breadth. Since no one wanted to reduce the "size" of the major, the potential course reduction meant choosing between the distributional requirements and major prerequisites in sophomore and freshman years. And since

---

[1]CSC Minutes, 3 February 1962, 7 March 1963.

only 1.5 out of 5 freshmen found their courses "intellectually stimulating" under the present system, given the tenor of the Report on the Freshman Year, there was little doubt which choice would win out. What survived was the faculty's interest in honors work, independent specialization, and the graduate seminars which were drifting down into the majors, an emphasis which had, for some time, been openly endorsed at Harvard. In short order, the History Department received approval for a major that controlled all but three courses in junior and senior years. Clearly, the curriculum restrictions placed upon the major by the Course of Study Committee had become as conceptually unbased as those involving the distribution system[1]

Though the system of distribution was becoming unstuck and the system of majoring unhinged, there was no doubt whose objectives were to be preferred, as the matter of advanced placement made quite clear. The number of students receiving advanced placement, and thereby both advanced credit and distributional credit, increased every year, with the class of 1963 reaching a new peak. It made obvious sense for capable freshmen not to repeat work already accomplished, and it thus made sense to give them advanced placement credits when they arrived at Yale. However, to give distributional credit as well made sense only if the distributional system and the general education with which it was usually equated were seen and acknowledged as precursors to the major. It was, after all, perfectly possible to insist that the student who had mastered a basic language in secondary school (or even in the country of his birth) study that same language, or another one, at Yale. Might not

_____

[1]Letter from R. D. Masters, assistant professor of Political Science, to Dean Georges May, 5 November 1965, in Carroll Mss., Box 2B, folder marked Course of Study Committee Minutes, 1965-66; CSC Minutes, 23 April 1963, 29 January 1963, 14 February 1963, 15 October 1964.

The number of undergraduates taking graduate courses jumped from 41 in 1950-51 to 405 in 1961-62 (see CSC Minutes, 7 March 1963).

For comparisons with Harvard, see CSC Minutes, 26 October 1961.

the student who had passed basic, college-level physics in secondary school learn something valuable
from a year of chemistry taught by accomplished scientists in fabulously resourceful University laboratories? If the Faculty were serious that the distributional system was to provide experience in the
handling of various disciplines at the college level,
as well as to assure a breadth of basic knowledge,
distributional credits would not[1] have been tied to
advanced placement as they were.

In 1965, Professor E. S. Morgan, chairman of
the Course of Study Committee, circulated a formal
proposal to the Faculty:

> The object of the committee has been to take
> advantage of the increasingly advanced prepara-
> tion of entering students in order to give them
> a greater degree of freedom in the choice of
> courses and at the same time to raise the stan-
> dards of a Yale education. Adoption of the
> proposals would mean that a student may, by
> superior grades or advanced placement exams,
> reduce the number of courses needed for gradua-
> tion, but no student would be given distribu-
> tional credit. Prior preparation in a subject
> would simply enable a student to satisfy the
> [distributional] requirement at a higher level.

This suggestion was a clear reversal of the strong
tendency to regard the breadth supposedly assured
by the distribution system as excellent preparation
for the major. This imbedded approach had tended
to turn the distributional credits into unpleasant
hurdles in the path to the major and graduation,
hurdles which the student naturally resented and
had resented at least since 1955. In fact, so closely
had the distributional credits and the majoring
requirements become intertwined that, to pick an
extreme example, the Divisional Major in the History
of Science and Medicine had to be elected before
the beginning of the freshman year, since it dictated
the entire course of study, including the

---

[1]Dean's Report, 1959-60, p. 2; CSC Minutes,
19 November 1964, and attached letter from Professor
Folsom.

distributional requirements, over four years at Yale.
Now, by means of Morgan's proposal, the Course of
Study Committee was attempting to return the axis
of breadth to its former place as a justifiable end
in its own right. However, this approach was not
acceptable to the faculty. The Deans were reputed
to believe this arrangement would place Yale at a
grave disadvantage in recruiting the best students
from the secondary schools. The professors objected
to the possibility that a freshman with no foreign
language experience could satisfy the language requirement with a single year's introductory study, and
they simply insisted that some kind of distributional
credit be given for exceptional secondary school
work. The faculty was just not interested in breadth
for its own sake, and if the present distributional
system could not be made to function without disturb-
ing the major, it was just a matter of time before
it would have to be revised or eliminated.[1]

The roots of the solution to the Course of Study
Committee's problems and the seed of the denouement
which resulted in the Guidelines of 1966 lay in a
suggestion made by the new Dean of Yale College,
Georges May. He off-handedly proposed that the distribution requirements be expressed negatively, that
is, as limits upon concentration. The idea was not,
however, pursued immediately, and the Committee continued to grapple with various distributional schemes.
One ended up favoring the social sciences at the
presumed expense of classics and philosophy, and
it was discarded as making it impossible for those
Departments to carry a full staff and try out men
at junior levels. A four-hour meeting with Kingman
Brewster, now President of Yale, elicited the comment

---

[1]CSC Minutes, 4 January 1962; memo to Department
Chairmen, Directors of Undergraduate Studies and
Deans, from Georges May and Edmund S. Morgan, 12
November 1965, in Carroll Mss., Box 2B, folder marked
Minutes 1965-66; memo to the Course of Study Committee
from R. C. Carroll, 6 December 1965, in Carroll Mss.,
Box 2B, folder marked Minutes 1965-66; CSC Minutes,
9 December 1965. Some members of the Faculty argued
that failure to recognize superior secondary school
work would deprecate the efforts of these schools
and generally lower standards.

from one committee member to the effect that some
problems can be logically proved to be insoluble,
and that perhaps the distributional requirements
were one of them. Then the chairman of the Committee
on the Teaching of Science proposed yet again that
the distributional requirements be arranged to force
each student to take two full courses in science,
perhaps with the stipulation that calculus might
be substituted for one. Eventually another hesitant
suggestion to express the distributional requirements
as limitations on concentration was made in a jocular
effort "to give the narrow specialist a break."[1]

The Course of Study Committee began the year
1965-1966 debating a possible basic skills requirement
in mathematics, only to find that the Math Department,
unlike the science Departments, did not want one
such requirement, much less two of them. The Department feared staffing difficulties for the vastly
increased teaching load, and it worried that the
level of the required course would be too low. In
other words, the mathematicians were content instructing only those with both aptitude and expressed interest. Shortly thereafter, the science Departments
agreed to abandon the use of the distributional
requirements as a means of forcing students into
general education courses in the sciences. Responding
to pressure from the diplomatic Dean, who intervened
personally in still-another effort to get outstanding
scientists interested in teaching undergraduates,
the scientists finally agreed to a "free market"
and stipulated only that freshmen not be permitted
to take more than one course in any one Department,
and that all students be required to take some courses
outside the Division of their major. This concession
made it possible for all to agree "that no specific

---

[1]CSC Minutes, 19 November 196, 17 December 1964,
15 April 1965. The students had already registered
their objection to the science requirement through
the Student Advisory Board. See CSC Minutes, 18
October 1965.

distributional requirements be imposed, other than one preventing unreasonable concentration."[1]

As a result of this consensus, the revision of the distributional requirements was simplicity itself. As published for the freshman of the class of 1970 in the Programs of Study Bulletin, they read:

> 1. A Freshman may take no more than one course (or two term courses) in a single department and no more than three courses (or six term courses) in a single division (there are three divisions: Natural Sciences, Social Sciences, and Humanities . . .).
> 2. Every student during his four years at Yale, must take at least eight courses (or 16 term courses) outside the department of his major, of which at least six courses (or twelve term courses) must be outside the division of his major.

"The purpose of these requirements," the Bulletin continued, "is . . . to spread your courses widely among departments in the Freshman Year in order to ensure exposure to a variety of ideas and ways of thinking. . . . [But] in choosing your Freshman courses . . . you should give attention to the prerequisites for any major in which you feel a particular interest."[2] The final sentence was necessary because most of the natural science and some of the social science majors required a sequence of courses taken in chronological order for four years, and because all students were urged to give some consideration to selecting a major. Those who received college credit for advanced work done in school in any subject outside the intended major Department were free but

---

[1]CSC Minutes, 23 September 1965, 14 October 1965, 13 January 1966; memo to members of the Course of Study Committee dated 11 January 1966, Carroll Mss., Box 2B, folder marked Course of Study Committee Minutes 1965-66; Faculty Record, 27 January 1966; personal interview with Georges May, 25 November 1980.

[2]Programs of Study Bulletin, 1966-67, p. 3.

"not encouraged," to reduce the number of required courses outside that Department. This meant that the distribution system was no longer to function as an effective mechanism to delay a student's choice of major. Suggestions about aiming "for the maximum of novelty" and trying out some subjects "never tried before" did not alter the underlying premise. All in all, the statement which rang most assertively had to do with choosing a major:

> To study a subject in depth can be the most rewarding and most liberating educational experience open to you. . . . Although no one should specialize to the neglect of distribution, knowledge advances by specialization, and you can gain some of the excitement of discovery by pressing close to the outer limits of human knowledge in some one field.[1]

There are several explanations for the willingness of the Course of Study Committee to abandon the distributional requirements in their positively expressed form. President Brewster mentioned one:

> The change removes the design of a balanced educational fare from the traditional pulling and hauling of legislative debate among competing departments on the floor of the faculty. Such legislative process has long dogged the issue at Yale and elsewhere . . . the temptation to compromise has too often led to patently irrational required patterns.[2]

In particular, the change removed the need for protracted negotiations with the sciences, who in the past had wanted the protection of the distributional system, and made it unnecessary to argue whether bad teaching or bad counselling accounted for the low enrollments in the basic science courses. Along the same lines, the need to protect the Philosophy Department and the Classics Department, both traditionally sheltered by the distributional requirements, had apparently disappeared. Enrollments were up in philosophy, and the chairman of the Classics Department had expressed his belief that no Department

---

[1]Ibid., pp. 11-12, 9, 11.

[2]Pres. Report, 1965-66, pp. 33-34.

benefitted from being favored: Too often the result
was inadequate teaching. Thus, those who had had
protection no longer wanted it, and those who wanted
it had finally agreed they would function more effectively without it. A "free market" would test the
attractions of all.[1]

Another explanation was the increased specialization among the faculty. The professors were simply
more oriented than ever toward their subjects and
Departments. The teaching of introductory courses
was always problematic and had been since the demise
of the freshman core curriculum. Now the Departments
were thrown on their own self-interest to attract
new students in the way they felt best. The more
students they could eventually interest in their
majors, the more budget they would be allocated,
the more courses they could offer and therefore the
more students they could attract. The importance
of good introductory courses in this scheme was self-
evident.[2]

The negatively expressed distribution requirements had yet another attraction for the Course of
Study Committee. Some of the Committee's control
over the curriculum had already passed to the residential colleges. The college seminars or discussion
groups were largely organized by the college Masters
and Fellows, who also exercised considerable influence
on the admission of students, the choice of instructors, and the selection of subject matter. The science Departments, for example, complained to the
Course of Study Committee that the college discussion
groups were an inappropriate way to introduce basic
science subject matter; but there was little the
Committee could do. Similarly, what assurance could
there be that the subject matter of Economics 10

---

[1]CSC Minutes, 11 February 1965, 9 December 1965.

[2]Letter from R. D. Masters to Georges May, 5
November 1965, Carroll Mss., Box 2B, folder marked
Minutes 1965-66. Actually, the faculty were not
entirely happy even with this solution, which made
them feel a bit guilty, and there came into being
a committee concerned primarily with teaching in
the College.

taught in a free-wheeling college seminar matched
that purveyed in the more controlled, more heavily
populated lecture hall? Negatively expressed distribution requirements were a neat way to escape those
curricular responsibilities the Course of Study Committee had already lost the power to enforce.[1]

A further reason for the Committee's action
was that it was entirely in harmony with the spirit
of the 1962 Report of the Committee on the Freshman
Year, which was the governing policy document of
the era, in at least two significant ways. First,
the desirable "creative experience" which the Report
had emphasized was in fact a hard concept to realize
since it was so broad in scope that it embodied much
more than the mere stimulation of new subject matter.
At the same time, the concept could be interpreted
to be quite limiting, for the Report had specified
that a "creative experience" was available in the
further pursuit of familiar material. In either
version, the "creative experience" was clearly uncon-
nected with the distributional requirements. Second,
the Report's emphasis on early concentration was
at variance with the whole concept of distribution,
even in the guise of the best possible preparation
for later specialization. The Report had suggested
the placement of qualified freshmen in college discussion groups (as indeed happened), and its tone
strongly endorsed an Early Concentration Seminar
for freshman. Not coincidentally, the Course of
Study Committee had had to award both the social
science and the English distributional credits for
this single course--which only emphasized the dilemma
it had now solved. In sum, the distributional requirements were not on the whole compatible with the Report
on the Freshman Year.[2]

Lastly, those with the greatest vested interest
in the distributional system were gone. Griswold
was dead, and by 1966, DeVane, after twenty-five
years service as Dean of Yale College, was completely
retired. Both, whatever their other differences,

---

[1] CSC Minutes, 2 December 1963.

[2] CSC Minutes, 29 January 1963, 8 April 1965.

184

were ardent supporters of liberal education in the
very broadest sense. Unlike Griswold, President
Brewster was not a PhD, especially not in the humanities. A Yale College graduate who had been a Harvard
law professor, Brewster was primarily a university
man. Dean Georges May, who had been appointed to
succeed DeVane just before Griswold died in April
1963, was not a Yale graduate at all. He had been
trained in the universities of France--non-residential
and non-collegial. Neither man was particularly
committed to the distribution system.[1]

Despite all the excellent reasons which recommended the revised distributional requirements expressed negatively as restrictions upon over-concentration, there was no concealing the fact that,
standing alone, the revisions did not represent any
kind of a definition of a liberal education or of
a proper course of study aimed at effecting a liberal
education. The Faculty freely admitted that "one
of the distinguishing features of a liberal education
is that it has no single definition . . . that each
student [must] design his own program of studies,
suited to his own particular needs and interests.
. . ." Still, the Faculty was unwilling completely
to abandon its traditional devotion to the ideal
of liberal education: "Educated men by no means
agree about everything that a liberal education should

---

[1]Georges May had been chairman of the Course
of Study Committee and was a member of the Committee
at the time of his appointment as Dean. As Dean,
a major objective was to improve the teaching of
the science courses in Yale College. In his view,
altering the distribution system to achieve this
end was an experiment worth trying. President
Brewster was, however, initially leery of abandoning
the distribution system, fearing that it could never
be reinstated even if the Faculty eventually decided
that course of action would be desirable. Personal
interview with Georges May, 25 November 1980.
For DeVane-May transition, see Griswold Mss.,
Box 20, folder marked Yale College Deanship Committee
(1962, 63). DeVane remained as a Professor of English,
in which role he taught in the Early Concentration
Seminars for freshmen. Upon Griswold's death on
April 19, 1963, Kingman Brewster, the Provost, became
Acting President of the University.

include, but nearly all would agree on the following propositions."[1] There followed a set of Guidelines designed to help the student plan his own liberal program of study. Their promulgation was, however, somewhat contradictory, for the Faculty had previously admitted that liberal education had no single definition and therefore, logically, no definition at all. However, the Guidelines were, even as a blurred outline, a reaffirmation of the ancient liberal faith. Oversimplified and in brief, they read:

1. An educated man should be able to express himself clearly in his own language, both in speech and in writing. It is a frequent illusion to suppose that you can think clearly if you cannot write clearly. . . . [The normal course of action is to take at least one course requiring written papers subject to criticism for clarity. English courses were the most obvious, but there were appropriate selections in Classical Civilization, History and Philosophy. In addition, a course in English was generally advisable.] You will be missing one of the rewards made possible by your own increased skill unless you follow or accompany the study of writing by the study of literature.

2. Besides attaining skill in English, you should be able to understand, speak, read and write a language other than your own. Mastery of a foreign language will increase your subtlety of mind and sharpen your sensitivity to the use and meaning of words in your own language. . . .

3. The study of a foreign language and literature will help to overcome geographical provincialism, but there is such a thing as temporal provincialism. An educated man should seek historical perspective. . . . Ideally, you should study the art, artifacts, and ideas both of the modern and of the ancient world. But if you must choose between the two, it would be wise to begin with the ancient.

4. A man should not consider himself educated today unless he has an understanding of the

---

[1]Programs of Study Bulletin, 1966-67, pp. 1-3.

mathematics that underlies many of the basic
fields of study. Mathematics is not only necessary for an understanding of most subjects in
the natural and social sciences, but it proves
a useful tool in some of the humanities. . . .

   5. As you should couple the study of languages and writing with the study of literature,
so you should couple mathematics with the sciences. . . . These are areas where human reason
and imagination have made their most dramatic
progress in the last three hundred years and
especially during our own century. Indeed,
the creative effect of the sciences so dominates
modern culture that no person in this century
may consider himself educated without an understanding of science. . . .

   6. To understand the duties and problems
facing you as a human being among other human
beings, you should become familiar with at least
one of the social sciences. . . . An educated
man should have some understanding of what men
have learned and are learning about living
together. . . .[1]

---

[1]Ibid., pp. 4-8. As a sample, the text of Guideline 1 follows:
   "1. An educated man should be able to express
himself clearly in his own language, both in
speech and in writing. It is a frequent illusion
to suppose you can think clearly if you cannot
write clearly. Words are the basic tools of
thought. If you cannot use them skillfully,
you will be handicapped not only in communicating
your ideas to anyone else but also in developing,
defining, and understanding them yourself.
You should therefore take at least one course,
and preferably several, that will require you
to write papers and have them criticized for
clarity of expression by the instructor. The
most obvious department in which to look for
such courses is English. Examples are English
15, 25, 29, and 77. But several other departments offer courses that give strict attention
to writing. Among them are several courses
in Classical Civilization, History, and Philosophy.
   "In whatever department you study writing,
it would be well to take at least one course

Any close examination of this inspirational
rhetoric quickly shows it to be conceptually flawed,
in minor and major ways. As a petty example, one
doubts that even talented Clasics majors learned
to speak Latin or ancient Greek as Guideline 2 recommends. And one wonders how much classroom effort
or private homework was devoted to clear expression
in speech, an objective of Guideline 1. More sub-
stantively, in considering the same Guidelines, does
one doubt that Einstein thought clearly, when he
himself admitted that words got in his way; or that
Beethoven was muddleheaded before the score of the
Fifth Symphony? Finally, as has been pointed out
before with regard to the 1945 Reforms, there is
no logical, necessary connection between the subject
matter recommended by the Guidelines and the educational attributes that subject matter is alleged
to develop. As a clear example, there is good cause
to doubt that anthropology, a subject under Guideline

---

in English literature. Although language is
an essential tool for any kind of study, you
will not fully understand its possibilities
and the avenues of thought and feeling it can
open, unless you can appreciate the use made
of it by its greatest masters. You will be
missing one of the rewards made possible by
your own increased skill unless you follow or
accompany the study of writing by the study
of literature."
The Course of Study Committee was unwilling
that the Guidelines be interpreted as regulations,
thereby restricting the new freedom recommended by
the Report on the Freshman Year which permitted
"greater flexibility of pace and specialization."
Twice the Committee reaffirmed
"that the guidelines were in fact guidelines
and not requirements, and that in the exercise
of interpretation of the rules [advisors of
all kinds] should use their own good judgment.
Were the guidelines to be interpreted as pro-
scriptive [sic] rules, ... the new system
would lose much of its value."
See CSC Minutes, 24 February 1966. The Committee
restated this position for the College Deans again
on 5 May 1966. See CSC Minutes, 5 May 1966.

6, is any more effective at developing an understanding "of the duties and problems facing you as a human being" than, say, a reading of Shakespeare's plays. Or again, will an historical study of the democracy in Fourth Century Athens, which quite resembles ours, do more to prevent "temporal provincialism" than an archeological expedition to the "lost" cities of South America or even a brief visit to backwoods New Guinea? Probably not.

It is asking too much of a series of Guidelines drafted by committee in a matter of weeks that it present a philosophically cohesive response to the problematic definition of liberal education which has puzzled great thinkers over the centuries.[1] On the other hand, there is much self-evident truth in what the Yale Faculty had to say, as one instinctively senses. Focusing once again on purpose makes clear why this is so. The suggestion is that the matter of purpose has crept into the wording of the Guidelines without open acknowledgment. It is indeed true that the use of words promotes clarity of thought when that is the intention of the writer; it is also true that a foreign language can create subtlety of mind, if that is the purpose of its study; likewise, an examination of today's primitive society in the Amazon can destroy fallacies about modern human cultures. The point is that what the Faculty put forward as a necessary connection is not a necessary connection, unless the student and teacher adopt the appropriate purpose. And it is only when the fundamental purpose is liberal that liberal education is achieved. It makes no difference whether distributional requirements are expressed negatively or positively to the student genuinely interested in a multi-faceted view of reality, which is intended to liberate him in the sense that a comprehensive approach makes him freer to move around accurately, safely and realistically in a very complex world.

---

[1]The Guidelines were largely written by Edmund S. Morgan, the historian who was chairman of the Course of Study Committee, with the active assistance of Dean May and President Brewster, who involved himself deeply in this project. Personal interview with Georges May, 25 November 1980.

189

In the sixties, as in the thirties, Yale College never quite abandoned some structure to its course of study. The Guidelines would not be without considerable effect in a later era of notable turmoil and anti-authoritarianism. The Faculty had not utterly abandoned the pursuit of liberal education, but neither had it been willing to restrict, if it could have, the demand for "greater flexibility of pace and specialization." Although the Guidelines did preserve some sense of structure, one cannot escape the fact that the Faculty had, in the final measure, transferred the responsibility for the definition of a liberal course of study to the student, thereby largely abrogating its historic prerogative. As the sixties and seventies wore on, the Faculty would begin to surrender other perquisites: The grading system would be softened, the right to approve the subject matter of the college seminars would become token, and, especially symbolic, representation on the Course of Study Comittee would be surrendered to the undergraduates. Inevitably, the reassertion of faculty authority and leadership would come about, and with it, in the late 1970s, tighter control of the course of study. But the full flourishing of the liberal ideal awaits a university-wide willingness to accept a wider conception of appropriate subject matter and a correspondingly broader definition of the concept of the curriculum.

Chapter VIII

THE REFORMS OF 1978

The half decade which followed the promulgation of the Guidelines of 1966 was a time of turmoil and turbulence at most of the nation's universities, and Yale was not an exception. During this period, the University, like the country, was enmeshed in the whole question of governance, and the Yale College Faculty's once unquestioned control over the course of study no longer went unquestioned. The Faculty, as we have seen, had already voluntarily abrogated a portion of that control when the Guidelines transferred responsibility for the final definition of a liberal education to the student and his advisors. The process of transfer, once started, was not so easily limited or reversed. Further, the new "responsible" undergraduate enrolled at Yale pursuant to the recommendations of the 1962 Report on the Freshman Year was indeed capable of making decisions and not surprisingly felt he was thereby entitled to a voice in those affecting his own college career. From the point of view of the curriculum, the key question of the era at Yale was not what, exactly, should constitute the course of study, but who, specifically, should constitute it.

In the late sixties, the undergraduates were increasingly involved in determining their own course of study, and they were increasingly effective in revising it to their own, not-always-admirable ends. But, as the decade turned, their undeterred successes were signally slowed. The Guidelines, which had been undertaken as a faculty-instigated experiment and not in response to student pressures, were reviewed and reaffirmed in 1971, an event which in itself measured the turning of affairs. So did the refusal of the Faculty to adopt the Report of the Study Group on Yale College, which had proposed extensive and even radical reforms of the undergraduate curriculum. Eventually, in response to clear evidence that the students were complying less and less closely with the Guidelines, the Faculty enforced, by means of the Reforms of 1978, a new rigor within the system of distribution that would have been unthinkable a decade before.

Still it is a mistake to conceive of the Reforms of 1978 as innovative. In the discussions which led to them, the faculty rejected a proposal that would have significantly reorganized the course of study, structuring it with reference to selected subject matter rather than the standard academic disciplines. Instead the Faculty chose to proceed within the familiar principles of distribution and concentration. Accordingly, the Reforms of 1978 did not really attempt to reverse most of the influences that have clearly over the years eroded that system of "delicate balance" and rendered it less effective in the service of the liberal ideal. Consequently, though Yale had never entirely capitulated to the demands of professional, utilitarian or specialized education, neither had Yale successfully defined a modern conception of liberal education or captured it in the College course of study. To do so in the modern era remains both a challenge and an opportunity.

In the late 60s the Course of Study Committee was presiding over a curriculum which threatened, for many reasons, to drift entirely beyond its control, something it had never ever permitted. One of the places where it had already largely slipped was in the area of the college seminars. These discussion groups had been part of President Griswold's effort to enhance liberal education, using the twelve residential colleges as vehicles. Early in his administration, President Brewster endorsed this approach, commenting that insufficient use was being made of Yale's "special asset." Brewster felt the colleges should be brought directly into the main business of Yale College, that is, educating undergraduates; and he set out to raise funds for this purpose-- $200,000 per year on an experimental basis.[1] He also appointed a committee, known as the Hall Committee, to determine how best to implement this objective. Brewster at this time had no concern about dissipating the course of study:

> Intellectual development is not limited to the curriculum. It finds stimulus in the bull

---

[1]Pres. Report 1965-66, pp. 34-35; Pres. Report 1966-67, pp. 28-30.

session, the group with a cause, and in a host
of other organized and semi-organized extracurricular pursuits. And not all development is
intellectual, let alone academic. The student
is above all a living person, who thinks but
also feels; who needs activities, ways of growth
and forms of expression that could not possibly
all be provided even by the best curriculum
. . . the quality of the faculty, the quality
of the extra-curricular life, the quality of
Yale as a residential community--all will determine how well the university years do in fact
develop intellectual, personal, and moral talents.
. . .[1]

The Hall Committee recommended, with the enthusiastic endorsement of the students, that the residential colleges should take an innovative role in
setting up courses, to be given for regular college
credit, in an effort to satisfy "the intellectual
curiosity and diversity of interest of the present
undergraduate generation." These experimental courses,
usually offered for a single year, taught in seminar
format, sometimes by non-academic instructors, and
offered to a limited enrollment, were supposed to
provide "some leavening of the curriculum." The
Hall Report of 1968 was a frontal attack on the Yale
College Faculty's conception of and control of the
curriculum, and while the Faculty had no choice but
to accept the intent of the Report, it did succeed
in amending it to require, first, that all instructors
in the new college seminars who were not members
of the Yale College Faculty be approved by the appropriate Department, and, second, that all college
seminars be subject to the approval of the Course
of Study Committee in the same way as any new offering
in the standard curriculum. Nevertheless, there
was no disguising that student-inspired concerns
for "relevance" had triumphed in some measure over
the traditional academic disciplines.[2]

---

[1]Pres. Report 1967-68, pp. 17-18.

[2]Faculty Record, 2 May 1968; Yale Alumni Magazine,
July 1968, p. 8; Yale Daily News, 25 April 1968,
26 April 1968.

The whole host of college seminars which came
into being--by 1971 they numbered 140--caused the
Course of Study Committee problems about categorizing
them for purposes of the major, the distribution
system, and the Guidelines. And since the Hall Report
had established a supervisory Special Committee on
Teaching in the Residential Colleges, a group which
included students, the Course of Study Committee
in effect was required to review the approvals previously given by a committee with overlapping authority. In short, with regard to the college seminars,
the Course of Study Committee began to function as
a sort of second level quality control group, a function which was not entirely unnecessary since at
least one potential instructor was an individual
who had been denied an appointment as a visiting
professor by the appropriate Department and since
one proposed seminar, **Interpersonal Relations**, featured "T-Group" sessions under the guidance of an
available psychiatrist. Fortunately, students were
effectively limited by enrollment pressure to one
college seminar at a time.[1]

Lest the Faculty's acquiescence to the Hall
Report and the resulting bastardization of the traditional disciplined, structured, and departmentalized
curriculum by the college seminar seem absurd, it
might be well to make a brief survey of the University
community and identify some of the trends and events
which, in the late sixties, were fragmenting it.
Change and confusion were rife, collision and conflict
omni-present. The 1962 Report on the Freshman Year
had marked the beginning of a vigorous effort to
diversify the student body. This effort had been
explosively expanded by the decision of the Yale

---

[1]Faculty Record 27 May 1971, 18 December 1969,
13 March 1969. Of the 140 courses offered at the
time in the college seminar program, all but 12 were
full, and most were over-subscribed. In two-thirds
of them, there were 25 "first-choice" applicants
and in a few as high as 100. See Faculty Record,
27 May 1971.

Corporation to admit women.[1] Initially, Yale had
not intended to decrease the number of men admitted,
an objective that eventually proved financially
unrealizable. Consequently, together with women,
came the problems of deciding whether there should
be male/female admissions quotas or whether Yale
should be "sex-blind." Student agitation about pari-
entals, women's rights, and sexual harrassment followed right along. Then the trend to student diversity was further reinforced by the Corporation's decision to admit students without regard to financial
need. This policy, which had the side effect of
discriminating against the children of Yale alumni,
met vocal opposition, though it increased the general
capability of the undergraduates.[2]

President Brewster had gone on record that a
Yale education was not bounded by the curriculum,
and the undergraduates, always ready to involve themselves in extra-curricular activities, found some
un-traditional ones. They protested a decision to
deny tenure to a popular assistant professor of philosophy and succeeded in getting the Administration
to review the whole matter of faculty promotion.
The so-called Bernstein affair was the marked opening
of a "new era in which students demanded and deserved
respect for their views."[3] The undergraduates engaged
in sit-down strikes and forceably detained University
employees. They called for the expulsion of ROTC,
not only from the curriculum, but from the campus.

---

[1]Faculty Record, 14 November 1968. Brewster
recommended the admission of 250 freshman women
together with 250 transfer students as a first step
toward an eventual total of 1500. Earlier Yale had
investigated the possibility of making some kind
of arrangement with Vassar College. See Faculty
Record, 28 September 1967. An interesting analysis
of the increased diversity of the Yale undergraduate
body, particularly in its academic preparation,
appears in a memo from Kenneth Kenniston to Raymond
Suplinskas, 1 May 1969, May Mss., Box 17, folder
222.

[2]Pres. Report, 1970-71, p. 11.

[3]Pres. Report, 1967-68, p. 20.

When they questioned the entire governance of the
University, President Brewster announced the formation
of a Study Commission, which produced the Dominguez
Report.[1] Finally, there were the Black Panther trial,
May Day 1970, and Brewster's decision that for one
week the giving and attending of classes as well
as what would be taught therein would be at the individual discretion of both faculty and students.
It was small wonder that Yale's President later publicly confessed that he had feared for the very sur-
vival of the University, a thought he also admitted
had never before occurred to him.[2]

Like the University, Yale College had to accommodate itself to student pressure while attempting
to separate worthwhile suggestions from self-serving
demands. In early 1967, Dean Georges May reported
to the Faculty that the Student Advisory Board wanted
a voice in the quality of their education in general
and in faculty appointments in particular. May denied
the Chairman of the Yale Daily News permission to
attend Faculty meetings, but he did agree to supply
an agenda and report afterward on what had happened.
In response to student demand, the Faculty voted
the abolition of number grades and replaced them
with the use of honors, high pass, pass, and fail.
Later the Faculty agreed that failing grades would
not be recorded. Acceding to student "suggestions,"
fairly early on, the Faculty reduced the number of

---

[1]Faculty Record, 11 November 1969; Faculty Record,
30 January 1969; Faculty Record, 2 October 1969;
Faculty Record, 17 April 1969.

[2]Faculty Record, 23 April 1970; Pres. Report
1969-70, pp. 1-5. Brewster's comments on the Black
Panther trial are on pp. 4 and 8-10. The President's
Report of 1968-69, dealing with (a) student government
and university government, (b) black power and arrangements for the study of black experience, (c) protection of dissent and the prevention of disruption,
gives eloquent testimony to the travail which besought
the University.

satisfactorily completed term courses required for
graduation from 40 to 36.[1]

And then there was the matter of student representation. It will be remembered that, when the
distribution requirements were rewritten in 1966,
the Faculty established a committee to oversee teaching in the colleges. This group became the standing
Committee on Teaching and Learning. Since good teaching was an important student interest, the Student
Advisory Board quickly set up a parallel student
committee. At the beginning of the 1968-69 academic
year, a Joint Committee on Teaching and Learning
was created. At the same time, students were given
three seats on the Course of Study Committee and
three seats on the Executive Committee of Yale College,
the group which made exceptions from standard academic
requirements and handled disciplinary problems in
the name of the Dean. Finally, students were invited
to attend Faculty meetings as observers. The only
area the Faculty was never willing to accept as a
matter of joint concern was the making of academic
appointments. No compromise affecting this ancient
prerogative was ever made.[2]

The enlarged Course of Study Committee had to
address a considerable number of confusing issues
in this confusing time by means of confusing
approaches involving confused responsibility. The confused responsibility stemmed partially from the fact
that the purposes of the Joint Committee on Teaching

---

[1]Faculty Record, 5 January 1967; Faculty Record,
27 April 1967; Faculty Record, 2 November 1967;
Faculty Record, 9 April 1970; Faculty Record, 16 April
1970; Faculty Record, 15 February 1968. One of the
reasons students advocated a non-numerical grading
system was that letter grades made it difficult for
draft boards to make the calculations upon which
exemptions were based. For much the same reason,
the students supported a program which enabled an
undergraduate to be certified as a teacher upon graduation. Teaching was, of course, a draft exempting
job. See Faculty Record, 8 December 1966.

[2]Faculty Record, 3 October 1968; Faculty Record,
30 May 1968; Faculty Record, 24 April 1968.

and Learning much resembled those traditional ones
of the Course of Study Committee which went beyond
the routine approval of new courses, namely the function of the curriculum as a whole, its administration,
and the quality of its delivery. The Course of Study
Committee had been so busy handling its "routine"
work that it had not had time to guard its former
prerogatives, even though it had recently reorganized
itself to handle its "regular" work by subcommittee,
supposedly leaving the full committee free to deal
with matters of educational policy. To further confusion, the Committee on the Teaching in the Colleges,
established at the time of the Hall Report, functioned
as a sort of subcommittee of the Course of Study
Committee, though it actually was not, officially
or in terms of membership. Quickly, the Course of
Study Committee decided not to redo all the work
done by this other group, though it never really
escaped the supervisory responsibility and attendant
problems.[1]

A brief review of some of the matters brought
before the Course of Study Committee immediately
shows the complexities of the issues it was expected
to deal with as well as the extent of their departure
from tradition. There was the possibility of a five-
year BA program, suggested because so many students
dropped out for a year anyway. Alternatively, there
were the combined BA/MA programs, which militated
in the opposite direction. Apparently, even the
length of the course of study was no longer a settled
issue.[2] The Committee had to face the problem of
how many Graduate School courses would be accepted
for undergraduate credit,[3] and, when the first holder

---

[1] In 80 years, the Yale catalogue listing grew
from 60 courses to nearly 1600. See Report of the
Study Group on Yale College, 1972 (the Second Dahl
Report), p. 100, Yale Archives. Faculty Record,
28 September 1967; Faculty Record, 24 April 1969.

[2] Faculty Record, 6 March 1969; CSC Minutes,
7 January 1971. The five year BA program would also
serve to protect the student from the draft while
he was "dropped out."

[3] CSC Minutes, 1968-70, passim. At the time
of discussion, undergraduates were allowed to take
up to four term courses in a professional school.

of the DeVane Professorship had to fulfill his obligation to offer an undergraduate course, there was some question of what constituted an undergraduate course.[1] The non-numerical grading system caused all sorts of problems about calculating averages, honors, the Dean's List; about awarding prizes; and generally about evaluating what any grade meant.[2]

A key example of the situation which confronted the Course of Study Committee was student interest in redefining the major. In the first place, there were student demands for new majors such as Afro-American Studies, the Study of the City, and Environmental Studies. Somewhat sketchily, these demands were accommodated despite the fact that many members of the faculty recognized that these new majors lacked the coherence and rigor of the more traditional disciplines.[3] In the second place, the Faculty had abandoned the concept of requiring a departmental or comprehensive exam, permitting each Department, instead to substitute another "final exercise"--a situation which promoted a variety of generally less demanding requirements.[4] And, in the third place, the Faculty had dropped its limitation upon the number of courses which had to be taken outside the Department of the student's major. This permitted a previously forbidden level of concentration.[5] Despite

---

[1]CSC Minutes, 14 January 1971.

[2]Faculty Record, 30 May 1968.

[3]Faculty Record, 12 December 1968, 28 May 1970. The Afro-American Studies program was originally proposed under the Divisional Major rubric. But since Divisional Majors tended to connote honors quality programs, George W. Pierson suggested dropping the term Divisional, and the Faculty concurred. The Studies of the City program seems to have been authorized but never actually offered.

[4]Faculty Record, 2 November 1967.

[5]Faculty Record, 6 June 1969. Students continued, of course, to be required to take courses outside the Division of the major, but they were no longer required to take courses within the Division in other Departments.

this relaxation of the structure of the major, the undergraduates remained unhappy. In 1969, 66 percent of them felt they could design a better program of study than the one they were involved in; 39 percent continued to feel that the major was not flexible enough; and 36 percent claimed they had been deterred from enrolling in an otherwise attractive major because of its inflexible requirements.[1] As late as the Fall of 1970, the Joint Committee on Teaching and Learning was strongly suggesting to the Course of Study Committee that the major be recast to allow still greater flexibility and to promote "relevance."[2]

The attack on the structure of the major during this period was probably inevitable, given the tenor of the times, but it is worth suggesting that one of its causes lies in the juxtaposition of the recommendations of the 1962 Report on the Freshman Year regarding admissions with the academic flexibility made possible by the 1966 adoption of the Guidelines and the simultaneous relaxation of the distributional requirements. The 1962 Report had advocated admitting individuals with particular interests. And when these individuals took advantage of the curricular freedom encouraged by the Guidelines, the result was not the pursuit of serious scholarship but the triumph of personalized academic goals. Intellectual relevance was entirely an individual matter, and the Faculty supposedly had no basis for or right to insist upon impartial standards. That the faculty had been partially responsible for maneuvering itself

---

[1]CSC Minutes, 24 April 1969, 29 May 1969. The Student Committee for Investigating the Structure of Majors proposed (1) complete freedom for students to choose courses; (2) expanding the advisory system; and (3) making more factual information available concerning post-graduate opportunities.

[2]Faculty Record, 1 October 1970, 29 October 1970. The later meeting shows that the major was regarded as an area of faculty control under challenge at a time of diminishing academic professionalism among the students.

into a position so destructive of its basic function did not help assuage its damaged self-esteem.[1]

The stature of the Faculty of Yale college had, in this half-decade, been under siege for several other institutional reasons, that is, for reasons unrelated to undergraduate demands which would, therefore, tend to have more substance and longevity. In the first place, there was an unmistakable transfer of power from the Yale College Faculty to the University Administration. The already unwieldy size of the Faculty had been further increased when it had been formally merged with the Graduate School Faculty into the Faculty of the Arts and Sciences.[2] Necessarily, in a group so large, effective power began to be exercised by a smaller group, the Executive Committee of the Faculty of the Arts and Sciences, which included the President, the Provost, the Directors of the University Divisions, the Dean of the Graduate School and the Dean of Yale College. Although President Brewster emphasized that the maintenance of a separate Yale College Faculty and Dean would assure good leadership for the College and more attention to the distinctive needs of undergraduates by the professors who taught in both the College and the Graduate School, there is some doubt that these factors outweighed the financial control of the Executive Committee asserted through the budget-making process. More and more, Faculty meetings came to resemble opportunities for the Administration to introduce programs or seek support for them, and

---

[1] I owe this reasoning to A. Bartlett Giamatti, History of Scroll and Key: 1942-1972 (New Haven: The Society, 1978), pp. 30-33.

[2] In 1971-72, the Yale College Faculty in the ranks of lecturer and above totalled 772. See Report of the Study Group on Yale College 1972 (Second Dahl Report), p. 109. At the time of the Panther trial, there was considerable confusion about which professors were entitled to be admitted to Faculty meetings. See, for example, Faculty Record, 23 April 1970. Four hundred thirty-two faculty members were in attendance that day. See also Faculty Record, 30 September 1971.

for the faculty to lobby for their own particular interests.[1]

In the second place, the College Faculty's stature had been hurt because it had lost some measure of its unquestioned control over academic apointments. Following the student-instigated Bernstein affair, President Brewster had appointed a Faculty Committee, some members of which were tenured, some not, to review Yale's system of academic appointments. The Ad Hoc Committee on Policies and Procedures on Tenure Appointments produced a report, which concluded:

Neither unusually effective teaching nor unusually significant contribution to the community's well-being can compensate for a total absence of the most tangible and enduring demonstration of a scholar's distinction--that is, written work of outstanding competence.

The report went on to recommend that the initiative in making tenure appointments remain with the Departments and suggested a methodology for evaluating

---

[1]Pres. Report, 1965-66, p. 11. An open exercise of this power was manifest later when the Faculty was considering the Second Dahl Report. In his annual report, Brewster disclaimed any intention of telling the Faculty how to deal with the Report, but at the same time, he did say that it would have to be dealt with in some way and set a time limit for action. See Pres. Report, 1971-72, p. 3. On the other hand, the Faculty, being so unwieldy, begged at times to be led. For example, the Committee on Teaching and Learning invited President-designate Giamatti, immediately after his selection, to present his views to them, and shortly afterwards the new President was requested to appoint a new "Dahl Committee" to study Yale College. This Giamatti declined to do. See Minutes Teaching and Learning Committee and letter from Michael E. Zellner to Giamatti, 16 March 1978, Taft Mss., folder marked Teaching and Learning Committee, 1977-78.

faculty teaching.[1] Significantly, the Executive Committee of the Faculty of the Arts and Sciences did not accept these recommendations, proposed some of their own, and obtained the approval of the Corporation for an indecisive compromise. Eventually, tenure decisions ended up being reviewed by non-departmental peers and Divisional committees, rather than Departmental committees, a procedure which Brewster believed strengthened the entire faculty. Faculty control over its own destiny was not, however, simultaneously strengthened.[2]

The third factor which diminished the stature of the Yale College Faculty was its probably unavoidable decision to delegate its traditional responsibility for undergraduate discipline to the President. This "constitutional" question arose to pertinent

---

[1]Yale Alumni Magazine, November 1965, pp. 12-14; Faculty Record, 25 October 1965. For an account of the Bernstein affair, see Yale Alumni Magazine, April 1965.

[2]Pres. Report, 1972-73, pp. 4-5. The Faculty committee had rejected student evaluation of teaching for purposes of tenure decision and had suggested appointing a committee to study the matter of evaluating teaching and the improvement of teaching by both tenured and non-tenured faculty. The Executive Committee rejected the notion of a committee and suggested that honors graduates and PhD candidates be invited to submit written appraisals of their educational experience to the appropriate Department head. The Executive Committee also proposed that a written statement about the professor's teaching be included in the materials circulated at the time of tenure review. The Corporation, the Yale College Faculty, and the Graduate School Faculty all merely voted to accept the report and by so doing avoided a decision between its recommendations and those of the Executive Committee. Eventually, the Yale College Faculty set up faculty and student committees on teaching, established a series of departmental student advisory committees, and permitted student evaluation for the sole purpose of an instructor's improving his own teaching. See Faculty Record, 10 February 1966.

immediacy at the time of student unrest over ROTC in 1969 and at the time of the Black Panther trial in the Spring of 1970. Brewster believed that it would be more damaging in these times of crisis to admit to the students that he lacked the power to discipline them for disrupting the University than to disturb precedent by usurping a traditional Faculty prerogative. In both instances, the faculty concurred, and once again a measure of power slid from the Faculty to the Administration.[1]

Although the flood tide which lapped at the shores of the Faculty's prerogatives and position did not exactly turn in the academic year 1970-71, one senses the development of eddies in its former undeterred advance. The Course of Study Committee undertook to review the Guidelines and the distributional requirements with a sense of procedural calm that would have been impossible the year before, and this despite the fact that the undergraduates continued to press, particularly in the Committee on Teaching and Learning, for flexibility, relevance, and an unregulated selection of courses.[2] The Committee concluded that the Guidelines system had basically worked well. In discussions that intermittently covered two years, the Committee refused to accede to attempts to reduce the number of distributional requirements and rejected a suggestion that they be completed by the end of junior year. Yet another proposal that distributional credit not be awarded simultaneously with advanced placement credit

---

[1]The classic argument appears in Faculty Record, 23 April 1970. For discussion of ROTC problem, see Faculty Record, 30 January 1969.

[2]Faculty Record, 1 October 1970. When Dean May asked the undergraduate members of the Course of Study Committee what effect the Guidelines had on them, he was told, "You believe the catalogue Freshman Year, but after that you forget it." See CSC Minutes, 5 November 1970. On the other hand, after Georges May announced his intention to retire as Dean, when students were asked by the Committee on the Deanship to suggest appropriate candidates, not a single name was received. See Faculty Record, 5 February 1971.

college-level work done before admission to Yale
was defeated because the Admissions Office still
felt that that oft-suggested procedure would damage
relations with the secondary schools and harm the
whole advanced placement program. An effort to reduce
the number of courses which had to be taken outside
the Division of the major was defeated as was a proposal for an experiment called "Undirected Studies,"
basically a very tentatively proposed modification
and expansion of the Scholars of the House program.[1]

What the Course of Study Committee did recommend
was to split the three existing distributional areas--
the humanities, the sciences, and the social sciences--
into four unnamed Groups, basically by subdividing
the languages and literatures (including English)
from the other humanities. Course classifications
were to be made by the Dean, and some courses were
cross-classified in two or more groups. All undergraduates were still required to take twelve credits
outside the Group of their major, and freshmen were
not permitted to take more than four term-courses
in a single Department, nor more than six term-courses
in a single distributional group. Furthermore, all
freshmen were forced to take at least two term courses
in Groups I and/or II, and two term courses in Groups
III and/or IV.[2] This curricular restructuring was
largely a reaffirmation of the status quo, which
in itself was a significant assertion of faculty
authority given the environment in which it was made.
But, for some, it did not go far enough. The new
Dean, and former chairman of the Course of Study

---

[1]CSC Minutes, 4 December 1969; CSC Minutes,
14 January 1971; CSC Minutes, 28 January 1971; CSC
Minutes, 5 June 1970. "Undirected Studies," for
50-100 students, featured no specific course requirements and relied upon an oral exam and an independent
project to evaluate the student's entire academic
accomplishment.

[2]CSC Minutes, 28 January 1971; CSC Minutes,
25 February 1971; Yale College Programs of Study,
1971-72, p. 13; Faculty Record, 11 March 1971. Students were enrolled as follows: 5721 in Group I;
6130 in Group II; 5852 in Group III; and 4378 in
Group IV.

Committee, Horace D. Taft, pointed out that numerous professors "were perturbed that several of the Guidelines were not being observed by the students," and the Dean predicted that unless the counselling system altered the patern of course selection, the Faculty would take further action. Still, the changes which were instituted were intended, first, to broaden each student's exposure to the various facets of knowledge; and, second, to attempt to delay any arrant specialization until after an exploratory freshman year. As such, the alterations were an effort to counter student interest in random electives or an over-concentrated specialization, both of which were clearly not examples of Yale's liberal ideal. This particular assertion of Faculty control over the curriculum was directed in a deeply traditional fashion. That and the fact that it occurred at all are what makes it significant. The specific changes themselves were relatively unimportant.[1]

Despite this successful defense of curricular structure in the Course of Study Committee, a return to business more or less as usual was not, however, in the offing. When "an overall fresh look at the goals of undergraduate education and the programs to achieve these goals" was proposed to President Brewster, he imnediately appointed a Study Group on Yale College, "to return to the Yale community within the year with their best thoughts about what Yale College should be trying to accomplish and how it should go about it." The Study Group was chaired by Robert Dahl, a professor of political science who had served on the Course of Study Committee in the mid-fifties and who in the mid-sixties had led the ad hoc committee which dealt with the University's procedures for promotion and tenure.[2] It is important to understand that as part of an extremely broad mandate, Dahl's Study Group was specifically charged to be concerned with financial feasibility. Once

---

[1] CSC Minutes, 1 April 1971.

[2] Pres. Report, 1970-71, pp. 18-19; Faculty Record, 22 April 1971. In addition to Dahl, the committee included William Kessen, Jonathan Spence, and, ex-officio, Deans Taft and Elga Wasserman.

again, Yale was desperately short of money, and had
been since the mid-sixties. Thanks to the crises
and confusion that permeated the end of the decade,
a $388 million fundraising campaign had to be aban-
doned in the planning stages, and Yale's financial
crisis had only grown worse. Thus, despite the President's free-wheeling instructions to Dahl to suggest
a badly needed "coherent, purposive articulation
of the goals of education at Yale . . . [and] a
rethinking of the objectives and functions of college
education," the Study Group was tacitly encouraged
to produce ways that were less expensive.[1] At this
present historical remove, it is simply impossible
to decide whether Brewster was using the Study Group
to find a new, economical educational pattern or
to convince the faculty in general of the seriousness
of the fiscal crisis, thereby preparing them for
the necessary sacrifices. Probably the President
intended to do both.

Although the Second Dahl Report, as it came
to be known, was never accepted by the Faculty,
neither was it formally rejected. Consideration was
distracted and indefinitely deferred by more urgent
concerns. It served, finally, as a basis for further
committee work, for plenty of discussion; and it
did do its part in causing the Faculty to realize
the seriousness of the University's plight. Nevertheless, the Report is fascinating, both because
it documents the educational situation at that moment
and because it delineates the high water mark of
the unstructured spirit of the late sixties.

The Study Group considered the goals of undergraduate education, the proper scale of Yale College,
the faculty, the students, the setting of undergraduate life, and the structure and process of learning.
Its report, like the 1962 Report on Freshman Year,
dealt with matters far beyond the formal course of
study and perhaps even the informal curriculum.
For example, the Study Group questioned the assumption
of the 1962 Report that Yale students should be

---

[1]The President's Report of 1966-67 was essentially a preliminary sketch of a vast capital campaign
which ended up being delayed until 1973-74. Quotation
from Report of the Study Group on Yale College (Second
Dahl Report), p. 5.

scholars and teachers, and suggested a redefined admissions policy which would seek to admit those of any age, sex, or income who would most benefit others later on, those who would benefit most from Yale's particularities, those who would contribute most to other students.[1] The Study Group also recommended the building of two new residential colleges and the subsequent conversion of the freshmen dormitories on the Old Campus into two further colleges, for a grand total of sixteen. The thought was that what little remained of the Freshman Year should be done away with entirely and that the Dean of Yale College should assign students with similar interests to the same residential college in order to allow special intellectual characteristics to develop among the colleges, though never at the ultimate expense of overall diversity.[2] Finally, the Study Group recommended a revised academic calendar, which would enable the student to get his BA degree not after the existing eight terms but in six "extended semesters," with a year off campus for private study or work in society. This proposal was openly advanced as a possible solution to the University's financial problems, a means to increase tuition revenue without expanding facilities.[3]

---

[1]Ibid., pp. 12-13, 40-50.

[2]Ibid., pp. 55, 60. In fact, John Hay Whitney, '26, had already given Yale the money for two new colleges (which have never been built). See Pres. Report, 1970-71, p. 16.

[3]Report of the Study Group on Yale College 1972 (Second Dahl Report), pp. 110-116. Discussion of the Dahl Report immediately centered around this calendar proposal since it affected all segments of the community in immediately tangible ways. Eventually, Yale did adopt a voluntary summer term (voluntary for both students and professors), but during the trial period, it never generated sufficient revenue to end up being taken seriously. The summer term was allowed to lapse and the time was devoted to remedial work and foreign language training. The shortened calendar, for Fall and Spring terms, instituted during the trial period of the Summer term, remains, however, in effect. See Pres. Report, 1972-73, p. 11; Faculty Record, 15 December 1977.

On curricular matters, the Dahl Report was equally innovative. It criticized the elective system and the concept of the "college as cafeteria." It reaffirmed the principles of concentration and distribution as the hallmarks of a proper college education, depth distinguishing it from the secondary school and breadth from the graduate school. The Study Group was aware, though, of the limitations of the present system: It pointed out that if the scholar-teacher of the Yale faculty forgets that he is teaching undergraduates and not candidates for the PhD degree, no system of distribution and concentration will accomplish anything "more than exposing students to fragments of scholarly learning." And the Study Group noted that undergraduate teaching was clearly the second priority among the Yale faculty.[1] Although the Report suggested that students should have the option of non-departmental concentration, it also suggested that the Departmental Major combine undergraduate and graduate courses, particularly for those who wanted to omit a year en route to graduate school. The Report recommended strengthening introductory courses and suggested the creation of a Committee on Curriculum Planning to "engage the interest of Faculty members in devising profound and appealing ways of studying the areas of breadth." The Report recommended the elimination of the Divisional Majors, Directed Studies, the Scholars of the House program, and the Early Concentration Seminars. On the other hand, it proposed creating a Dean's fund to support non-departmental activities.[2]

The innovative and controversial central proposal of the Study Group was to divide the College into two divisions, the entering division and the degree division, the function of the first being to accommodate advanced placement, to assure breadth of study, to introduce novelty, and to assure an experience in a special interest seminar. After completing

---

[1]Report of the Study Group on Yale College 1972 (Second Dahl Report), pp. 17-18, 15, 32.

[2]Ibid., pp. 74, 73, 98-99, 89, 104-105, 105-106.

the requirements of the entering division and preparing an acceptable Proposal for a Degree, the undergraduate would move to the degree division, which would supervise and certify the completion of the concentrated work outlined in his Proposal for a Degree. The whole system was to be supervised by a hierarchy of Mentors, members of the faculty on a rotating basis, affiliated with the residential colleges, to advise, counsel and chastise students somewhat like the tutors at Oxford and Cambridge. The whole was an attempt to strike a balance between flexibility and inflexibility in curriculum design and in planning the individual student's particular course of study. The concept had roots in the general education programs at Harvard, Chicago and Columbia, and therefore in the 1953 Report of the President's Committee on General Education; it was another effort to develop academic rigor outside the departmental structure of the University; and it was also an effort to assure good instruction by individualizing it and making the system that delivered it flexible. Unfortunately, the Dahl Report's central proposal also adopted some of the defects of the earlier proposals. Specifically, the faculty saw themselves as academics, not personal counselors; too little account was taken of the faculty's interest in protecting its future by scholarly effort; there was inadequate financial leverage outside the Departments; and the institutional separation of the preparatory years from the years of concentration only exacerbated the tendency to regard the early years as unpleasant hurdles, both for faculty and students, on the way to the real purpose of college academic life. In addition, the faculty believed the mentor system increased the influence of the residential colleges at their expense and overly catered to the academic interests of undergraduates.[1]

In considering the Yale College Faculty's tepid response to the Dahl Report, it is interesting to speculate why the collective reaction was so inert. In addition to the obvious hesitancy attendant upon any proposals as radical as the Dahl Report's, particularly where there was no time to build a

---

[1]Ibid., pp. 77-94.

constituency favoring them, I suspect there are two
key reasons: First, the concept of the hierarchy
of Mentors moved the focus for defining liberal education entirely away from the Faculty; second, the
proposal was inimical to the interests of the Departmental Majors, which had been considerably attacked
of late and whose requirements were just beginning
to be redesigned, reaffirmed and reasserted by the
departmentalized faculty.

When the Faculty adopted the Guidelines of 1966,
a large portion of the responsibility for defining
a Yale liberal education had shifted to the student
and his residential college advisor. Overall compliance with the Guidelines was indeed monitored
for the Faculty by the Registrar, but in individual
instances the student and his advisor decided for
themselves, as indeed the Course of Study Committee
had wanted them to. In some cases, undergraduates
found even this freedom too limited, and they pressed
for more. Thus, it is possible to see the Dahl
Report's system of Mentorships as an effort to strengthen the counseling system in the face of student
demands for an elective system. On the other hand,
and from a faculty perspective, the Dahl proposal,
though it did not specifically repudiate the Guidelines, implicitly ignored them, leaving it entirely
to the student and his mentor to structure the student's course of study, within or without the University, within or without the traditional disciplines.
The Guidelines, which were, after all, the Faculty's
only vehicle for asserting what a liberal education
seemed to them to be, simply played no significant
part in the new concept. And that the Faculty would
not accept. If they were unwilling to enforce undevi-
ating compliance with their own definition of liberal
education, which they were, they were equally unwilling to abandon the effort completely to the student
(and his Mentor) by agreeing to "unstructure" a curriculum which had been structured always, publicly
and pointedly. In this sense, the recommendations
of the Dahl Report were at variance with Yale's historic pattern and did not therefore commend themselves.

The second reason the Faculty rejected the Dahl
Report involved the system of the major. Though
excessive concentration in a particular subject has

been a frequent target of curricular reformers over
the years, nevertheless, there are real intellectual
advantages to the systematic disciplines and to the
departmental organization of university academic
life which they inspire. President Brewster put
it thus:

> The discipline as the organizing principle
> of academic organization finds its most persua-
> sive justification at two points: the making
> of appointments to the faculty, and the confer-
> ring of undergraduate honors and the highest
> academic degrees. The best assurance of rigor
> in both of these critical actions derives from
> being able to hold to a standard of excellence,
> made objective and recognizable by the ability
> to make comparisons with the best of the craft
> throughout the world.[1]

The system of the major was where the concept
of a discipline impinged upon undergraduate work.
And the system of the major had been singularly successful over the years—if anything too successful—
in accomplishing its objectives, particularly when
it was not abused for professional or vocational
ends by the undergraduates. The professional work
of the faculty fitted best into the system of majoring,
and the independent work which capable students undertook in honors programs and in Scholars of the House
was impressive as well as valued. Thus, when the
Dahl Report suggested a total revision of the conception of the major, that recommendation went counter
to a, if not the, fundamental technique of undergraduate instruction, one which I believe the faculty
had no intention of abandoning. The fact that, in
the end, the financial crunch was dealt with by
faculty attrition which the faculty reluctantly
accepted as unavoidable, supports this view. So does
the fact that at this time the Faculty voted to review
systematically every non-departmental program.[2]

Furthermore, the faculty, as part of its whole
effort to maintain control over the curriculum, had
figured out new ways to strengthen and improve the

---

[1]Pres. Report, 1965-66, p. 12.

[2]At the opening of the 1973-74 academic year,
the Faculty of the Arts and Sciences in absolute

212

more popular majors. In the late sixties, the Course of Study Committee discussed the concept of both narrowing and broadening the major in the interests of flexibility and pertinency. The idea was to reduce the absolute requirements to a relatively few "core courses" in the discipline while widening the area covered by "related courses." The departmentally required "core coures" would prevent over-concentration in some sub-sub specialty of the discipline, while the "related courses" would accommodate a student's personal interest in tangential areas. The revision of the Guidelines in 1971, which altered the distributional requirements from twelve courses outside the Department of the major to twelve courses outside the Group of the major supported the tendency to broaden the work of the last two years.[1]

The improvement and redefinition of the major is but one example of the Faculty's slow reassertion between 1970 and 1978 of its authority over undergraduate academic life, the non-adoption of the Dahl Report being the point where events began to move almost exclusively in the direction of Faculty control. In this period, the Course of Study Committee acted as an increasingly strict quality control group, gradually tightening its definition of the acceptable until a new insistence upon the traditional academic excellence may be discerned. The Study of the City

----

numbers had decreased 8-1/2 percent since 1970-71, though it was 22 percent larger than it had been in 1963. See Faculty Record, 20 September 1973.

The review of non-departmental programs was to take place once every five years; see Faculty Record, 30 November 1972.

[1]An examination of the Program of Study Bulletins in the years 1971-74 shows that some Departments, Economics and History for example, seem on their own to have adopted this approach. An example of its articulation is memo from Kenneth Keniston to Raymond Suplinskas, 1 May 1969, May Mss., Box 17, folder 222.

major, for example was abolished.[1] The grading system was revised to letter grades, and later the Registrar was instructed once again to record failures.[2] The Faculty rejected a student proposal that general honors be abolished and did not accept a recommendation from the Joint Committee on Teaching and Learning that the course load for the degree be reduced to thirty-two.[3] It was decided that acceleration credits for advanced placement could not be used to support "sudden" decisions to graduate a full term ahead of schedule, and the Departments were given a much larger voice in approving the instructors of the college seminars.[4] These discussion groups themselves had been shrunk in number; their instructors had been increasingly professionalized; and when the whole program was reviewed, the Faculty chose virtually to ignore the seminars as a necessary and somewhat inconsequential evil not worth fighting about. Most professors thought the seminars were second rate and generally chose not to teach one of them. Consequently, their subject matter was seldom transferred to the standard curriculum.[5]

---

[1]Faculty Record, 10 April 1975.

[2]Faculty Record, 9 March 1972, 11 December 1975. The Registrar also began to note when students had withdrawn from a course after mid-term. The Faculty did adopt a provision allowing for one credit/fail option per semester, which was supposed to allow for experimentation in an era of academic pressure. See Faculty Record, 6 March 1975. Brewster praised this move, saying that it "curtailed the cynical search for 'gut' courses." Brewster was acknowledging that academic over-pressure was unhealthy and that exploration enjoyed a place in a college experience which was intended to be more than "a career oriented, pre-professional scramble." See Pres. Report, 1974-75, pp. 4-5.

[3]Faculty Record, 21 February 1974, 2 May 1974.

[4]Faculty Record, 1 May 1975, 16 December 1976.

[5]Faculty Record, 7 December 1978, 15 December 1977, 3 March 1977. Only 5-1/2 percent of the

By the mid-seventies, the Faculty was once again sufficiently dominant in matters concerning the course of study to begin to consider it from an overall perspective. President Brewster believed the key issue was to decide between "the claims for structure in the student curriculum, on one side, and the desire to make students feel some responsibility for the fashioning of their own course of study on the other." After reviewing the history of the Guidelines and asserting that they were "not a counsel of permissiveness on the part of the Course of Study Committee" the President went on to express his opinion that:

> There are probably too many students now graduating from Yale College who have avoided the breadth of exposure which a liberal education requires, either because of a fanatic zeal to over-concentrate in their field of special interest, or out of a desire to avoid areas which seem strange, boring, or difficult for them."[1]

Brewster's position was based on and bolstered by a Report on the Effectivenes of the Guideline System, the so-called Jubin Report. This document showed that between 1970 and 1975 the percentage of students who had complied with the Guidelines and earned credit for four terms of foreign language had declined from 86 percent to 65 percent and further that those who had completed two term courses in a natural science had fallen from 75 percent to 59 percent. Intriguingly, the Report also documented a high correlation between academic excellence and a wide distribution of studies. Transmittal of the Jubin Report focused

---

instructors were from the Yale College Faculty. By May 1978, the number of college seminars had shrunk to 52. See Faculty Record, 11 May 1978. The University's financial stringency bears some of the responsibility as funds for the seminars were reduced by no longer channelling them to the Yale College faculty. See Faculty Record, 1 May 1975.

[1]Pres. Report, 1975-76, pp. 11-13.

the agendas of the Course of Study Committee and
the Committee on Teaching and Learning for the next
two years.[1]

Ironically, the Committee on Teaching and Learning, which over the past decade had been more respon-
sive to undergraduate pressures for flexibility,
relevance, and student involvement was at this time
more aggressive than the Course of Study Committee
about "stiffening the distributional requirements."
The Teaching and Learning Committee actually discussed
reinstating the pre-1966 system of required distributional categories; they also discussed the possibility of identifying specific courses which would
be suited for the purposes of fulfilling the distributional requirements.[2] The Course of Study Committee,
on the other hand, proceeded more traditionally,
appointing a subcommittee to address the question
of giving greater structure to the first two yeas
of undergraduate study. The Gaudon Subcomittee was
instructed that it should ignore problems directly
connected to the major, that the advisory system
lay beyond its purview, that it should begin with
"a commitment to the principle of distribution, one
way or another," and that "any attempt to determine
what particular subjects ought to be taken by every

---

[1]"Some Observations on the Proposal of the Course
of Study Committee and the Committee on Teaching
and Learning for the Augmentation of the Distributional Requirements," p. 3, Taft Mss., folder marked
Distributional Guidelines 1977-78. This document
was drafted by Dean Taft. The Jubin Report itself
is in the same folder. Ms. Jubin was of the opinion
that no form of persuasion would have any effect
on voluntary compliance with the Guidelines. Neither,
she felt, would improved science courses. See CSC
Minutes, 3 November 1977.

[2]The Committee on Teaching and Learning also
discussed such old chestnuts as the possibility of
not permitting advanced placement credits to satisfy
distributional requirements, and the Committee was
surprised to find that the foreign language Departments were not anxious to have a foreign language
requirement. Minutes of 21 October 1977, 8 November
1977, 29 November 1977, 24 January 1978, Taft Mss.,
folder marked Teaching and Learning Committee.

undergraduate was probably too complex and difficult."[1]
In the spring of 1977, the Gaudon Subcommittee, seeking guidance, asked the entire Course of Study Committee to answer two questions:

1. Is it desirable to design a system which builds upon categories different from the standard departmental ones? That is, should requirements be instituted which foster a different kind of definition and distribution than is currently achieved by the departmentally-oriented distribution requirements?

2. Do we want "hard" or unavoidable distributional requirements such as mathematics, foreign language, writing?

In response the full Committee voted informally. They split on question 1 but agreed, in response to question 2, on the need to avoid specific, inflexible course requirements.[2]

Eventually, the Gaudon Subcommittee proposed that certain courses offered in Yale College be designated as satisfying requirements within distributional areas selected by subject matter rather than by academic discipline. For example, some of the proposed classifications were systems of thought, non-modern or non-western civilizations, and social systems. This suggestion did not, however, survive discussion in the full Course of Study Committee or in the Committee on Teaching and Learning. Both Committees finally agreed:

That any assignment of courses to such [non-departmental] categories was subject to wide

---

[1]CSC Minutes, 4 November 1976, 18 November 1976. This Committee also looked at an old chestnut, a proposal for a basic math requirement which met the traditional opposition, namely that the Math Department was uninterested in unmotivated students and unproductive teaching. See CSC Minutes, 24 February 1977.

[2]CSC Minutes, 7 April 1977.

variations in individual judgment and was therefore in the end inevitably arbitrary. Such
assignments within a single department, using
the published course descriptions, would often
be obliged to ignore departmental priorities.
. . . Furthermore, the selection of a limited
group of courses as appropriate for the fulfillment of such requirements would imply that the
courses not selected made no contribution to
breadth in studies, a proposition that is difficult to defend on a course-by-course basis.
. . .[1]

The Committees also rejected the concept of creating
special courses to satisfy distributional requirements
"along the lines of various general education programs
taught at other universities," believing that "this
approach would not easily comport with Yale's traditional departmental and inter-departmental style."[2]
Both Committees judged it best to retain the College's
current curricular framework intact while augmenting
the two distributional requirements which had been
adopted in 1966 and revised in 1971. The new third
requirement read:

In meeting the Distributional Requirements
for the bachelor's degree, the student must

---

[1]"Some Observations on the Proposal of the Course
of Study Committee and the Committee on Teaching
and Learning for the Augmentation of the Distributional Requirements," pp. 3-5. The categories proposed by the Gaudon Subcommittee were (1) abstract
or quantitative methods; (2) systems of thought;
(3) languages (other than English); (4) English language and literature; (5) modern Western civilizations;
(6) non-modern or non-western civiizations; (7) social
systems; (8) the natural (physical and biological)
world.

[2]Ibid., p. 5. One cannot help wondering how
much the Gaudon Subcommittee was influenced by
Harvard's refashioning of its undergraduate curriculum
during this period. For example, a copy of Harvard's
Dean's Report of 1975-76, which discusses reforms
underway at Cambridge, is located in Taft Mss. folder
marked Gaudon Subcommittee.

earn at least two course credits in each of
the four Distributional Groups by the end of
the student's fourth term of enrollment.

The effect of this new regulation was to force each
Yale undergraduate to complete a full year's work
in each of the four distributional groups (instead
of the previously acceptable three), unless advanced
placement in one or more areas exempted him from
that particular requirement. And the new regulation
also mandated that the undergraduate achieve the
proposed additional breadth by the end of sophomore
year.[1]

The rationale propounded by the Dean for imposing
distributional requirements of any sort is intriguing
because it casts light on the faculty's current conception of a Yale liberal education. Three main
reasons were advanced:

First, the bachelor's degree should certify
"demonstrated competence in a reasonable distribution of studies," approximately measured by
the four distributional Groups.
Second, demonstrated competence in the four
areas of distribution was a "plausible requirement" toward meeting the educational objective
of acquiring that knowledge which it is appropriate for an educated man to know.
Third, imposing distribution early in a student's career was useful to him in understanding
educational options, in expanding his

---

[1]Ibid., pp. 5-6. The Jubin Report showed that
many undergraduates were delaying their compliance
with the less restrictive distributional requirements
of 1971 to junior and even senior year, and sometimes
to the point where they were forgiven by the Dean's
Office. And although it was not generally mentioned,
the Faculty had already, in a development reminiscent
of the mid-fifties, quietly changed the freshman
distributional requirement to permit greater than
normal concentration in a single distributional Group,
if that concentration were in foreign language or
a science lab course. Compare Programs of Study
Bulletins 1975-76 and 1976-77.

comprehension of the "relevance of different fields
of study to each other and his own interests," and
in providing the student with a solid basis for making
choices "concerning his future studies and perhaps
even a career."[1]

The Reforms of 1978 have been hailed as far
reaching, and perhaps from the point of view of the
Faculty's revived willingness to impose any regulation,
particularly regulation in the interests of a liberal
education, they were.[2] But from a conceptual point
of view, seen in the context of the history of the
curriculum since World War II, they were not all
that substantial. In this connection, it is worth
examining what the 1978 Reforms did not accomplish,
or even attempt to accomplish. In the first place,
they did not attack many of the forces which were,
in Griswold's phrase, "browning the edges" of liberal
education. They made no changes which would help[3]
stop the increasing specialization of the major;
and they did little to deter the encroachment of

---

[1]Ibid., p. 6.

[2]Yale undergraduates on balance were clearly
opposed to the Reforms of 1978. See CSC Minutes,
9 March 1978. Neither was the faculty unanimously
in favor of the Reforms. See Faculty Record, 2 March
1978, 20 April 1978.

[3]For example, the Course of Study Committee
approved a major in Near Eastern Languages and Literature and another major in Theatre Studies. See
Faculty Record, 4 March 1976. Previously, the Committee had approved a "psychology track" within the
philosophy major and a "philosophy track" within
the psychology major. See Faculty Record, 18 April
1974. Earlier, the Committee had permitted similar
"tracking" between biology and psychology. See
Faculty Record, 1 June 1973. And in the late sixties,
the Committee had authorized a special major in linguistics and a special major in administrative science,
mathematics and statistics. See Faculty Record,
15 June 1968, 12 December 1968.

professional studies into the undergraduate curriculum.[1]
Graduate school procedures also continued to manifest
themselves in the College course of study.[2] Thus,
the Reforms of 1978 did not try to deal in any effective way with the problems of professional and graduate school pressures upon Yale College.

In the second place, the Reforms of 1978 did
nothing to increase faculty attention to the system
of distribution and divert them from preoccupation
with the major. The faculty did continue to question,
in a familiar fashion, the ability of the science
Departments to handle the increased workload generated
by the strengthened distributional requirements,
and they also questioned those Departments' willingness to adapt and improve the quality of their introductory offerings. The social science Departments
did continue to look for an effective way to develop
junior and senior courses which were not simply "mini

---

[1]For example, the Faculty approved a new major
in Applied Mathematics. See Faculty Record, 4 March
1976. And another major in Applied Physics, given
jointly by the Department of Physics and the Department of Engineering and Applied Science. See Faculty
Record, 6 March 1980. Undergraduates continued to
be allowed to take a maximum of four profesional
courses for credit toward the BA degree. See CSC
Minutes, 4 November 1976. There was also the instance
of the Teacher Training Program, which was instituted
in the sixties. The Course of Study Committee
reviewed this program and found it acceptable undergraduate fare in the Fall of 1976. Teacher Training,
which had places for thirty students, required each
student to complete a Yale College major. In his
junior year he received one term-course credit for
"observing" in a local secondary school for four
hours per week. In senior year, he received three
term-course credits for nine weeks of practice teaching. It was alleged that most of the instructors
in this program were members of the Yale College
Faculty, even those who taught methods courses.
See CSC Minutes, 7 October 1976.

[2]Of 1151 members of the class of 1977, 16 qualified for the simultaneous award of the MA degree.
See Faculty Record, 13 May 1977.

221

graduate courses,"[1] but the Reforms made no effective attempt to cope with the continuing explosion of knowledge and the increasing differentiation and specialization of its disciplined pursuit.

In the third place, although the Course of Study Committee offhandedly discussed other ways of implementing a liberal education--better counselling, for one example and better quality science and math courses for another--the fundamental acceptance of the traditional crossed criteria of depth and breadth was never seriously questioned.[2] Similarly, the Reforms of 1978 did not examine the ingrained perception of the distribution system, and the general education with which it was equated, as preparatory to the major. This unconscious focus was indicated by the fact that the propriety of awarding distributional credits simultaneously with advanced placement credits was never seriously debated and also by the fact that all attempts to delay the expected satisfaction of the distributional requirements beyond sophomore year were ultimately rejected. So strong and instinctive was the predisposition to regard the distributional system as preparatory to the major that the matter of the major and its relation to the rest of the course of study was never evaluated at all, since it was, by definition, beyond the purview of the Gaudon Subcommittee.[3]

These outcomes, which were not favorable to those interested in a liberal curriculum, were probably inherent in the rather limited charge originally given to the Gaudon Subcommittee and in the specific targeting of the Subcommittee's efforts toward improving the first two years of undergraduate education.

---

[1]CSC Minutes, 23 February 1978. See also Faculty Record, 7 February 1980.

[2]CSC Minutes, 27 October 1977. This discussion shows that the sciences continued to remain somewhat apart from the rest of the Yale community, much the way they were at the time of the 1945 Reforms.

[3]CSC Minutes, 4 November 1976. Also CSC Minutes, 16 February 1978. For specific charge to the Gaudon Subcommittee, see CSC Minutes, 18 November 1976.

But even more significantly, the question of purpose
and the matter of intention, were, in the case of
the 1978 Reforms, no more discussed than they ever
had been. The preliminary proposals of the Gaudon
Subcommittee, as outlined in a report which was never
completed, transmitted, or formally rejected, makes
this clear. They deserve analysis: The draft is
a fascinating document. "We feel strongly," wrote
Professor Gaudon, "that each individual department
or program has a duty towards the College as a whole,
and should demonstrate in a practical and imaginative way its own commitment to general education."
Apparently, the Departments were not fulfilling their
duties or following through on their responsibilities:

> We feel that counselors and advisers should
> not be recruiting agents for their own subjects
> and should help the students to build a coherent
> and varied program, not limited by the narrow
> needs of professionalism. . . . Breadth does
> not necessarily foster incoherence. No subject
> has to be boring. The subcommittee takes a
> rather poor view of the specialists who believe
> that it is impossible to teach intelligent,
> but uninformed students without talking down
> to them. We also think that a teacher who is
> able to communicate his enthusiasm to non-
> specialists should not be treated as a second
> grade citizen in the academic community. . . .

As Gaudon saw it:

> The traditional opposition between education
> as acquisition of knowledge and as formation
> of the mind still dominates discussions. . . .
> Although accumulation of knowledge is no longer
> given priority . . . enforced specialization,
> based on acquisition of knowledge, is widely
> practiced, sometimes at the expense of the pro-
> claimed ideals. . . . We would like to suggest
> that an education can only be based on the acqui-
> sition of a variety of intellectual tools and
> a certain amount of knowledge. We would also
> like to suggest that the problems of communi-
> cation between human beings can be helped by
> an increased awareness of other people's points
> of view, their ways of thinking or of expressing
> themselves, and also by an ability to understand

the implications and shortcomings of one's own position. This is perhaps the main purpose of a _liberal_ education.

Gaudon then classified, as we have seen, the "indispensible components of a general education" into seven distributional categories which specifically did not correspond to the departmental organization of the Faculty, and he went on to define the proper responsibilities of the Departments:

> On the purely negative side, no program for the major should be so heavy with prerequisites, compulsory courses and related "electives" that the whole notion of a liberal education is put in jeopardy. . . . On the positive side, the notion of introductory courses and courses for non-majors should be examined by each department. . . . We recognize that there are disciplines in which there is no clear sequence of courses. However, when a course is aimed at beginners or non-specialists, especially in the sciences, there is no reason why the intellectual level (as opposed to the technical) should not be extremely high. Imaginative courses for non-specialists would certainly attract students, and would be equally rewarding for their teachers. Fulfilling distributional requirements has no meaning other than administrative. In the classroom, interest and a sense of discovery ought to prevail.
> Should this report be approved . . . departments would be required to [identify] courses which could be specially listed as meeting the distributional requirements. . . . It is hoped . . . that established scholars would find it an interesting challenge to share their knowledge with intelligent freshmen and sophomores, in a non-cryptic language.[1]

---

[1]Memo to Subcommittee on Distribution and Guidelines from Jean Gaudon, 8 May 1977, pp. 2-5, Taft Mss., folder marked Gaudon Subcommittee 1977-78. Professor Gaudon was a French scholar, educated in Europe, with an interest in film-making as a serious discipline. There is some evidence that the Faculty was reacting to its perception of his report rather

Professor Gaudon was, in effect, suggesting that the Faculty classify its plethora of course offerings with regard to their purpose. He wanted to identify and if necessary develop those most suitable for the purposes of a liberal education which, in the perceptions of the moment, was equated with the distribution system. That the Faculty declined to make such a differentiation, and in fact professed the impossibility of so doing makes clear once again that a formal discussion of purpose is not yet possible in the context of the scientific approach which still dominates the modern university. For to say that all courses were equally suited to liberal education is the logical equivalent of maintaining that all were equally unsuited.

It had been suggested to Professor Gaudon and his Subcommittee that they avoid a philosophical approach. Nevertheless, Gaudon pointed out that:

> The mere transposition of philosophical terms into administrative ones is not in itself a solution. . . . No administrative framework is free from ideological assumptions . . . a re-writing of . . . requirements and guidelines can only be a cosmetic operation, if it is not accompanied by other measures. . . .[1]

In other words, the Subcommittee, and for that matter Yale College, was in need of a new philosophy of liberal education. More accurately, the philosophy available was inadequate, for President Brewster had devoted the last President's Report of his tenure,

---

than to the report itself. Gaudon was something of an outsider (he has subsequently returned to France), and his foreign training was thought by some to predispose him to the core curriculum approach being advocated at Harvard. Thus, it may just be that Gaudon's suggested categorization was effectively equated with the development of a few general education surveys of the type the Yale Faculty historically distrusted. Personal interview with Dean Howard Lamar, 21 November 1980.

[1]Memo to Subcommittee on Distribution and Guidelines from Jean Gaudon, p. 1.

to a "self-conscious articulation" of "the values
of liberal learning."

"The most fundamental value of a liberal education," said Brewster, "is that it makes life more
interesting," and he went on to expand this notion:

> Liberally educated people share the excitement
> of the effort to reduce [the mysteries of the
> universe] to rational explanation by the appli-
> cation of logic to fact. They can enjoy the
> effort to articulate human experience by rigorous
> and precise literary and historical expression.
> They can perceive revelations in expressive
> and symbolic form, in creative letters, in music,
> and other arts. In these terms, even if you
> "do nothing with it," a liberal education makes
> life much more interesting than it otherwise
> would be.[1]

Brewster believed that any individual's sense of
place, sense of self and sense of judgment were
"enhanced" by a liberal training. Their development
and refinement constituted the objectives of a liberal
education:

> A society which does not have some members
> of each generation blessed with these senses
> will soon cease to be civilized. . . . [They]
> do, after all, contribute to a person's ability
> to take the measure of problems and people,
> to see possibilities and recognize impossibili-
> ties, to avoid the pits of dismay and the giddy
> heights of hubris. . . . Of course a liberal
> education does not guarantee wisdom. . . . But
> liberal learning does increase the chance of
> wisdom. . . .[2]

Clearly, the liberal ideal was being honored as always.
Yet Yale's President was far less articulate about
the means to achieve these most desirable ends:

> Yale College has long held out against pre-
> mature professionalism and excessively narrow

---

[1]Pres. Report, 1975-76, pp. 4-5.

[2]Ibid., pp. 6-7.

concentration. The goals mentioned cannot be achieved unless there is a broad exposure to a variety of intellectual experiences.
One dimension of this variety is in terms of subject matter. . . . Exposure to the distinctive ways of applying the human mind to major areas of natural and human experience is [also] fundamental to liberal education. . . . [1]

In addition to broad exposure Brewster listed three other fundamental means: learning by discussion; developing the capacity for expression, and, through the device of the major, gaining a sense of the requirements and limitations of mastery. "Without puffing," said Brewster, "I think it can be said that Yale College provides an excellent opportunity for a liberal education on all four of these grounds. . . ."[2]

At no point, it is worth noting, did Yale's President attempt to make a direct, logical, explicit connection between the goals of liberal education as he evocatively outlined them and the four means he set out for achieving them. Like the rest of the Yale community, Brewster simply assumed the connection. He defined liberal education in terms of Yale's established methodology, in other words in terms of a particular set of means for achieving the goals, and then accepted that because Yale pursued those means, it was reaching the liberal goals. The argument is, however, conceptually flawed, being tautological. The fact is that the four means Brewster outlined, that is, broad exposure, discussion, expression, and a developed sense of mastery, may be easily utilized, as has been pointed out before, to achieve an effective specialization. All four-- and particularly broad exposure--are, it is true, necessary conditions; but they are not sufficient conditions for assuring a liberal education. In the interchange between teacher and learner, some consideration must also be given to relating the specific knowledge within the particular discipline

---

[1] Ibid., pp. 8-9.

[2] Ibid., p. 9.

to knowledge outside the discipline. The instructor
must make some effort to convey not only facts and
information, but a sense of his discipline's distinguishing methodology. He should be willing to explain
the human relevance of what he knows, and to discuss
with his student the value dimensions of the knowledge
he is imparting. Lastly, the instructor must attempt
to get the student to understand how what he has
learned can be useful, not in any limited vocational
or technical sense, but useful to a fulfilled human
life. In other words, Brewster was oversimplifying;
for if the quintessential teaching/learning interchange does not take place across this broader range
of concerns, broader than the mere conveyance and
receipt of knowledge as factual data, the liberal
goals Brewster outlined will be achieved only hap-
hazardly, or simply not at all. This is true, even
if the subject matter involves the humanities and
even if, as George W. Pierson pointed out in the
outline of the Planned Experiment in Liberal Education,
the information purveyed originates in a handful
of different disciplines. Whether or not any particular collection of subject matter, any course
of study, could, by itself, assure the delivery of
a liberal education was, therefore, open to question.
Thus, Yale College, like most institutions of higher
learning in America, did indeed need a new educational
philosophy, despite the fact that the Faculty did
continue, openly and expressly, to urge and to honor
the liberal ideal. However, Yale, unlike many of
those other institutions, had succeeded in permitting
nothing to preclude an undergraduate's obtaining
a liberal education, an accomplishment achieved primarily by the faculty's championing of the ideal
and by its unremitting insistence upon distribution
and exposure, the absence of which would more than
likely have doomed any hope of achieving the liberal
education Yale prized. This meant that Yale was
well situated to lead the search for a renewed conception of liberal education and to find effective
ways of transmitting it in the full realization that
the course of study was not, and could not be, the
sole vehicle.

Chapter IX

CONCLUSION

The difficulties Yale increasingly experienced
in the years after World War II in the process of
clearly defining and adequately designing a liberal
course of study are not an anomaly in American higher
education. In fact, the history of the whole general
education movement in the twentieth century supports
the contention that Yale's particular history is
quite typical, and not at all atypical, of the
national pattern. Yale, for example, is a clear example
of the extensive trend toward adopting concentration
and distribution systems which appeared around the
turn of the century. This approach was meant to
counteract the popular elective system and the
increased emphasis upon specialized study which often
accompanied it. Yale did not pursue the development
of the general survey or orientation courses that
became popular around the time of the First World
War, though the establishment of the Common Freshman
Year with its predilection toward emphasizing good
teaching and exposure to a broad core curriculum
could be said to have had similar purposes. Yale
was too established and too traditional to take part
in experiments like those at Bennington, Sarah
Lawrence, and Reed College, or, in public institutions,
like the founding of the General College of the University of Minnesota or the Experimental College
at the University of Wisconsin. However, Robert
M. Hutchins, who instigated a public dialogue with
John Dewey on the philosophy and purposes of higher
education, was a former Yale Dean when the debate
began.[1]

---

[1]Three excellent brief reviews of the history
of general education can be found in McGrath, General
Education and the Plight of Modern Man, chap. 3,
pp. 20-50; in Sloan, "The Teaching of Ethics in the
American Undergraduate Curriculum, 1876-1976," pp.
237-248; and in Frederick Rudolph, The Curriculum:
A History of the American Undergraduate Course of
Study Since 1636 (San Francisco, Washington, London:
Jossey-Bass Publishers, 1977), chap 7, pp. 252-264.
The major history is Thomas, The Search for a Common
Learning.

In more recent times, that is, since the Second World War, the analogy between what happened at Yale and elsewhere is even closer. As we have seen, Yale participated in the surge of interest in general education which swept the country after the war following the publication of the Redbook. One estimate was that half the colleges in the country, Yale among them, experimented with some form of general education in the decade which followed the war.[1] This period at Yale included the successful expansion of the Directed Studies program and the development of the eventually unacceptable recommendations of the President's Committee on General Education. At Yale, and across the country, the mid-fifties appear to have been the height of the interest in general education; for, after the launching of sputnik in 1957, emphasis quickly shifted to scientific studies and technological research. At Yale, these years saw the splintering of Directed Studies, the adoption of the concept of areas of concentration selected in freshman year, increasing stress on the distribution system and finally its transformation into the Guidelines of 1966.

Although experiments have continued,[2] it is only very recently, according to Sloan, that general education has

> experienced a resurgence among those involved
> in reconceiving a "liberal core" in the under-
> graduate curriculum as a means of countering
> excessive specialization and curricular frag-
> mentation . . . this is a problem endemic to
> the modern university, and reform efforts
> intended to deal with it wax and wane with cyclic
> regularity. . . . It remains to be seen whether
> the most recent attempts in this regard will
> preserve at their center any notion of "the
> educated person" . . . or whether they will

---

[1]McGrath, General Education and the Plight of Modern Man, p. 126.

[2]Some of these are enumerated in Gerald Grant and David Riesman, The Perpetual Dream: Reform and Experiment in the American College (Chicago and London: The University of Chicago Press, 1978).

devolve, at best, into a streamlined refurbishing of the old system of distribution, or, at worst, into the politics of departmental representation.[1]

This articulation indeed fits Yale where, as we have seen, the Reforms of 1978, which have been trumpeted as a reinvigoration of the liberal curriculum, are, in fact, a tightening of administrative controls as a way of reaffirming the system of distribution and concentration in a modernized form.

The assertion that Yale is a representative example in the post-war story of liberal learning is buttressed by a closer look at the three pioneers of the general education movement: Columbia, Harvard, and the college of the University of Chicago. All four stories are similar. At Columbia, for example, in 1954, the college revised the traditional credit system, which had permitted undergraduates to take a general degree, and instituted instead a requirement that all students select a major and complete it. Shortly thereafter, the required two year <u>Contemporary Civilization</u> course, the 1929 creation of which was one of the landmarks in the general education movement and which once attracted the teaching talent of professors such as John Randall, Jr., Charles Frankel, Gilbert Highet, and others, was modified. The second year of the famous course was made largely optional, and undergraduates were permitted to enroll in standard departmental courses. Finally, in 1975-76, the second year of <u>Contemporary Civilization</u> simply became one of a large group of electives. McGrath attributes this relaxation of the traditional requirement to

difficulties regarding the purpose of the course, pressure from the social science departments for students to begin work in their disciplines in the sophomore year, and difficulty in recruiting senior faculty to the staff. . . .[2]

---

[1]Sloan, "The Teaching of Ethics in the American Undergraduate Curriculum, 1876-1976," p. 247.

[2]McGrath, <u>General Education and the Plight of Modern Man</u>, pp. 28-34.

Interestingly, Columbia, like Yale, was not successful, when the idea was suggested after the Second World War, in implementing a two year general science sequence to parallel Contemporary Civilization and its companion Humanities course. Instead, the sciences developed multiple tracks within the standard disciplines. The intention was to accommodate different kinds of students with different interests, each of whom was entitled to work at his own pace. The commonality in the curriculum was quickly eroded by this approach which also isolated students who were often intent only on their limited, specialized goals. Irresistably, graduate school techniques and requirements forced their way down into the college curriculum. And the multiple track approach rapidly spread from the sciences to the social sciences. Staffing the general education courses became an increasing problem, just as it had in the Directed Studies program at Yale, since many department chairmen urged bright doctoral candidates who were teaching many of the general education courses to join a department instead. The idea was to enhance the career of the young academic by enabling him to devote himself entirely to a single discipline. The combination of all these forces resulted in the "decay of general education at Columbia."[1]

In the early sixties, when Yale was implementing the recommendations of the Report of the President's Committee on the Freshman Year, the Dean of Columbia College, concerned about the way things were headed, appointed the sociologist Daniel Bell as a "committee of one" to review the general education program. Bell's report, which was published as The Reforming of General Education, was characterized by a practical tone, and it was quite specific about outlining manageable course curricula. Bell was also quite detailed about the institutional and staffing limitations that had to be dealt with. He suggested that a thorough reform in the whole program was needed. As a basis for the reform, Bell began by rejecting the notion that any body of knowledge could be held in common by a community of educated men, and he suggested instead a concentration on "the centrality

---

[1]Ibid., pp. 31-35. Also Bell, The Reforming of General Education, pp. 197-273.

of method" as the organizing concept. This approach
led Bell to propose that a "third tier" of general
education courses be given in senior year, after
the undergraduates had achieved a modicum of mastery
in the disciplines they had chosen to major in.
His intention was to place the subject that the student had specialized in in a broader context, specifically a conscious awareness of the differing
methodologies that characterize different disciplines.
And that awareness was to be what educated men would
hold in common.[1]

The response to Bell's imaginative proposal,
which was published the very year the Yale Faculty
adopted the Guidelines of 1966, was complete disinterest. Nearly a decade later, Lionel Trilling, the
literary critic, who was a gifted Columbia teacher,
commented:

> From my long experience of Columbia College
> I can recall no meetings on an educational topic
> that were so poorly attended and so lacking
> in attention and vivacity as those in which
> the Bell report was considered. If I remember
> correctly, these meetings led to no action what-
> ever, nor even to the resolve to look further
> into the matter. The faculty simply was not
> interested.[2]

Bell's report included an incisive description
of the fate of the general education program which
had been instituted at Harvard after World War II.
The 1945 General Education in a Free Society served
as the basis for the program from 1949 until 1962.
Originally, Harvard had intended that six of the
sixteen courses required for graduation be general
education courses, that is, courses distinct in purpose and content from specialized courses. At least
one general education course had to be selected from
those offered in three curricular categories: the

---

[1]Bell, The Reforming of General Education, pp.
197-273.

[2]Quoted in McGrath, General Education and the
Plight of Modern Man, pp. 35-36. Daniel Bell left
shortly afterwards for Harvard.

natural sciences, the social sciences, and the humanities. At Harvard, as at Yale and Columbia, this approach was least successful in the sciences. From the very beginning, undergraduates who intended to major in the natural sciences were exempted from the science requirements of the general education program, and within a decade every undergraduate was permitted to substitute departmental courses for the previously required general education offerings in science. In April 1966, again a key year, the Harvard faculty adopted a more flexible system of general education, which reduced the number of required general education courses to three, and, more significantly, allowed students to skip the basic introductory general education courses. Promptly, general education offerings proliferated, and they came to be less and less distinguishable from standard departmental courses. Finally, in 1971, the Harvard faculty permitted the substitution of any two departmental courses for the appropriate general education course, so that the only surviving general education "requirement" was in fact merely the insistence that each student get some exposure in each of the three great curricular divisions. In other words, the Harvard faculty, like Yale's, ended up relying solely on a rudimentary system of distribution to advance liberal learning and was equally unable to establish criteria for distinguishing general education courses from departmental courses.[1]

The erosion of the general education program at Harvard had one of its causes, and one aleady encountered at Yale, in the failure adequately to incorporate the natural sciences. There were also staffing difficulties, another familiar problem, since the famous professors who initially agreed to teach the basic general education courses grew stale and eventually returned to their specialties. Introductory departmental courses came more and more to resemble the general education courses which they paralleled, and increasingly the students, particularly those receiving advanced placement, wanted to move directly into specialized study, and they

---

[1]McGrath, General Education and the Plight of Modern Man, pp. 36-42; Bell, The Reforming of General Education, pp. 186-190.

wanted the beneficial stimulation of instruction in small groups. The Freshman Seminars, introduced in 1959, were designed to accommodate both pressures within the general education program. These groups, which the proponents of Directed Studies in New Haven had immediately reacted to as competition for top undergraduate talent, typically consisted of eight to ten students and met weekly, sometimes with a well-known professor whose interest had been attracted. Some seminars went far into specific, specialized topics; others investigated a single subject from a wide variety of perspectives. Like Yale's seminar-style discussion groups in the residential colleges, Harvard's Freshman Seminars were given only for a year or two and then abandoned for new offerings. The resulting turnover in faculty, which was considerable, can be viewed either as a sign of the program's vitality or as a sign of the senior professors' essential disinterest in long-term involvement in what was, after all, deliberately conceived as an adjunct to the general education program.[1]

The words "decline," "erosion," "decay," and the like have been applied to the history of the general education programs at Columbia, Harvard, and Yale; but those trends were not limited to the older universities on the Eastern Seaboard. The college of the University of Chicago, in the hands of educational theorist and Yale graduate Robert Hutchins, had developed a radical program of general education. Originally, Chicago's course of study consisted solely of a series of integrated courses covering the major fields of knowledge. The underlying assumption was that specialized education should rest upon and not be confused with broad intellectual development. During the forties and early fifties, all undergraduates enrolled in essentially the same complement of courses, taught by a college-affiliated faculty that stressed teaching and curriculum improvement. In part because of the departure of Hutchins and in part because of Chicago's unusual pedagogical methodology--the variable entrance requirements, placement in courses by examination, and the typical two year course of study--the program could not be

---

[1]Bell, The Reforming of General Education, pp. 183-186.

sustained once the national enthusiasm for general
education evaporated in the mid-fifties. In 1957-
58, a system of majoring was introduced, and a standard four year BA program was adopted. The faculty
that had previously been associated with the college
was not prepared to teach the specialized courses
now specified for junior and senior years. Efforts
to interest the scholars in the graduate division
of the university were not particularly successful
because the two faculties were suspicious of one
another. Still, an awkward model emerged: General
education was emphasized in the first two years,
and specialization in the last two, a conception
not unlike the 1953 proposals of President Griswold's
Committee on General Education. But at Chicago,
as at Yale, the forces of specialization outweighed
the needs of general preparation. In 1966, the college of the University of Chicago was divided, from
an academic point of view, into five "area colleges":
The undergraduate might specialize in physical science,
biology, social science, or the humanities; or he
could enroll in the "collegiate division" and concentrate on "civilizational" studies, that is, on a
broad education somewhat like what was earlier
required of every student. Even within the specialized
"area colleges," there remained a flavor of interdisciplinary work, an emphasis upon intellectual
method, and an interest in common understanding.
Yet in the end, a single fact illuminates what happened: In one recent year, only 53 students out
of a total enrollment of 1632 were affiliated with
the "collegiate division."[1]

If Yale's experience can be shown to be in some
measure representative of the whole fate of liberal
learning in the American college, and I believe it
largely can be, what then can be said of significance
about the future of liberal education at Yale, and
elsewhere, that might perhaps give encouragement
to those particularly interested in education for
the good life? In the first place, it seems to me
important consciously to recognize that the curriculum
of learning and the course of study are not synonymous,

---

[1]Ibid., pp. 190-91; McGrath, General Education
and the Plight of Modern Man, pp. 42-48.

and that liberal education occurs in both places. No amount of attention to the details of regulating the course of study, no fine tuning of the "delicate balance" between depth and breadth, for example, will in and of itself assure an undergraduate's receiving a liberal education." For one reason, the course of study is only part, though generally the most significant part, of the curriculum; and it alone cannot accomplish what the curriculum as a whole should be designed, as far as possible, to accomplish. For a second reason, as I think has been demonstrated, regulating the course of study will not and cannot assure that the non-professional, non-specialized, non-utilitarian education currently passing as liberal education will not be perverted by the student, or his teacher, to less elevating ends. Neither will any teaching methodology such as the seminars, reading lists, discussion groups, independent study or comprehensive examinations that have been recommended in the past; or the computers, integrated learning systems, or telecommunications that will no doubt be recommended in the future.[1]

This is not to say that much could not be accomplished by a committee intent to improve a supposedly liberal course of study. For one thing, it might closely examine the basic role and fundamental purpose of the major in a liberal education, especially with a view to determining if the major might serve some

---

[1]Yale seems to be moving toward reinstituting a basic foreign language requirement in addition to the Guideline which recommends the study of a foreign language and which is frequently and legitimately circumvented by studying foreign literature in translation. Although an understanding of the nature of language can be part of a liberal education (see, for example, Ernst Cassirer, An Essay on Man [New Haven and London: Yale University Press, 1944], chap. 8), and although such an understanding may be advanced by cultivation of a foreign tongue, a basic foreign language requirement may also serve simply to facilitate a career in the Foreign Service. Whitehead has commented that the main defect of "the educational method of the literary curriculum" is "unduly to emphasise [sic] the importance of language." Whitehead, The Aims of Education, pp. 48-49.

terminal, integrative function. Such a consideration
of the major has not been officially undertaken,
or to my knowledge even suggested, at Yale College
for several decades. For another, the committee
might well review individual course outlines to assure
that some attempt is being made to assist undergraduates in making meaningful interconnections between
the subject matter of the particular course at hand
and others. It might also question whether the
instructor has made sufficient effort to explicate
the characteristic methodology of his discipline
as well as the normative dimension of the information
he imparts. In short, close attention might be paid
to the quintessential exchange between student and
teacher, and some effort might be made to insist
that students be led toward some understanding of
the usefulness of what they are learning to the good
life. Last but not least, an innovative course of
study committee might well examine ways to evaluate
the teaching performances of the faculty as effectively as their contributions to scholarship and
the advance of knowledge are evaluated. The importance of the teaching function to a liberal education
is not lessened by the difficulty of quantifying
it or developing satisfactory criteria for appraising
it.

A second major consideration is this: Even
the college which focuses on its curriculum in the
broadest sense as a vehicle for transmitting a liberal
education will continue to have to shape that education within limits beyond its control. At Yale,
we have seen the necessity to negotiate with students
about their education, and also to conform to the
needs of the high schools, the graduate and professional schools, the government, and employers. To
counteract all these pressures, there survives, essentially, the concept of the college as a community
with a special, educative purpose, a notion which
is closely allied to a definition of the curriculum
which is far wider than the course of study. In
earlier, easier times, Dean DeVane asserted this
position with characteristic elegance:

The American college of liberal arts and sciences
is vital, and will continue to be so, because
it brings together young people at a crucial
time in their lives under very favorable

238

conditions, and gives those youngsters a happy combination of freedom and regularity. The college provides something for all the necessities and appetites of youth to feed upon: it hastens living. The formal learning of the student is by no means negligible--and through the studies an intellectual frame is provided which gives meaning and pattern to the whole venture. But one of the immense values of college to youth is the opportunity provided each of them in their classes, on the field and river, in their daily contacts and night conversations, in their competitions, rivalries, and cooperative ventures, to find themselves and their places among their fellows--their weaknesses and their strengths, what they can do, and what is beyond them, where they stand in history as well as their place in the contemporary world. In four years they learn what it takes the self-educated man a lifetime to learn. Yale College offers these opportunities in superlative form, and the fact that it is a national institution, both in the geographical distribution of its alumni and students and in its great prestige enables it to keep before its students that "vision of greatness" which Whitehead asserts is a necessity to an institution which aspires to educate youth for great place and magnanimous living.[1]

The demands of students tend to be immediate and insatiable, and certainly not all of them are reasonable; but student interest in involving the faculty in the community life of the College, manifested primarily by expecting faculty members to be interested in teaching undergraduates and leading them to meanings, does merit attention. When, for example, the Yale College faculty expressed their

------

[1]Dean's Report, 1949-50, pp. 7-8. A. Bartlett Giamatti, the current President of Yale, appears to espouse somewhat the same reasoning, at least as quoted in the Yale Daily News: "The mission of Yale College is 'to allow people to educate themselves to be ethically sensitive, intellectually acute, and civically humane.'" Yale Daily News, 12 December 1980.

disinterest in the Mentorship system recommended
by the 1972 Study Group on Yale College, believing,
it was said, that they were untrained as counsellors
and that their proper function was lecturing, research
and scholarship, the members of the faculty, in their
disinterest, were expressing an attitude that was
unfavorable to the interests of liberal education,
however else they judged the overall merits of the
recommendations of the Second Dahl Report.[1]

A third major issue in considering the future
of liberal education is the need overtly to recognize
the extent to which the scientific spirit has pervaded
the university. This study has repeatedly shown
that the sciences have been integrated with the other
Departments of Yale College only with difficulty.
If, however, one conceives of the periodic efforts
to promote liberal education and/or the humanities
as a rearguard action in the College against the
conquest of the rest of the University and most of
the academic world by scientism and the scientific
approach, it then becomes apparent that it is the
sciences and not the rest of the College that are
integrated into, congenial and compatible with, the
fundamental outlook and purposes of the modern university. Since the scientific spirit dominates the

---

[1] "Although it was clearly recognized . . . that
proper implementation of the guideline system would
require increased effort by the faculty in the advis-
ing and supervising of individual students, later
rejection by the faculty of the 'Report of the Study
Group on Yale College' was clear evidence that, in
fact, the majority of the faculty felt neither prepared nor qualified to devote substantial effort
outside the classroom to this kind of activity.
This attitude did not imply any lack of concern about
the problem or any reluctance to devote time and
effort to appropriate educational ventures. Rather,
it reflected a judgment by many faculty members that
their time is best spent in the classroom and the
laboratory--and that personal counseling is best
done by persons especially trained for this function."
Dean Horace D. Taft, "New Distributional Requirements
for Yale College," Yale Alumni Magazine, November
1978, p. 22.

modern world as well as the modern university, this domination is ultimately appropriate. What is not appropriate is that the scientific spirit should exclude the ethical spirit, the aesthetic spirit, the poetic spirit, or worse yet, infuse their intrinsic methodologies with a diluted scientism. Liberal learning must have roots in all of them.

It is particularly important to recognize the dominance of the scientific attitude at Yale for three reasons: First, the scientific approach excludes, erroneously I believe, consideration of much of the curriculum which lies beyond the formal course of study and which I have argued is significant for liberal education;[1] second, this exclusion is resisted, sometimes enthusiastically, by the students whose interest in a broader curriculum is manifest in their attention to extra-curricular activities and their participation in the residential college seminars and the offerings of the other Schools of the University; third, the emphasis upon the humanities at Yale, traditionally central to the purpose of the College, can be best understood when their centrality is seen as an instinctive reaction to the dominance of the scientific approach. This infrequently recognized function of the humanities, which are deeply revered and consciously protected,[2] has probably prevented Yale from succumbing entirely to the prevailing scientific spirit and abandoning the liberal ideal in fact if not in name. Many years ago, and the situation has not substantially changed, DeVane put it thus:

> Since the founding of the College the studies known as the humanities have been the core of the educational system at Yale. The particular subjects in this area have changed and the emphases are remarkably different. Still today, in my opinion, the most substantial and valuable education we can give to a youth who comes to

---

[1] See, for example, Huston Smith, "Excluded Knowledge: A Critique of the Modern Western Mind Set," in Education and Values, ed. Douglas Sloan (New York: Teachers College Press, 1980).

[2] See George W. Pierson, "The Humanities and Moral Man," Yale Alumni Magazine, October 1965.

Yale College lies in the disciplines of literature, history, and philosophy. . . . If these
studies are complemented by some acquaintance
with the sciences and the social sciences on
one side, and by the fine arts and music on
the other, the student will have had the kind
of fundamental education most needed in America
today and tomorrow. It might be added that
Yale is almost unique among the great universities of the country in the value it places upon
the humanities.[1]

One might make the case that it is the centrality
of the humanities and the strength of the College
as a residential educative community that have left
Yale free to make available, though it can no longer
assure, if it ever could, a liberal education. And
the same two factors, it might be said, also leave
Yale free to assert a new theory of liberal education
if and when it is conceived.

A fourth consideration for the future of liberal
education is the need to address the question of
whether the departmental organization of a university
faculty, which initially paralleled the several,
well-defined scholarly disciplines, continues to
be useful. We have seen how departmentalization,
which originated as an administrative, bureaucratic
compromise when the emerging university was insti-
tutionalized,[2] repeatedly frustrated efforts to
develop interdisciplinary programs and a viable conception of subject matter integration.[3] Must the

---

[1]Dean's Report, 1948-49, p. 9.

[2]Laurence R. Veysey, The Emergence of the
American University (Chicago and London: University
of Chicago Press, 1965).

[3]In late 1980, the Yale College Faculty voted
to abandon the HAL program, the first and longest-
lived interdisciplinary effort of the modern era.
Fewer students were interested in enrolling in the
program, but the main problem was actually the lack
of interested professors. The Director of the program
said, "We have had a problem keeping prestigious
and distinguished faculty teaching HAL courses year

valued professionalization and scholarly production of the faculty be irrevocably tied to a budget-based, departmental organization? The continuing divisions and recombinations of the disciplines suggest otherwise. So, at Yale at least, does the movement of power from the Faculty to the Administration. So does the absurdity of lumping huge synoptic disciplines like history together with minute, empirical disciplines like administrative science into one conceptual category because for half a century that has been the traditional mode of thought. It would seem that both smaller and larger conceptualizations would be appropriate for practical financial and management purposes, particularly since, in Yale's case, the negatively expressed distributional requirements have effectively ended inter-departmental maneuvering for a preferred position in the College course of study, if not elsewhere.

As Jean Gaudon pointed out to the Course of Study Committee in the late seventies, developing a new scheme of administration will not necessarily solve the plaguing difficulties of developing adequate theoretical bases for interdisciplinary studies, a still unsolved problem identified as early as 1943 by George W. Pierson's draft of the "Planned Experiment in Liberal Education." Nor will even a restructuring of the whole University solve the more fundamental need to articulate at Yale or elsewhere a coherent conception of liberal education for our times. This fifth consideration for the future of liberal learning is of over-arching importance, for the fact of the matter is that such a philosophical underpinning does not exist, even at Yale, as President Brewster's final report to the Yale community in 1976 makes clear. And while I am certainly not prepared to assert any adequate philosophy of liberal education, I am prepared to assert that liberal education will not flourish without some agreement on the integrating principle of the curriculum. The alternative is liberal education by happenstance

---

after year. We have to be able to provide . . . a program of continuous quality for the next two years," which apparently could not be consistently done. See Yale Daily News, 6 November 1980 and 5 December 1980.

243

and inadvertance. This need was identified by President Alexander Meiklejohn of Amherst as early as 1922. An educator, who was deeply committed to liberal education, Meiklejohn believed that the growth of science had destroyed any conception of the unity of knowledge and his challenge to liberal educators was nothing less, as Sloan has put it, than to "discover and defend a philosophical foundation for the curriculum that would by definition challenge the very conception of knowledge and knowing dominant in the university." This challenge, I believe, survives as the essential challenge today, and a meaningful future for liberal education depends upon its solution.[1]

---

[1]Thomas, <u>The Search for a Common Learning</u>, pp. 70-73. The quotation is from Sloan, "The Teaching of Ethics in the American Undergraduate Curriculum, 1876-1976," p. 240. Meiklejohn's article, "The Unity of the Curriculum" appeared in <u>New Republic</u> 32, pt. 2 (25 October 1922), pp. 2-3. Sloan goes on to say, on pp. 247-248, "The main problem that has continued to plague both the teaching of ethics and general education has been the modern tendency to regard only scientific knowledge as genuine and to look upon other concerns as somewhat out of place in the university. . . . Unless this problem is addressed, one would expect continuing problems for the present [general education] movement. In the meantime, the vision of a meaningful general education will continue to appeal to many who would insist on raising questions concerning the moral uses of knowledge and who seek a concrete arena within which personal and social ethics can be taught in relation to the whole curriculum." See also Daniel Bell, "A Second Look at General Education," <u>Seminar Reports</u> 1 (7 December 1973).

BIBLIOGRAPHY

The Yale Archives, located within the Sterling Memorial Library, are a boon to any historian interested in the University. The formal records of the University itself, as well as its various components, Yale College in particular, eventually find their way to this depository, as do Yale memorabilia, manuscript collections, and the personal papers of important Yale personages. Official Yale University records less than twenty years old are not available for research unless permission is granted to the researcher by the University office that created the particular record.

Chief among official University documents used by this study are the Presidential papers of Charles Seymour (1937-1950) and A. Whitney Griswold (1950-1963). Registers, which greatly ease the effort of locating documents, exist for both collections, which consist of boxed groups of ordinary, labeled file folders. The Seymour boxes are arranged alphabetically but are not numbered. The Griswold boxes, much larger, are also arranged alphabetically and number 102. The papers of President Kingman Brewster (1963-1977), which fill over a thousand boxes, are not yet organized or open to the public. Other official records at the Archives include the Minutes of the Yale Corporation (the University's Board of Trustees) and the records of the various committees of the Corporation, the most pertinent to this study being the Educational Policy Committee. The Archives also possess bound copies of the annual Reports to the President by various University officials, particularly the Deans of the various Schools and the Dean of Yale College. The bound Record of the Board of Permanent Officers, a group generally consisting of the full professors elected to the Yale College Faculty is also in the Archives. The Record since 1956 is, however, located in the Yale College Dean's Office. Until the Second World War, the Board of Permanent Officers played a significant role in faculty appointments, though later, as the Faculty grew and as tenure procedures were increasingly codified, the Board's function has come to be largely symbolic.

The Archives maintains an extensive collection of official University publications such as the _Yale_

Alumni Magazine and the President's Reports, issued
annually to the Yale community over the years under
various titles. The Archives also maintains collections of the yearly Yale University Catalogue (which
lists the faculty) and the yearly Undergraduate Course
of Study Bulletin, which in 1965-66 was renamed the
Yale College Programs of Study (and often called
the Blue Book). Student publications like the Yale
Daily News and Yale Literary Magazine are available.
Publications of this sort which I have consulted
are listed below under Collections of Yale Publications. Documents I have termed Reports and Pamphlets
Prepared for General Circulation are accessible by
means of the Archives' card catalogue, as are what
I have called Other Reports. The former were widely
and systematically distributed among the faculty,
sometimes in printed, or if not printed, in staple-
binding format. The latter group of reports were
distributed, at least initially, to much more limited
groups. In both cases, copies sometimes exist elsewhere, for example within Presidential papers. Nevertheless, the footnoted indication "Yale Archives"
means that the document is indexed in the Archives'
card catalogue.

     I have naturally made extensive use of the
Records of Yale College. The Faculty Record, essentially the bound minute books of the Yale College
Faculty meetings, is kept in the vault at the Yale
College Dean's office. When referring to the Faculty
Record, which dates back many decades, I have merely
given the date of the appropriate meetings, the minutes of which are filed chronologically over an
extremely extended period. Access to this invaluable
record is controlled by the Dean of Yale College.

     The working files of the Deans of Yale College
are transferred from the Dean's office vault to the
Archives at the discretion of the then-current Dean.
At present, Dean Howard Lamar has elected to retain
only those of his immediate predecessor, Horace D.
Taft (1971-1978). The records of Deans William C.
DeVane (1938-1963) and Georges May (1963-1971) are,
therefore, located in the Archives. The Archives
also have the files of Richard C. Carroll, who was
Associate Dean of Yale College from 1939 until 1968.
Registers have been prepared for all three collections.
Permission to use the records located in the Yale
College Dean's office was given to me by the current
Dean.

Finally this study has relied heavily on the minutes, usually mimeographed, of the Course of Study Committee. These minutes are unofficial documents (for example, they were seldom formally approved at the beginning of meetings). Generally they served to make a written record and to inform absent Committee members about discussions they had missed. Generally distributed to all members of the Course of Study Committee, the minutes were also sent to ex-officio members of the Committee, the Dean of Yale College in particular, but not, for example, to the President or other University officials. Suggested curriculum revisions, study conclusions, and written proposals were often distributed together with the minutes and filed accordingly. The Minutes of the Course of Study Committee are accessible as follows:

> From 1939-40 to 1966-67, copies of the minutes are in the files of Richard C. Carroll, catalogued in the Archives as Records: Yale University: Dean's Office, Dean of Undergraduate Affairs, R. C. Carroll.

> The year 1967-68 is located in Records: Yale University: Dean's Office, Box 37. (There is, of course, no Dean of Yale University, and the unspecified Dean is the Dean of Yale College, William C. DeVane.)

> The years 1968-69 and 1969-70 are located in Yale College: Records of the Dean: Georges May, Box 17.

> The minutes for the years 1970-71 to 1976-77, which are not wholly complete, are presently located in the files of Dean Taft, which are currently in the vault at the Yale College Dean's Office. Dean of Undergraduate Affairs Martin Griffin also has an incomplete file of this period and a virtually complete file for the year 1977-78.

> In my footnotes, to save confusion, I have simply listed CSC Minutes and the appropriate date.

> Other Standard Abbreviations which I have adopted are:

247

<u>Pres. Report</u> refers to the annual report of the President to the Yale community, whether the document was actually titled Report of the President, President's Report, Report to the Alumni, or something less conventional.

<u>Dean's Report</u>, with the dean unspecified, refers to the Report to the President by the Dean of Yale College. Reports by other Deans identify the Dean's School or affiliation.

<u>CSC Minutes</u> refers to the informal minutes of the Course of Study Committee.

<u>Griswold Mss.</u> refers to the Presidential papers of A. Whitney Griswold (1950-1963).

<u>Seymour Mss.</u> refers to the Presidential papers of Charles Seymour (1937-1950).

<u>Carroll Mss.</u> refers to the Records of Yale University, Dean's Office, Dean of Undergraduate Affairs R. C. Carroll (1939-68).

<u>May Mss.</u> refers to the records of Dean (of Yale College) Georges May (1963-71).

<u>Taft Mss.</u> refers to the files of Dean (of Yale College) Horace D. Taft (1971-1977).

Unpublished Sources

Reports and Pamphlets Prepared for General Circulation

Directed Studies Program (annual pamphlets).

1945 Report of the Committee on the Course of Study (adopted by Faculty, Spring 1945).

1947 Report of the Course of Study Committee, 20 December 1947.

1953 Report of the President's Committee on General Education.

1955 Report of the Committee on the Course of Study to the General Faculty of Yale College, April 1955.

Report of the Study Group on Yale College, 1972.

Yale Studies for Returning Servicemen (descriptive pamphlet).

Official Records

Board of Permanent Officers Record.

Faculty Record.

Minutes of the Yale Corporation.

The President's Report (also known as the Report of the President or Report to the Alumni).

Records of the Educational Policy Committee of the Yale Corporation.

Report to the President (annual) from the Dean of the Engineering School.

Report to the President (annual) from the Dean of the Freshman Year.

Report to the President (annual) from the Dean of the Sheffield Scientific School.

Report to the President (annual) from the Dean of Yale College.

Interviews

Lamar, Howard, 20 November 1980

May, Georges, 24 November 1980.

Mendenhall, T. C., 23 December, 1980.

Pierson, George W., 10 June 1980, 6 January 1981.

Corespondence with Author

Gabriel, Ralph H.

Mack, Maynard.

Mendenhall, Thomas C.

Manuscript Collections

The Papers of Charles Seymour, President 1937-1950.

The Papers of A. Whitney Griswold, President 1950-1963.

Records of Dean of Yale College, Horace D. Taft.

Records of Dean of Yale College, Georges May.

Records of the Yale University Dean's Office (William C. DeVane).

Records of Yale University Dean's Office, Dean of Undergraduate Affair, R. C. Carroll.

Minutes of the Course of Study Committee

1939-1967: located in Records: Yale University: Dean's office: Dean of Undergraduate Affairs, R. C. Carroll, 1939 to 1955-56 in Box 2; 1956-57 to 1963-64 in Box 2A; 1964-65 to 1966-67 in Box 2B.

1967-1968: located in Records: Yale University: Dean's Office, Box 37.

1968-1970: located in Yale College: Records of the Dean: Georges May, Box 17.

1970-1977: located in the files of Dean Horace D. Taft. Office of the Dean of Yale College.

1977-1978: located in the files of Dean of Undergraduate Affairs, Martin Griffin. Office of the Dean of Yale College.

Other Reports

Joint Program for Internships in General Education.

Report of the Director, Yale Studies for Returning
    Servicemen.

Report of the President's Committee on Foreign Area
    Studies, 18 October 1944.

Report of the Pesident's Committee on Modern Foreign
    Languages, 15 May 1944.

Report on Sophomore Year of Directed Studies, by
    T. C. Mendenhall, 7 July 1949.

Report on British Schools and Colleges, Summer 1952,
    by T. C. Mendenhall.

Collections of Yale Publications

Undergraduate Course of Study Bulletin.

Et Veritas (a publication of Dwight Hall).

Yale College Programs of Study Bulletin.

Yale Daily News.

Yale Alumni Magazine.

Yale University Catalogue.

Yale History

Buck, Polly Stone (Mrs. Norman S.). We Minded the
    Store: Yale Life and Letters During World War
    II. New Haven: Buck, 1975.

Chittenden, Russell H. History of the Sheffield
    Scientific School. New Haven: Yale University
    Press, 1928.

Committee of Post Doctoral Seminar. The Department
    of Education at Yale University, 1891-1958.
    New Haven: n.p., 1960.

Crocker, Richard E. "The Directed Studies Program:
An Experiment in Education," Et Veritas, April
1948.

DeVane, William C. "American Education After the
War." Yale Review, Summer 1943.

_____. "Changes in the Curriculum." Yale Alumni
Magazine, December 1945.

_____. Higher Education in Twentieth-Century
America. Cambridge: Harvard University Press,
1965.

_____. "The New Program in Yale College." Journal
of Higher Education, 2 (1 November 1945).

Editors of the Yale Daily News. Seventy-five: A
Study of a Generation in Transition. Foreword
by A. Whitney Griswold. New Haven: Yale Daily
News, 1953.

Furniss, Edgar S. The Graduate School of Yale:
A Brief History. New Haven: Yale University
Press, 1965.

Giamatti, A. Bartlett. History of Scroll and Key:
1942-1972. New Haven: The Society, 1978.

_____. "'Nature Justly Viewed': Yale's Scientific
Heritage." Yale Alumni Magazine, October 1979.

Griswold, A. Whitney. Essays on Education. New
Haven: Yale University Press, 1954.

Havemeyer, Loomis. Undergraduate Yale in the Second
World War. New Haven: Yale University, 1960.

Kelley, Brooks Mather. Yale: A History. New Haven:
Yale University Press, 1974.

Mack, Maynard. "Directed Studies." Yale Alumni
Magazine, May 1949.

Osterweiss, Rollin G. Three Centuries of New Haven,
1638-1838. New Haven: Published under the
auspices of the New Haven Colony Historical
Society, 1953.

Pierson, George W. "Democratic War and Our Higher Learning." _Yale Alumni Magazine_, December 1942.

_____. "The Elective System and the Difficulties of College Planning, 1870-1940." _Journal of General Education_ 4 (April 1950).

_____. _Yale College: An Educational History: 1871-1921._ New Haven: Yale University Press, 1952.

_____. _Yale: The University College: 1921-1937._ New Haven: Yale University Press, 1955.

Report of the President's Committee on General Education. New Haven, 1953.

Wharch, Richard. _School of the Prophets: Yale College, 1701-1740._ New Haven: Yale University Press, 1973.

Whitehead, John. _The Separation of College and State: Columbia, Dartmouth, Harvard and Yale 1776-1876._ New Haven: Yale University Press, 1973.

Discussions of General Education and the Nature of the University

Bell, Daniel. _The Reforming of General Education: The Columbia College Experience in Its National Setting._ New York: Columbia University Press, 1966.

_____. "A Second Look at General Education." _Seminar Reports_, 1 (7 December 1973).

Broudy, Harry S. "Tacit Knowing as a Rationale for Liberal Education." In _Education and Values._ Edited by Douglas Sloan. New York: Teachers College Press, 1980.

Cassirer, Ernst. _An Essay on Man._ New Haven and London: Yale University Press, 1944.

Cremin, Lawrence A. _Public Education._ New York: Basic Books, Inc., 1976.

_____. _Traditions of American Education._ New York: Basic Books, Inc., 1977.

DeVane, William C. "American Education After the War." _Yale Review_, Summer 1943.

Dewey, John. _Democracy and Education._ New York: Free Press Division, Macmillan Publishing Company, Inc., 1966.

Grant, Gerald, and Riesman, David. _The Perpetual Dream: Reform and Experiment in the American College._ Chicago and London: The University of Chicago Press, 1978.

Harvard Committee. _General Education in a Free Society._ Cambridge: Harvard University Press, 1945.

Hirst, P. H. "Liberal Education and the Nature of Knowledge." In _Education and Reason._ Edited by R. F. Dearden, P. H. Hirst, and R. S. Peters. London: Routledge & Kegan Paul, 1972.

Hutchins, Robert Maynard. _The Higher Learning in America._ New Haven: Yale University Press, 1936.

Kerr, Clark. _The Uses of the University: With a Postscript 1972._ Cambridge: Harvard University Press, 1972.

Lowell, A. Lawrence. "The Choice of Electives." In _At War with Academic Traditions in America._ By A. Lawrence Lowell. Cambridge: Harvard University Press, 1934.

McGrath, Earl J. _General Education and the Plight of Modern Man._ Indianapolis, Ind.: The Lilly Endowment, Inc., n.d.

_____. _Values, Liberal Education and National Destiny._ Indianapolis, Ind.: The Lilly Endowment, Inc., 1975.

Mill, John Stuart. "Inaugeral Address at St. Andrews." In *James and John Stuart Mill on Education*. Edited by F. A. Cavanagh. Westport, Conn.: Greenwood Press, Inc., 1979.

Newman, John Henry (Cardinal). *The Uses of Knowledge*. Edited by Leo L. Ward. Arlington Heights, Ill.: AHM Publishing Corp., 1948.

Ortega y Gasset, José. *Mission of the University*. Edited and translated by Howard Lee Nostrand. New York: W. W. Norton & Company, Inc., 1966.

Phenix, Philip H. *Realms of Meaning: A Philosophy of the Curriculum for General Education*. New York: McGraw-Hill Book Company, 1964.

Pierson, George W. "The Elective System and the Difficulties of College Planning, 1870-1940." *Journal of General Education* 4 (April 1950).

Plato. *The Republic of Plato*. Translated with introduction and notes by Francis MacDonald Cornford. London: Oxford University Press, 1941.

Sidorsky, David. "Varieties of Liberalism and Liberal Education." *Seminar Reports*, 5 (Spring 1977).

Sloan, Douglas. "The Teaching of Ethics in the American Undergraduate Curriculum, 1876-1976." In *Education and Values*. Edited by Douglas Sloan. New York: Teachers College Press, 1980.

Smith, Huston. "Excluded Knowledge: A Critique of the Modern Western Mind Set." In *Education and Values*. Edited by Douglas Sloan. New York: Teachers College Press, 1980.

Thomas, Russell. *The Search for a Common Learning: General Education, 1800-1960*. New York: McGraw-Hill Book Company, Inc., 1962.

Veblen, Thorsten. *The Higher Learning in America*. New York: Hill and Wang, 1957.

Whitehead, Alfred North. *The Aims of Education*. New York: The Free Press Division, Macmillan Publishing Company, Inc., 1967.

Yale Faculty. "Original Papers in Relation to a Course of Liberal Education." American Journal of Science and Arts 15 (January 1829).

History of Higher Education

Bledstein, Burton J. The Culture of Professionalism: The Middle Class and the Development of Higher Education in America. New York: W. W. Norton, 1976.

Cremin, Lawrence A. American Education: The Colonial Experience: 1607-1783. New York: Harper & Row, Inc., 1970.

Haskins, Charles Homer. The Rise of Universities. Ithaca, N.Y.: Cornell University Press, 1957.

Hawkins, Hugh. Between Harvard and America: The Educational Leadership of Charles W. Eliot. New York: Oxford University Press, 1972.

Hofstader, R. Anti-Intellectualism in American Life. New York: Vintage Books, Random House, 1965.

James, William. "The PhD Octopus." Harvard Monthly 36 (1903).

Jencks, Christopher, and Riesman, D. The Academic Revolution. Foreword by Martin Trow. Chicago: University of Chicago Press, 1977.

McCaughey, Robert. "The Transformation of American Academic Life: Harvard University, 1821-1892." Perspectives in American History 8 (1974).

Meiklejohn, Alexander. The Liberal College. Boston: Marshall Jones, 1920.

Rudolph, Frederick. The American College and University: A History. New York: Vintage Books, Random House, 1962.

_____. The Curriculum: A History of the American Undergraduate Course of Study Since 1636. San Francisco: Jossey-Bass Publishers, 1977.

Rudy, Willis. The Evolving Liberal Arts Curriculum:
An Historical Review of Basic Themes. New York:
Teachers College Press, 1960.

Sloan, Douglas. "Harmony, Chaos, and Consensus:
The American College Curriculum." Teachers
College Record 73 (December 1971).

Veysey, Laurence. The Emergence of the American
University. Chicago: University of Chicago
Press, 1965.